Rogue Traders

Brick Tower Press
Habent Sua Fata Libelli

Brick Tower Press
1230 Park Avenue
New York, New York 10128
Tel: 212-427-7139
bricktower@aol.com • www.BrickTowerPress.com

Library of Congress Cataloging-in-Publication Data
Skyrm, Scott E.D.
Rogue Traders
ISBN 978-1-59019-001-2

1. Biography & Autobiography : Business 2. Business—Corporate
History 3. Business & Economics : Investments & Securities -
Commodities 4. Business—Capital Markets 5. Business & Economics :
Business Ethics

First Printing, April 2014

Rogue Traders

Scott E.D. Skyrm

TO MY FAMILY

ACKNOWLEDGEMENTS

I wish to thank Andrew Spencer, who continues to work tirelessly with me on my books; Robert Linton, who taught me everything I know about the money markets; and Harold Holappa, who provided me a great education on CDOs; and special thanks to Andy Ansel, Andrew Colbeck, Scott LaShelle, Trip Mestanas, Jean-Luc Savignac, and Jennifer Skyrm for proofreading.

Contents

Introduction 9

Chapter One,
David Heuwetter and Drysdale, 1982 15

Chapter Two,
Howard Rubin and Merrill Lynch, 1987........................... 43

Chapter Three,
Joe Jett and Kidder Peabody, 1994.................................... 71

Chapter Four,
Nick Leeson and Baring Brothers, 1995......................... 105

Chapter Five,
Brian Hunter and Amaranth, 2006.................................. 143

Chapter Six,
Jérôme Kerviel and Société Générale, 2008.................... 175

Chapter Seven,
Thomas Hayes, RBS, UBS, and Citigroup, 2009............ 205

Chapter Eight,
What's Next?.. 239

INTRODUCTION

Ever since the earliest days of commerce, businesspeople have organized themselves into partnerships. They formed groups with a common interest and worked together as a single unit, assuming both the risks and rewards of the business. It was a natural way of achieving a common goal. If the business succeeded, all of the partners made money. If it flourished, the partners even sometimes became rich. However, success wasn't assured, and if the business failed, they all suffered together. In addition to a multitude of other industries, this was the model that dominated how Wall Street firms operated up until the 1980s.

For most of their existence, all financial firms were organized as partnerships. It was a collective sink-or-swim environment in which everyone benefited or suffered, depending on the firm's success or failure. There was no formal management structure, at least through the lens of modern-day standards. Instead, it was a relatively simple division of labor. Partners oversaw the areas that they knew best, and business lines developed and thrived based on the success of the individual partner in charge.

Wall Street firms were run by well-known personalities, many of whom were listed in the New York City social registers. Bankers worked at the same firm for the duration of their careers, rarely jumping ship just for the lure of more money. And it wasn't just about business. Social structures grew from the longevity of people working so closely together. Partners belonged to the same social clubs, vacationed together, and even entertained at each other's homes.

There was always a senior partner at the helm wielding the entirety of power. He decided which deals the firm participated in, the amount of risk they assumed, and what new businesses they would pursue. All of the partners shared the profits and losses, but the senior partner decided what percentage of ownership each partner was entitled to.

On the trading floor, a partner was always in charge; he was a veteran trader who had spent years at the firm. Given the amount of money they gambled when they bought or sold, the head trader was keen to keep a close eye on those underneath him. The other traders were well aware that the partner in charge risked his own money on every trade they made. Some traders would say that a good head trader could sense when someone was losing money just by looking at their face and their reaction to the market. If the head trader didn't like how the market looked on a Friday, he might go around the desk and tell the traders to cover up their shorts before the weekend. No one wanted to take any unnecessary risks. And because the head trader was married to the long-term financial health of the firm, he had a vested interest in it.

Client relationships were held as the highest priority. Firms were dedicated to their clients, regardless of market conditions at any one particular point in time. The customers were loyal too. They might not even check a price they received from their preferred securities dealer. They knew them, they trusted them, and they believed that they would never be ripped off. It was a symbiotic relationship; that meant decisions were always made with an eye on the long-term interests of clients.

The partners themselves kept a substantial amount of their own money at the firm. The upside was that profits flowed directly down to the partners, a reward for the time they had put in and their dedication to the business. One problem, at least from the perspective of the partners, was that while the profits flowed directly down, so too did the liabilities. It meant that if the partnership sustained a significant loss that was greater than its capital base, creditors were legally entitled to go after the partners personally.

The system worked well for many years, despite—or perhaps because of—the risks associated with unlimited liability. With their own money on the line, the partners closely monitored the risks they were taking. Decisions were made with the intention of limiting the downside while still making a profit. At the same time, knowing that their life savings hung in the balance provided an incentive for the partners to work towards the best interests of the firm in the long run.

Beginning in the 1960s, the business began to change. Corporate America realized that it could save money if it encouraged investment banks to compete for its business. It was a move away from the relationship banking of the past. It wasn't just about bringing a banking deal to the market and selling it to clients anymore; now securities had to be competitively priced and traded. This ushered in an era of increased competition.

When securities firms began competing on a transaction-by-transaction basis, past business had no bearing on future business, or current business for that matter. The financial world's motto was becoming one of "What can you do for me today?" Securities firms entered into a new world of risk-taking and of making secondary markets for their clients. In other words, if a customer wanted to sell a security, the securities firm would show the customer a bid. Sometimes it meant buying the security itself and holding it in its own account. When you're holding securities, it means having a view on the direction of the market. In other words, it means taking risk.

Then, on May 1, 1975, the Securities and Exchange Commission issued a decree that would change forever the landscape of the financial markets. On the day that came to be known as "May Day," sales commissions were no longer a predetermined, fixed amount. As of that day, brokerage commissions were open for negotiation between the securities firms and their clients. That change opened up the world of stock brokerage to the same market force that drove the rest of the economy—competition. The result was lower costs for both retail and institutional investors, but it also drove Wall Street firms to find new ways to make money.

There had always been a problem associated with the partnerships, and that was a perpetual lack of capital. The investment bank's ability to underwrite stocks and bonds and finance securities was tied directly to the size of its capital base, which was always tied directly to the net worth of the partners. The higher the partners' savings, the more capital the firm had to work with; lower bank balances meant less capital.

When a partnership was flush with wealthy partners, the capital base was not much of an issue. But as partners retired or died, their ownership interest went with them. In order to stem the loss of capital resulting from departures, there were often arrangements in place whereby the exiting partner was moved into a limited partnership role, meaning he took his personal funds out in stages. It gave the firm time to name new partners and replace its capital reserves to the previous levels.

But as the economy grew, securities underwritings became larger, and partnerships had an increasingly harder time maintaining enough capital. At the same time, investment banks were branching out into new areas outside of underwriting: opening retail branches, getting into securities trading, and asset management. The partnership structure was just too small to support the demands of the growing securities business.

The 1970s and '80s saw the private partnerships morph into public corporations. Upper management no longer consisted solely of the owners of the business, but of management that was technically hired by the shareholders. The midlevel managers running the trading desks were encouraged to take on more risk. Traders at securities firms were now in the business of buying and selling for their own accounts, and the focus of many firms became that of proprietary trading. The employees were now playing with other people's money. Making money and taking risk became the new face of Wall Street.

At the same time, complexity was increasing exponentially. Financial instruments like repo, mortgage-backed securities, interest- and principal-only STRIPS, futures, and options all led to more forms of derivative instruments being processed, created, traded, and sold to customers. The markets were changing rapidly, and oftentimes the gray-haired leaders in the corner offices on Wall Street did not truly understand what the twenty-five-year-olds on the trading floor were buying and selling. But the returns didn't lie, and that's all that truly seemed to matter at the end of the day. As John Gutfreund, the former CEO of Salomon Brothers, said, "The world changed in some fundamental ways, and most of us were not on top of it. We were almost dragged into the modern world."

Beginning in the 1980s, it was not uncommon to find that a freshly hired trainee—a kid literally right out of college—knew more about the new financial instruments than the CEO of the firm that hired him. In some instances, the kids were learning about the finer points of newly invented instruments before their managers knew they even existed. These were the new breed of traders scattered across the trading desks. The firm expected them to make money pedaling these exotic securities that were rife with risk and uncertainty. Truth be told, the traders were expected to conform to the firm's risk management policies while many of the people enforcing the policies didn't understand the products to begin with. And few certainly understood the massive risk that some of these new instruments carried. It was potentially a recipe for disaster.

The partnership structure that had incentivized the employee-owners to take conservative risks was beginning to disappear. Risks were being taken by low-level employees in banks with thousands of employees. What's more, few of those on the trading desk had much of their own money at the institution. There was little reason to avoid risk; the traders had no skin in the game, so to speak. The system rewarded those traders who took huge risks and made equally huge profits.

On the other side, traders who lost huge amounts merely lost their jobs, only to get second, third, and even fourth chances. Ironically, big-name traders who lost vast sums in a very public way oftentimes were the beneficiaries of multiple job offers. Other firms were eager to jump in on the foray of profits that could be made on Wall Street, and a big name translated, at least in their minds, to big profits. The next time, it was reasoned, he wouldn't have such bad luck.

Change in the finance industry is seemingly never-ending. Perhaps the greatest transformation came at the turn of the twenty-first century, which ushered in the era of the colossal bank. The walls between investment banking and commercial banking were removed, and large banks scooped up those Wall Street trading franchises. Banks were now on both sides of the Glass-Steagall fence, engaging in businesses that were new to them. The global behemoths' trading floors were now run by career bank administrators; lifelong commercial bankers became the ones overseeing the trading of increasingly complex financial instruments.

Global trading operations at the mammoth banks had grown to a point where they were next to impossible to manage. With thousands of risk-taking employees spread out over multiple continents, trading twenty-four hours a day in every financial instrument known to man, there's no humanly possible way to keep order. The old conservative nature was now entirely gone, replaced with a new era populated by young and aggressive traders who were eager to make large sums of money using vast sums of bank capital, and they were managed by career commercial bankers. What could go wrong?

As we shall soon see, a lot could go wrong.

The individuals whose stories compose the contents of this book are some of the smartest people you'll ever read about. They had an intimate understanding of the markets and how best to make money from them, but they also had an equally in-depth knowledge of some of the flaws in the markets—or sometimes flaws in the systems at the banks themselves. They used their knowledge to make money. And when that failed, they often used their knowledge of how the system was structured to hide their losses. And when *that* failed, there was no turning back.

I don't want to suggest that these actions are typical Wall Street behavior. Far from it, in fact. The reason these men are called "rogue traders" is because they are anomalies compared to the vast majority of honest traders who make their living in the financial industry, myself included. But it's important to understand that there are immoral people out there among the honest ones, wolves disguised as sheep. The best way to differentiate the two is to understand what the rogue traders did, and how they managed to do it. After all, those who don't learn from history are condemned to repeat it.

Chapter One

David Heuwetter and Drysdale, 1982

Given that there are few better ways to start off a day than with a hearty breakfast, it only seems fitting that we begin our story with that all-important meal. According to culinary legend, the luxurious breakfast indulgence known as eggs Benedict got its start from, of all things, a hangover cure. The dish was the brainchild of Lemuel Coleman Benedict, a well-known man from an equally well-known, old-money New York family.

Benedict had built himself a reputation as a dashing young man about town who was popular with the ladies. He was descended from one of the original English families to have settled the island of Manhattan, yet was stricken with an unhealthy love of liquor. One morning following a night of hard drinking, the ill-feeling Benedict staggered into his regular breakfast spot on an otherwise ordinary morning in 1894 at the Waldorf Hotel, then located on Fifth Avenue and 33rd Street, which was to later become the world-renowned Waldorf-Astoria on Park Avenue.

Never being one to shy away from a large breakfast, Benedict ordered a pair of poached eggs, bacon, and buttered toast, plus a side of hollandaise sauce. When the order arrived, he stacked the bacon on the toast, topped it with the eggs, and slathered the whole tower in hollandaise. In the midst of his eating, the legendary chef Oscar Tschirky, who went by the moniker "Oscar of the Waldorf," happened by and inquired about the dish. After hearing the list of ingredients, Oscar decided to make the meal a part of his regular menu, though he substituted English muffins for the toast and a slice of Canadian bacon in place of the more pedestrian strips of bacon. And thus eggs Benedict was born.

Oscar of the Waldorf never confirmed the story of the breakfast's origins, though the story of Benedict's invention was first reported in an article that appeared in the *New Yorker* in 1942, and was later confirmed by his niece Ethyle Benedict. The Benedict family was slow to confess the story's less-than-gentile elements, as admitting having an infamous, hung-over son would certainly cast an unflattering light on the otherwise aristocratic family, and perhaps tarnish the man's reputation in both on his Wall Street career and in society.

Aside from his playboy reputation and love of large breakfasts, Benedict was known for his dark gray business suits and perfectly starched shirts with high white collars. His name often appeared in the New York society pages, frequently in reference to his generosity and for "looking after the interests of dancers." Lemuel was quite unlike the other members of his distinguished and private family. His flamboyant and outgoing style was in stark contrast to the more reserved attitudes of the Benedicts, a fact punctuated by Lemuel's decision to marry an opera singer in 1908 named Carrie Birdwell. Together, the newlyweds established themselves as major players in New York's trendy, well-to-do set.

There was a professional side to the man too. At the dawn of the twentieth century, Benedict was working at the stock brokerage firm James McGovern and Company, located at 7 Wall Street. When the firm's namesake retired at the end of 1904, Benedict joined forces with one of the firm's junior partners named Robert Drysdale to form Benedict, Drysdale and Company, and the new firm moved into the offices of its predecessor.

Benedict assumed the role of senior partner at the new company, having already made a successful name for himself on Wall Street, whereas Drysdale had only been with the firm for four years at the time, and was something of a baby in the industry at age twenty-nine. The young Drysdale would mature, however, into one of the most formidable financial forces of his day, and when he partnered with Benedict, the predecessor to Drysdale Government Securities Inc. was born.

The early years of the new firm were marked by success and growth. The company was a member of the New York Stock Exchange and its partners classified themselves as primarily commission-based stockbrokers. Everything was above board. The partners all served on various boards, as was customary, including such financial giants as the Corn Exchange Bank and the Washington Trust Company of the City of New York.

As the years progressed, Robert Drysdale was named senior partner of the firm in 1922 when Benedict retired from his post, though Benedict retained limited partnership interests. Two of Drysdale's children, Robert Drysdale Jr. and C. D. Drysdale, joined their father at the firm, making it into a Drysdale family business. Then in 1928 Benedict, Drysdale and Company officially changed its name to Drysdale and Company, and moved into a new office at 61 Broadway. Lemuel Benedict would die fifteen years later at the age of seventy-six, leaving behind a legacy forever linked to one of the world's best-loved breakfast treats and the beginnings of a Wall Street firm that would eventually change the financial markets forever. It was the beginning of what would become the epicenter for one of the biggest financial scandals to ever hit Wall Street.

In 1962 Robert Drysdale retired to become a limited partner of the firm and was replaced the following year by longtime partner William Bergan. When Bergan died the following year, Robert Drysdale Jr. was suddenly thrust into the role of senior partner. Perhaps it was because of that loss of its original identity and the departure of the Drysdales that created something of a power vacuum at the top of the organizational chart at the firm. A long succession of leaders followed, and the title was passed from one senior partner to another until in 1975, when David Wakeman III took control from his father and changed the partnership to a corporation, creating Drysdale Securities Corporation.

That change was much more significant than merely one related to title of the firm's classification; Drysdale joined the trend that was happening on Wall Street for years. As there are many financial benefits to forming a corporation, clearly the Drysdale partners no longer wanted the unlimited liability. Perhaps that was not surprising given the turnover in management that had been going on for ten years and the increased growth of trading for the firm's revenues.

Following the reorganization of Drysdale, the firm brought in entirely new management that included Joseph Ossorio and Albert Vacchiano, while David Wakeman III took a junior management role, becoming the vice president and treasurer. That new management team then hired a hotshot Wall Street trader who specialized in the trading of government bonds to run the firm's bond department. That hotshot's name was David Heuwetter.

Heuwetter was a bond-trading rock star of his day. He made a lot of money and had all of the trappings that went along with it. His massive apartment on Manhattan's swanky Upper East Side came with a $10,000-a-month price tag. Of course by today's standards that might sound like a bargain. But in the late 1970s, $10,000 a month was stratospherically expensive for rent, especially considering the fact that the median household annual income in the United States was just shy of $12,000. His wife—his second wife, to be more exact—fit the bill too, as she was a soap opera star named Rosalinda Guerra, also known as Ramona Gonzalez on the wildly popular *Ryan's Hope*.

But there was another side to Heuwetter, a less flashy component to his lifestyle. Rosalinda once described him as "quiet and serious," and he worked a schedule that would kill men. He was rumored to have worked twenty-three consecutive years—*years*—without taking a vacation. And he had remarkable business sense when it came to trading bonds. One former trader said of Heuwetter that he seemed to "have made a profit, no matter where they sold them."

With their new star trader at the helm, Drysdale was in the process of building up its market presence, and in 1979 established the Drysdale Options Corporation to house its options trading operation. The goal was to become a securities trading powerhouse.

The increased bond-trading activity didn't go unnoticed, suffice it to say; both the New York Stock Exchange (NYSE) and the Federal Reserve became worried that Drysdale's bond positions were getting too large, and they wanted those positions either reduced or eliminated altogether. The Federal Reserve had received tips from several market participants who thought Drysdale was trading far in excess of the firm's capital base, and many dealers had already refused to deal with the firm because of its renowned risk taking. The NYSE could ask Drysdale to limit the size of its bond-trading activities because it could make an argument that a bond-trading loss could affect Drysdale's ability to meet its stock exchange obligations. For the Federal Reserve, it was a different story. The Fed had no ability to restrict Heuwetter's risk-taking operations at all. Yes, that's true. At the time, the U.S. government bond market was completely unregulated. Hindsight is, of course, twenty-twenty, but looking back on that with perfect vision, officials should have seen the warning signs that were staring them straight in the eye.

* * *

Back then, there was virtually no regulation whatsoever governing the buying and selling of government-issued U.S. Treasury bonds, and, perhaps not surprisingly, these securities were typically traded and sold to investors by small firms. The Glass-Steagall Act, which split the banking industry into two distinct and separate entities, commercial banking and investment banking, simply did not apply to government or municipal bonds. Even when the Securities and Exchange Commission (SEC) began to push for more regulation in the 1970s, it left government bonds alone, thinking that if they were free from regulation, it enabled the Treasury to borrow money at the lowest possible cost. The Wall Street firms that engaged in the government securities market included the banks, investment banks, and small broker-dealers. The banks and large investment banks were regulated by an assortment of different government entities. For the smaller broker-dealers, the complete lack of regulation meant that approximately one-quarter of all of those trading government securities weren't registered with a regulator in any way, and those fortunate enough to be a part of that game were allowed to operate with minimal capital.

The regulation that the SEC did push for centered on the municipal bond market, when it brought charges against a host of municipal bond firms in 1975, citing high-pressure sales tactics, large markups on sales, and varied misrepresentations of the securities they were selling. It was determined that the municipal bond market definitely needed some oversight, and the SEC allowed the industry to create the Municipal Securities Rulemaking Board. The key word in that name is *municipal*, which is defined as state and local governments. In other words, U.S. government bonds were still free of regulation— making it the bond market's financial equivalent of the Wild West.

*   *   *

By the late 1970s, inflation began to grow increasingly problematic in the United States. It would hit a peak of 13.5 percent, which means that for every dollar something had cost last year, it required an additional thirteen and a half cents to buy it again this year. For those who have never experienced high inflation, it's not a good experience for any society. Something needed to be done to curb the skyrocketing inflation, and the institution charged with that task was the Federal Reserve.

The Federal Reserve System was established in 1913 with enactment of the Federal Reserve Act, and it was charged with regulating price stability (keeping inflation low) along with the goal of full employment (keeping employment high). For years, the Fed had accepted inflation in exchange for lower unemployment, and now, as they say, the chickens had come home to roost. In other words, it was finally time for the United States to pay for the "easy money" policies that had dominated the 1960s and 1970s. Prices were growing year after year to levels that seemed beyond the Fed's control. In order to combat the runaway inflation, the task was given to one person, namely the chairman of the Federal Reserve.

In 1979, that person's name was Paul Volcker. Two months after Paul Volcker was appointed Federal Reserve chairman, on the night of October 6, 1979, he made a drastic announcement that the Fed would increase the overnight fed funds interest rate substantially, from 11 percent to 12 percent, and he vowed to rein in inflation by targeting money-supply growth—a completely new approach that the Fed had never tried before. In other words, he pledged to slow down the printing of new money, but vowed to let short-term interest rates go wherever they wanted. And that direction was up!

The financial community nicknamed Volcker's surprise announcement the "Saturday Night Special," and it did have its desired effect, as the overnight federal funds rate shot up to a peak of 20 percent in June 1981. The move achieved the desired effect; by curtailing the growth of new money, runaway inflation started to turn, and within two years, inflation had dropped to 3.2 percent. Then, by October 1981, when Volcker began to loosen monetary policy again by pumping money back into the economy, interest rates declined accordingly. It was possibly the most successful execution of monetary policy in the entire history of the Federal Reserve. However, there were consequences for jacking short-term rates up so high and then dropping them down again; it meant extreme volatility in the bond market. Given that a 20 percent interest rate on a loan is by all accounts astronomically high, it's not difficult to understand why the bond market began a roller coaster ride from 1979 through 1982.

As volatile as interest rates were, it wasn't the only major change affecting the bond market in the late 1970s and early 1980s. Whereas Wall Street saw a huge growth in the market for government securities, a twist on an old concept began to emerge for traders of these securities. That new twist was called the repo market; repo, in this case, is short for repurchase agreement.

Stock traders have been short-selling stocks since the time stock markets came into existence. The premise is simple, but as the old saying goes, the devil is in the details. In a short sale, an investor believes the price of a particular stock is too high and about to drop, so the investor sells the stock with the intention to buy it back at a later date at a lower price. As any good investor knows, it's always best to sell when the price is high, and that's exactly what a short seller hopes to do. But there's a caveat to the short sale: When you sell something to someone, you need to deliver it to that buyer. Buyers don't like purchasing an investment and not actually receiving it. In order to deliver a stock that you don't own, you borrow it from another investor who owns it.

In the stock market, the borrowing and lending of stocks was originally called stock loan, but it had evolved in recent years to be called securities finance. Short sellers would call their bank or broker and arrange to borrow the stock for the period of time they're short. It's the same idea for bonds in the bond market, except the market for borrowing and lending bonds is called the repo market.

A repo is a widely used transaction for investing cash and covering short sales in the bond market, only it's typically done between large financial institutions as opposed to individual investors. Repos are typically loans that are repaid in a matter of days, with interest. That's the repurchase aspect of the repo: an institution is selling a security with the promise to repurchase it in the future. For short sellers, they're borrowing a security with the promise to return it later when they buy back their short sale. Interestingly, despite the fact that many average investors have never heard of a repo, it's the largest financial market in the world.

As it applies to the bond market, short selling typically involved borrowing bonds from the major money center banks and the largest investment banks. Up through the late 1970s, the short seller paid a fee in the range of fifty basis points to the bank, but by the late 1970s, the repo market began to change. Not only were large banks and investment banks trading in the repo market, there were also many of those small broker-dealers involved. Small, unregulated, and undercapitalized broker-dealers now had access to very cheap financing, with no limits on their trading through any regulation.

Returning to Volcker's massive interest rate hikes, the volatility of interest rates during that period in time meant that traders needed to find ways to minimize their risk of losing money. One of the best ways to hedge against losses from rising interest rates is to short-sell government bonds. As financial institutions began actively hedging their bond holdings, traders found themselves increasingly borrowing securities in the repo market. And that meant that the repo market itself was growing considerably in a very short time.

The repo market was quite possibly even less regulated than the nonregulated government bond market. There was no legal framework encompassing repos; the legal status of the transaction had never been tested in court, and there was no legal standard of how to classify the transactions in a bankruptcy. Were they a sale and repurchase? Were they a collateralized loan? Could they be immediately liquidated after a bankruptcy? Nobody seemed to know. But nobody seemed to care either.

So, let's try to keep track of it all: The market for government securities was unregulated in order to combat inflation; interest rates spiked, then shot back down; and a new market called the repo market had just developed. New types of securities transactions, a lack of regulation, and volatile markets—this was clearly a formula for disaster.

* * *

From 1979 to 1981, Drysdale Securities Corporation was having a good run. Interest rates were moving higher and David Heuwetter rode the short-selling repo market–enabled ride on Volcker's always-rising interest rates. In January 1982, under pressure from the New York Stock Exchange, Drysdale was forced to spin off its government securities business and establish Drysdale Government Securities Inc.

Richard Taafe, a former bond salesman from Kidder Peabody, would take on the role of president. His head trader was none other than Drysdale's own shining star, David Heuwetter, who also happened to own a vast majority of the new corporation. Drysdale sent out a letter to clients on behalf of its government securities spinoff announcing the formation of the new corporation, and adding that the new subsidiary had operating capital of approximately $20.8 million.

The announcement attracted neither clients nor counterparties with whom to trade, but that little setback didn't dampen the enthusiasm, as Drysdale still moved between twenty and thirty traders into the new office of Drysdale Government Securities. The fact that the office itself was an attic on the fifth floor above a dress shop probably didn't infuse a great deal of confidence in those traders, especially in light of the lack of enthusiasm in the grand announcement of the corporation's formation.

As a second attempt to attract business, Drysdale went back to the accountant who had orchestrated the spinoff in the first place, Warren Essner from accounting firm Arthur Andersen. He was asked to produce a more formal document that the corporation might use in its marketing efforts. The result was a letter from Arthur Andersen certifying that the subordinated debt and equity in Drysdale Government Securities was its audited opinion. In other words, Arthur Andersen was all but guaranteeing that Drysdale Government Securities had the capital that it claimed, and the accounting firm was willing to stake its own reputation on that fact—a move it would come to regret.

While Drysdale Government Securities had $20.8 million in capital, the firm failed to disclose the fact that $15.8 million of it was actually a loan from Drysdale Securities Corporation, and that $12 million was paid back soon after operations began, though that deficit was never reported by Essner. The remaining $5 million came in the form of securities that had been transferred in from Drysdale Securities Corporation. It would later be alleged that, in addition to those securities, the parent company also gifted the fledgling operation a $190 million deficit so that Drysdale could remove a loss from its own balance sheet, but that was never proven.

Financial discrepancies aside, with the certified statement in hand the new corporation was off and running, and at first things appeared well for the new bond-trading outfit. At Drysdale Securities Corporation, Heuwetter had made a great deal of money and was rumored to be using a secret and sophisticated computer-based trading strategy that was based on a computer program named Arnold. But it doesn't take someone with a supercomputer brain to understand what the firm was actually doing. The whole business model was based on taking advantage of the differences in market pricing conventions between outright Treasury bond short sales and the repo market.

In the case of buying and selling Treasury bonds outright, the process is pretty straightforward. The securities themselves are transferred from seller to buyer based on the bond's price plus the interest that had accrued up until that point. In other words, when you bought a bond, you had to pay the base purchase price as well as any interest that had accrued since the last coupon interest payment. With the high interest rates that were in place at the time, that accrued interest could be substantial, which meant that there was a lot of money added on when buying and selling bonds in between the bond coupon payment dates.

The repo market, however, worked on a different model. Because repo trades were typically only overnight transactions—or at most a couple of days—the accrued interest on the bond wasn't as much of an issue. It's important to remember that this was in the days before electronic trading with computers calculating things like accrued interest in a matter of nanoseconds. Back then, everything was done manually; someone in the back office figured out the accrued interest on a calculator. That amount of extra work involved in calculating the accrued interest over the course of a one-day trade just didn't seem to justify itself. As a result, the accrued interest for pricing bonds for repo trades was ignored.

It was David Heuwetter that found a way to play one system against the other and make a lot of money very fast. He realized that he could short-sell Treasury bonds in the outright market and receive the accrued interest on the bonds, then turn around and borrow the bonds in the repo market without having to pay that interest. It was, at its core, a superb way to get an interest-free loan regardless of interest rates. But Paul Volcker's jacking up of interest rates from 1979 through 1981 made the trade even more profitable.

Consider this scenario: If a trader short sold a Treasury bond that paid 10 percent coupon interest annually, the bond would accrue 2.5 percent in interest every quarter. After short-selling the bond in the Treasury market, the trader borrowed the bonds in the repo market, not having to pay out any accrued interest on the bonds. Say the trader short sold $100 million worth of bonds three months after the bond paid a coupon. That meant the trader had free use of $2.5 million. Expanding that out even further, if he upped the size of the trade to $5 billion worth of Treasury bonds at 10 percent rates, the bankroll he was taking in ballooned to $125 million.

Drysdale made a business of short-selling government bonds in the Treasury market in exchange for the price plus the accrued interest. In order to make good on their promise to deliver the bonds, Heuwetter and Drysdale acquired the securities from their clearing bank, Chase Manhattan Bank. Chase, in turn, would go out and borrow the securities itself from other dealers in the marketplace. Before the coupon payment date, Drysdale would buy back its short Treasury positions and return the securities it borrowed. Then, the firm would short-sell more bonds that had a lot of accrued interest on them, and the cycle would start anew.

When Heuwetter was developing the scheme in 1981, overnight interest rates were hovering around 15 percent. With $125 million to play with, Drysdale was able to finance the entire operation of Drysdale Government Securities. On top of that, Heuwetter could also generate upwards of $1.5 million in interest income every month. It seemed like a foolproof way to make a lot of money. But there's an old saying that applies here. Once you make something foolproof, the world goes and invents a better fool.

The scheme was working to perfection, and the money was rolling in, but the firm's operatives weren't satisfied, because, like all good Wall Street traders, they wanted more. To get more they had to put on larger position sizes—short sell more bonds—and that meant the need for more leverage. Enter the practice of leverage, using securities sold in the repo market as collateral against a loan to short-sell more securities. By leveraging its holdings to the brink, Drysdale managed to have positions between $6.5 and $7 billion in government bonds at its peak. Part of the firm's massive holdings included approximately $4.5 billion in short positions and $2.5 billion in long positions. Drysdale was short, at times, $3 billion more bonds than it owned, and that's only a financially stable model when interest rates are going up. As one Wall Street trader said of Drysdale, "It was the most astonishingly leveraged operation that I have ever seen."

Enter the New York Stock Exchange and the Federal Reserve, who were already looking at the size of Heuwetter's trading positions and didn't like what they saw. When the NYSE pressed Drysdale Securities Corporation to reduce the size of its positions, Drysdale's reaction was not to cut down on its trading, instead it merely set up Drysdale Government Securities Inc. and moved its traders there. Now, Heuwetter could grow the size of his trades as large as he wanted and run his own company to boot. As long as interest rates didn't fall, it was the perfect bond-trading business.

The success of this scheme was predicated on one simple fact, and that was that the bond market stayed relatively stable or that interest rates moved higher, causing bond prices to go down. Remember, Drysdale was short selling bonds and getting a free loan out of it. If the bond market rallied, and interest rates began to decline, Heuwetter would watch his profits disappear. Two out of three isn't bad when you're talking about baseball, but in the case of superstar trader David Heuwetter, he would have been well served to consider the downside of his trading strategy a little bit more.

And then the clock struck midnight for this bond-selling Cinderella. In October 1981, interest rates began a rapid decline as the inflation woes subsided. That meant a huge rally in the bond market, which was the one scenario that spelled imminent death for the Drysdale scheme. Throughout early 1982, losses began to mount, and instead of getting out, the Drysdale traders channeled their inner gamblers and started doubling down. Their thinking was that the market had to turn, and when it did, they'd be fine. Interest rates had been high for many years, and there was no reason to think Paul Volcker's new money supply–restricting approach would solve the nation's inflation woes. Heuwetter and Drysdale kept short-selling more bonds, and the losses kept piling up. When the time came where they could no longer keep increasing the size of their trades, the whole thing collapsed around them.

But it took some time for the aftershocks to fully bring down the house, and the dying corporation managed to limp its way through May of that year. The beginning of the end came on Sunday, May 16, 1982, during an evening phone call from David Heuwetter to an officer at Chase Manhattan Bank. Heuwetter gave him the unfortunate news that "we may have a problem" meeting the $160 million coupon interest payment due the next day on $3.2 billion in U.S. Treasury bonds. He hoped that Chase could see fit to loan Drysdale $200 million, just to tide it over.

There are few things in the world like a $160 million payment default to get bankers nervous, and Heuwetter's call set off a series of additional phone calls from one nervous Chase executive to another. It's hard to know what exactly was said over the wires, but as one executive later said, "The facts are that they didn't get a loan."

Without the loan from Chase, Drysdale had no way of making the coupon interest payments. With no way out of the trap it had made for itself, Drysdale collapsed.

* * *

History has demonstrated time and time again that events with disastrous consequences, like the fate that greeted Drysdale on that Monday morning, were the result of a combination of bad decisions and bad luck. It bears mentioning, however, that Heuwetter's strategy, though ultimately flawed in the long term, was not without its merits. Consider what would have happened had the bond market not taken such a dramatic upward turn. Through the use of leverage, Heuwetter had dramatically increased the firm's exposure to the market. The size of his trades could have resulted in substantial gains—or, at the very least, a break-even—had the market dropped again or even remained somewhat stable. Imagine how many times the market had rallied against him and Heuwetter had survived by holding out and waiting for it to turn. But this time Heuwetter's magic lottery numbers didn't come through. In the end, the fledgling bond firm was up against an impossible-to-meet coupon payment of $160 million.

On the eve of the official announcement that Drysdale Government Securities was insolvent, there were already waves of fear gripping the offices of Chase Manhattan Bank. Willard C. Butcher, the chief executive officer of the bank, called an emergency meeting attended by a collection of various Chase executives that same night. Because Chase had acted in the role of broker, or agent, for the failed Drysdale trades, there was concern that the bank might be seen as acting as the principal in the transactions. Had the bank been acting as principal, the bank would be liable to cover the entire loss. Luckily, the concerned executives assured Butcher that the bank was only acting only as agent.

The difference between acting as an agent and as a principal is significant. When acting as an agent, Chase's liability would be minimal; it was merely arranging the trades between Drysdale and other market participants. Those involved in the transactions would be relying on the credit of Drysdale as opposed to that of Chase, meaning that Drysdale would be solely liable for covering the losses. If, however, Chase had been the principal, it was guaranteeing the trades and would be responsible for assuming both the credit and default risks. Even though Chase was, at the time, the third-largest commercial bank in the country, covering Drysdale's losses would be a significant setback, equal to about 25 percent of its annual earnings. In today's world of high finance, there is a very clear declaration by any financial institution that it is merely acting as an agent. That fact is spelled out very clearly in documents. At the time of Drysdale's collapse, however, there was no such statement.

The old adage about there not being any such thing as a dumb question could have saved a lot of headaches at Chase. However, because nobody thought to actually ask the question, the bank's status as to whether Chase was an agent or principal was suddenly thrown into a big, messy pool of gray. Was the classification used by Drysdale enough to prove that Chase was the agent? There was no way to say for sure. The bank could have pursued a course of legal inquiry, but that would inevitably take years and there was no guarantee that Chase would emerge victorious. And what's more, there was a $160 million interest coupon payment due the next day. Decisions had to be made, and fast.

The opinions at the other Wall Street shops favored the idea that Chase was more than just an agent. Because Drysdale Government Securities was a relatively small firm that was a new kid on the block by the Street's standards, many in the market stayed away from dealing with it. But with Chase guaranteeing its trades, suddenly it was a whole new game. So whereas Chase thought it was serving as what is referred to as a blind broker—meaning it was just arranging trades between major brokers and Drysdale—those same counterparties were under the impression that they were dealing directly with Chase Manhattan Bank.

Interestingly enough, there were more than a few securities dealers who saw the situation and had walked away from trading with Drysdale, because those firms assumed the transactions were with someone other than Chase. There were those, too, who questioned Chase specifically as to the details regarding whom it was acting for. When questioned as to the identity of the third-party that Chase was clearing for, the bank refused to answer, and those brokers walked away. Still others asked Chase for written documentation saying that the bank was serving as the principal broker in the trade, something the bank also refused to do.

Despite all the naysayers who feared doing business with Drysdale directly, there were plenty of firms who ignored the potential warning signs and entered into transactions anyway. They assumed— always a dangerous thing to do, especially on Wall Street—they were dealing with Chase Manhattan Bank. It was those dealers who ended up on the wrong side when the Drysdale house came crashing down to the ground.

On Monday, May 17, after some of the smoke had cleared, Chase sent a team of auditors to the office of Drysdale Government Securities. Their mandate was twofold: They were to see if they could figure out what had happened and to determine what, if any, liability Chase had in terms of covering the losses. Willard C. Butcher called seven of the heads of major brokerage firms and banks to set up a meeting at six o'clock that evening. Thirty brokers and banks, those who had been involved with Drysdale in one way or another, showed up at Chase's conference room, all of them anxiously awaiting an explanation. They didn't like what they heard.

Butcher opened with his contention that Chase had been merely acting as an agent in the transactions. As such, the bank would not be sending coupon payments to anyone in the room. He maintained that his bank was in no way legally responsible for covering the payments, again citing the fact that it was not acting as principal.

The others in the room were livid. They argued that they had been under the impression that Chase was, in fact, their counterparty, and that they never would have done business with Drysdale had they known that wasn't the case.

As a peace offering, Chase offered to create a dedicated bailout fund that would hold $250 million to cover the pending coupon payments and other losses. Of that amount, Chase would contribute $90 million, with the remaining $160 million to be made up from the other investment banks involved with Drysdale. The idea did not go over well, and everyone left.

The next day, panic and fear gripped Wall Street. The word got around pretty quickly that Drysdale was done and, as such, wasn't going to be making coupon payments due to the Street. Few firms, however, considered it their own problem; at least that was the commonly held belief. The reality was that nobody knew exactly who had what exposure to Drysdale, which meant that nobody knew for sure who might be going down next. And that uncertainty prompted a market-wide pullback from all trading in the bond market. Though not known at the time, Drysdale's losses reached out to many of the largest firms on the Street, including Manufacturers Hanover Trust Company; U.S. Trust; Merrill Lynch, Pierce, Fenner & Smith; Drexel Burnham Lambert; Paine, Webber, Jackson & Curtis; Goldman Sachs & Company; Donaldson, Lufkin & Jenrette; New York Hanseatic; and Salomon Brothers. They were all owed coupon payments by Drysdale, but since no one knew for sure who was about to take a major loss, the entire market was suspect.

Even though the Drysdale unpleasantness did nothing to damage the reputation and credit of the United States or the bond market as a whole, the repo market essentially dried up. Few dealers were willing to do repo financing with other dealers or with their customers. That new development forced the Street and investors to sell many securities, driving prices down. One witness to the great sell-off said, "We're all in uncharted waters on this one. No one really knows what's going to happen."

Later that day, Paul Volcker agreed to host a meeting at the Federal Reserve Bank in New York to discuss the situation. However, he made it explicitly clear that representatives of the Fed would not endorse any specific solution on behalf of the Fed. They were attending more or less only as interested observers, who might have an opinion or two to share with the group. At the same time, the Fed's Open Market Desk issued a public statement announcing its willingness to stand behind the bond dealers by providing the necessary liquidity to support the repo market; in other words, it was willing to dump massive amounts of cash into the market.

The Federal Reserve Bank of New York called the meeting for the next evening, on Wednesday the nineteenth, scheduled at six o'clock. The heads of the largest Wall Street banks were requested to attend and discuss Chase's position about why they were not making the coupon payments. This Fed-orchestrated meeting was, in a sense, the first act of a repeating drama that would become a big part of Wall Street history over the next thirty years.

* * *

The Federal Reserve would arrange meetings between the major Wall Street banks twice again in later years. First, following the collapse of Long-Term Capital Management (LTCM) in 1998, and then again just before Lehman Brothers collapsed in 2008. LTCM was a Greenwich, Connecticut–based hedge fund management firm made up of what was considered at the time the best and brightest traders in the industry. The firm's investment strategy, like that of many hedge fund firms, was rooted in complex mathematical formulas that, if everything went as planned, generated huge profits. But nothing on Wall Street is quite so simple as that, and after Russia defaulted on its debts in 1998, the bond market did not act like it was supposed to—LTCM found itself severely overleveraged and out of cash.

The levee broke, and LTCM was facing approximately $1.85 billion in losses; this resulted in what amounted to a run on the bank at the end of September 1998. LTCM needed a buyer or a bailout, and it needed it fast. LTCM's capital was down to only $400 million, which is certainly not an insignificant amount, but next to the staggering $100 billion in assets that remained on its balance sheet, it was hardly a drop in the bucket. Long-Term Capital Management's "long term" had ended rather abruptly.

Fearing a nationwide panic in the market when news of LTCM's collapse became public, the Federal Reserve Bank of New York hosted the meeting where a bailout plan was agreed to, which was at the time completely unheard of. LTCM's major creditors—the major Wall Street banks—would finance a bailout package worth $3.625 billion. In return for their willingness to contribute, the firms would share a 90 percent ownership of LTCM proportional to the amount each contributed.

While not a wildly popular solution among LTCM's investors or among its traders, it was seen as the only solution. The market panic abated, and in time LTCM's positions were liquidated, generating a modest profit for the firms that participated in the bailout.

Then, in 2008, Lehman Brothers found itself in the unfortunate position of being heavily exposed to the real estate market, being highly leveraged just when the subprime mortgage market bubble burst. While Lehman's losses mounted in a hurry, the firm took its time trying to find a buyer until it was too late. Clients saw the writing on the wall and began withdrawing funds en masse. Lehman's stock price plummeted, as did its credit rating. It was unable to acquire the necessary funding to keep itself alive, and on Saturday, September 13, the heads of the major Wall Street banks found themselves again back at the Fed's offices, this time seeking a solution for Lehman.

Hank Paulson, then secretary of the Treasury, worked together with Ben Bernanke, the chairman of the Federal Reserve, and Timothy Geithner, the president of the New York Fed, mounting a search to find a viable solution, which included finding a buyer to keep Lehman alive. As no consortium came forth and no buyer emerged, on Monday,

September 15, Lehman officially declared bankruptcy. Some of the firm was quickly sold off to Barclays Bank, and the European operations were sold to Nomura. In the end, it was the largest bankruptcy in the history of the United States.

*   *   *

Back in 1982, the heads of the major Wall Street firms arrived at the New York Fed's office that Wednesday evening. Chase continued to maintain its position that the bank had only acted in the capacity of agent, and that it had no legal obligation to cover the coupon payments. On the other side of the table, dealers continued their own line of argument—that they believed that they were dealing directly with Chase. It was a standoff, and neither side was willing to budge.

At that point, the head of Merrill Lynch fired his own shot in the direction of the Chase executives. If Chase persisted in its steadfast denial of responsibility, Merrill would have no choice but to liquidate its entire portfolio of Chase Certificates of Deposit (CDs) and Banker's Acceptances (BAs), two major holdings that comprised approximately $736 million of Merrill's Ready Assets Trust Fund, also known as the RAT by Wall Street traders.

As the contentious arguments continued, Volcker emphasized the need for "getting money on the table." It was his way of saying that it was time for petty threats and arguments to end. It was now time for someone to do something to resolve the impending crisis. The meeting, however, ended with no solution, forcing the Fed to announce publicly that it stood ready to serve as the lender of last resort and assist any bank that ran short of cash.

Despite the reassurances from the Fed, there was still a great deal of uncertainty in the market, specifically that securities firms were losing their funding. Due to that fear, many customers were yanking their money out of banks and securities dealers, which in turn further added to the liquidity crunch in the market. Clearly, some of the smaller securities firms were looking down the barrel of imminent insolvency, especially given the long amount of time it might take to resolve the legal issues surrounding the Drysdale-Chase situation.

While the lawyers and accountants were sorting it all out, people began to realize there were significant risks around their repo transactions. Aside from the potential delay in getting any sort of resolution, there was also the prospect that Drysdale's repo transactions could be classified as "collateralized loans" by a bankruptcy court. If that were the case, those securities could not be immediately liquidated, further delaying any financial restitution. The counterparties involved could be left holding bonds for an indeterminate length of time, not knowing if they really owned them or not. As a result, no securities firm was considering entering into any new repo trades, which then meant the loss of financing for many of the smaller firms. On top of that, no bank would loan them money, given the uncertainty as to whom was owed coupon interest payments by Drysdale. The trickle-down effect was rapidly becoming an unstoppable avalanche.

The situation was so dire that Gerald Corrigan, the president of the Minneapolis Federal Reserve Bank, described the government securities and repo markets as "gridlock," warning that "panic was not far off." The Federal Reserve Board agreed with Corrigan, and realized it needed to contain the situation immediately. Rumors were running rampant, rumors of an impending financial disaster, rumors that were lacking in specifics because just the hint of a market crash fueled the already blazing fire of confusion and panic. The Federal Open Market Committee was seriously worried about what other banks might fail and what further disasters were looming on the horizon. To its mind, the entire financial system was teetering on the edge.

It bears mentioning that Chase Manhattan wasn't the only bank caught in the snafu wrought by Drysdale. Manufacturer's Hanover Trust and U.S. Trust had also participated in repo transactions with Drysdale, though not to the levels of Chase. Despite their limited involvement, however, all three banks were collectively caught with a major dilemma.

On the one hand, they could refuse to pay the coupon interest payments, thus contributing to other firms' looming bankruptcies and all the financial fallout that was sure to follow. If they were later found legally responsible for the coupon payments, their potential liability for damages would be incalculable. Assuming they survived the crash that would ensue following multiple insolvencies, they could potentially be sued for inordinate amounts of money.

On the other side of the risk-reward equation was the option of paying the coupon payments to the securities dealers who were owed money by Drysdale. That would put them among the ranks of creditors who had absolutely no control over the liquidation of Drysdale's positions. In other words, by making the coupon payments, they were essentially kissing all of that money goodbye forever.

It was, in every sense, a no-win situation.

On Thursday, May 20th, Manufacturer's Hanover Trust made an official announcement at 8:45 AM, forty-five minutes before the start of trading on the New York Stock Exchange. The firm acknowledged that it had been acting as principal for Drysdale, and as such it pledged to cover its portion of the coupon interest payments. The firm had calculated the amount it owed as $29 million, and immediately made the payments. This action, while potentially draining capital from the Manufacturer's Hanover reservoir, served to further isolate Chase Manhattan within the financial community. U.S. Trust followed suit at 10:15 AM that morning, announcing that it too had been acting as principal and would pay the interest due. It was a minimal loss for U.S. Trust, but the ramifications were enormous for Chase. The bank was now the lone holdout.

The Fed's Open Market desk injected another $4 billion in liquidity into the markets later that morning to help ease the continued financial gridlock. Several of the top minds at Chase got together to discuss their options. From that meeting came the belief inside the offices at Chase Manhattan that if the bank continued to stand its ground and refused to make the payments, it could very well bring the entire government securities market to a halt. Chase wasn't willing to let that happen.

At 11:45 AM—three hours after Manufacturer's Hanover had opened the floodgate—Chase Manhattan relented, publicly announcing its intention to cover the coupon interest payments, immediately paying out a total of $178 million, including the $160 million in missed payments that were due on Monday.

On the surface, it seems almost as if the Chase executives had been swayed by their own conscience to do what they were morally, if not legally, obligated to do. The less altruistic-minded might think it was due to the negative publicity it was facing after both Manufacturer's

Hanover and U.S. Trust made the payments. But the truth is, it was a combination of both those things, and with added pressure from the Fed, which stressed the moral implications inherent in the situation. If Chase refused to pay, there was a very possibility that it could single-handedly bring down the bond market.

The total Drysdale-related loss to Chase's earnings was later amended to over $270 million, though after taxes Chase was able to net the loss down to $117 million. That number was still large enough to largely wipe out any profits the bank had shown for the quarter. However, through an agreement with Drysdale Government Securities, Chase took over all of Drysdale's assets and operations, including the right to control the liquidation.

The crisis had been contained. The Fed congratulated itself for successfully navigating the minefield that had suddenly appeared before it; the Fed had, with limited intervention, averted a financial meltdown. But weeks later, trading activity in government securities was still very thin—investors were still skittish about the potential for another disaster, and the repo market was still effectively dead in the water.

Even though the panic subsided, a host of questions remained. There was clearly a lack of regulation and oversight in the government securities market, a topic that would generate a lot of discussion over the next couple of years. Was a repo transaction a collateralized loan or a sale and a repurchase? The elusive answer to that question boiled down to one's interpretation of the transaction itself. If it was a loan offered in exchange for collateral, then it was a collateralized loan, and, in the case of a bankruptcy, the securities were tied up in the bankruptcy. If a repo was simply a buyback transaction after a sale, repo transactions could be immediately liquidated in the event of a bankruptcy. No waiting months, or even years, for claims to be settled in court. But that circled back to the question of what, exactly, a repo transaction was. On top of it all, why was accrued interest not included on repo trades?

* * *

In June 1982, probes of Drysdale were launched by both the Securities and Exchange Commission and a Senate subcommittee. Washington was being harangued by cries for more government oversight and regulation within the securities industry, especially for the government bond market. Dr. Franklin Edwards, a renowned economist at the Columbia School of Business who held amongst other distinctions a Ph.D. from Harvard, prophetically said at the time, "Deregulation of the industry and the expansion of financial services have caused the competition to heat up, and this has caused banks to push beyond their areas of expertise." That statement has proven to be increasingly true in the twenty-five-plus years since its first utterance.

Philip Loomis, who at the time was an SEC commissioner, suggested that the time had come for those who traded in government securities to register with the SEC in the same way that stockbrokers were required to do. "It might be desirable," he said of the proposed requirement.

A colleague at the SEC was not quite so demure in his assessment of the situation. "How many incidents do you need before someone says that something has to be done?" asked Stanley Sporkin, former enforcement chief at the SEC.

The Association of Primary Dealers in U.S. Government Securities, a thirty-six–member organization of primary dealers, heard the cries for reform and got to work on developing solutions that favored self-regulation as opposed to governmental intervention. Its first proposal was that repo trades should include the accrued interest, something that most market participants had favored for a very long time. The rule was adopted on June 14, 1982, and the practice was further standardized by an order from the New York Fed that dictated full-accrual pricing be applied to all repo transactions involving bonds. But despite the Association's best efforts, its goal of autonomous self-regulation never fully materialized. There was still a noticeable lack in standardization of trading practices among government securities dealers, a shortcoming that screamed for government regulation. That was the only way to ensure a level playing field in the market.

Congress got involved, and certain members planned to bring to the floor a bill that would bring all government securities under the purview of a self-regulatory organization that would be called the Public Securities Rulemaking Board, modeled after the Municipal Securities Rulemaking Board. Tom Russo, in response to the proposed bill, published an op-ed piece in the New York Times in which he decried the government's reluctance to get involved. "Unless Congress holds hearings regarding the ramifications of the Drysdale affair and does something to prevent future defaults," he wrote, "we may not be so lucky the next time around." He went on to argue vehemently against the adoption of a self-regulatory agency, and eventually helped to draft a revised bill that gave the Federal Reserve the power to regulate government securities; the Senate modified the proposal, however, to give that power to the Treasury Department because of its interest in the market.

The dominoes continued to fall on Wall Street, and more government securities dealers collapsed, with many of those insolvencies linked directly to shady practices in the repo market, a fact that echoed with the reverberations of Stanley Sporkin's earlier question. Congress decided that enough incidents had transpired to warrant its direct intervention, leading to hearings in 1985 on the risks associated with the government bond market. Those hearings led to the passage of the Government Securities Act, which was signed into law by President Ronald Reagan in 1986. The new law empowered the Secretary of the Treasury to make rules that would ensure financial stability, regulate the custody and proper use of customer securities, and restrict the use of leverage in repo transactions. The Wild West days of the unregulated government securities market had come to an end.

There was still the issue of bankruptcy as it applied to repo transactions, which hinged on the interpretation of the transactions themselves, whether they were collateralized loans or simply repurchase transactions, as the name would suggest. The implications would be immense with regard to the development and growth of the financial markets. The entirety of the short-term funding markets relied on the practice of repo transactions, and the market could not continue without clarification. The decision came down on August 17, 1982. The Federal Bankruptcy Court of New York issued its opinion that repos were a buy-and-sell transaction, meaning they were explicitly not collateralized loans. The court realized the importance of being able to quickly liquidate securities in order to facilitate order in the market, forcing Congress to amend the bankruptcy code in 1984 to exempt repo transactions from the automatic stay provisions that restricted creditors from selling off collateral in the event of bankruptcy.

As for the major players in the crisis, their fates were largely determined by the courts. Drysdale Securities Corporation, the parent company, went out of business completely the following year, ending any investigations by the SEC. Dennis Ruppert, the former treasurer and comptroller of Drysdale Securities Corporation, was issued a lifetime ban from association with securities dealers in 1985. Joseph Ossorio maintained his own innocence in any wrongdoing, but decided in the end to plead guilty to three counts of security fraud. In an impassioned speech to the judge in 1984 he said, "I voluntarily plead guilty even though I do not believe I am guilty." He too received a lifetime banishment from the securities industry and was ordered to pay $10 million in restitution to former Drysdale clients. Warren Essner of Arthur Andersen was found guilty of preparing false and misleading financial statements. In his defense, he had no viable explanation for the exclusion of the information regarding Drysdale Government Securities' capital deficit of $15.8 million at the time of the firm's founding. Arthur Andersen, for its part, was indicted on criminal charges and ordered to pay $50 million to Chase. In 2001, the same firm would come under scrutiny and eventual prosecution for its alleged deliberate attempts to obstruct justice by shredding documents related to the Enron scandal that erupted in 2001.

Which brings us to David Heuwetter, the mastermind behind one of the most spectacular financial collapses of all time. At the relatively young age of forty, he'd risen to the top of his game, only to watch his world come tumbling down around him. He admitted in court that the charges levied against him were "substantially true" and said, "I had hoped that I could make up the losses." He pled guilty to charges of fraudulently trading billions of dollars worth of securities, conspiracy, and tax fraud. He was sentenced to three years in federal prison and four years of probation, as well as 400 hours of community service. He died on August 4, 2012, at the age of 71.

* * *

Regardless of your feelings on banks, broker-dealers, and hedge funds leveraging themselves to substantially magnify their profits and losses, the fact remains that leverage is a widely used investment tool at all levels of the game. The practice has risks associated with it, and those who choose to avail themselves of it understand and accept those risks. Much of the credit—or blame, depending on your perspective—for making leverage such an easy tool goes to David Heuwetter.

The repo market itself became *the* instrument that allows the use of leverage, and it offers lending institutions a quick way out when things go sour. Without the special treatment of repo in bankruptcies, allowing the other counterparty to immediately liquidate repo transactions, there would be significantly less leverage in the markets today. Again, depending on your perspective, that reality can be looked at in two distinctly different ways. Leverage has enabled firms to make untold fortunes for themselves and their clients. It has also brought down more than its fair share of financial stalwarts, including Long Term Capital Management, Bear Stearns, Lehman Brothers, and MF Global.

But regardless of your perspective, one thing is for certain—that the Drysdale collapse, and the ensuing rules and regulations that came as a result, had a major impact on the world's financial markets. The repo market, a major cog that moves the global financial markets as a whole, was made efficient as a result of the fallout from Heuwetter's actions and Drysdale's resulting collapse.

Finally, I had the opportunity to meet the architect of Drysdale's untimely demise. I was eleven years old at the time, and David Heuwetter had hired my father, James M. Skyrm, to run Drysdale's municipal bond department. It was in December of 1977, and we were taking part in our annual tradition of my spending a day at my father's work while I was on Christmas vacation. My father introduced me to Heuwetter, talking to me as if it were an unimaginable privilege to meet a man of Heuwetter's prestige and importance in the financial world.

When asked about how I was doing in school, I distinctly remember telling Heuwetter that I was doing very well in math. He asked me some math questions; perhaps it was a test of my skills, or maybe he just wanted to humor my sixth-grade ego. Whatever his motives, he was apparently satisfied with my answers, as he offered me a summer job when I was old enough.

I never got the chance to take him up on his summer job offer. My father left Drysdale a few months later. He never explicitly told me the reasons for leaving, only saying that he didn't like what he saw. At the time, I was disappointed that I'd probably lost my chance to spend a summer or two working for and learning from the great David Heuwetter. It would have been, I have no doubt, an extremely educational experience.

Assuming Heuwetter had allowed me to start working at either age fifteen or sixteen, then I would have been at Drysdale during the summer of 1981 or 1982. In other words, I would have been there immediately prior to Drysdale's implosion or immediately following. Either way, I'm glad I wasn't a part of it.

Chapter Two

Howard Rubin and Merrill Lynch, 1987

Anybody with a semblance of a financial pulse is all too aware that the world's economy took a drastic nosedive beginning in 2007, culminating in what many pundits label as the Great Recession. While in the midst of the monetary unpleasantness, the search for the causes of the crash seemed endless. It was, on the surface, a relatively simple question to answer. The housing market, which had been on a meteoric rise for several years prior, had suddenly crashed. Property values plummeted, houses were foreclosed on, and the term "underwater" came to be used to describe mortgage loans more often than not. And terms that many outside the financial sector rarely used before—subprime and CDOs—became synonymous with all that is evil and destructive in the world.

Though subprime loans are something that everyone is pretty familiar with, few people know much of anything about the financial instrument known as the CDO, short for Collateralized Debt Obligation. And that's incredibly surprising. How is it that something that had such a major impact on our lives is barely understood by the general public?

A CDO is the ultimate creation of the bond market. At first, it was thought to be the logical extension of securitization—the next step after securitizing mortgage loans. CDOs started out as a well-intentioned way of combining pools of loans, but by the mid-2000s, however, that intention morphed as CDOs became Wall Street's way of dumping all of its unwanted securities—everything from subprime loans to high-yield securities—into something that banks could off-load to investors, generating massive underwriting fees along the way.

The investors who bought into the CDO craze were getting high rates of return up front, but all the while they were assuming a tremendous amount of risk. In essence, they thought that they had found an investment gold mine, namely a low-risk investment with a high return. And just because they were intelligent enough to understand the complex structures, they were the ones lucky enough to earn those returns.

The high returns turned out to be teaser rates, rates high enough to get investors in the door with little concern for what might happen a few years down the road. The risks could have been—*should* have been—better disclosed when the bonds were sold to investors, but no one—not even the underwriters—really understood what was going to happen when the markets turned. Perhaps it's just impossible to predict what happens to newly created securities when their market first sells off. But what isn't impossible to say, in hindsight, is that CDOs became the second wave of losses sustained by investors as a result of the asset securitization.

Securitization was supposed to be the final incarnation of consumer credit. It's best thought of as the process of combining many individual assets into one unified security. The original mortgage-backed securities (MBS) are the perfect example. Take a few hundred—or better yet, a few thousand—mortgage loans issued by a bank or savings and loan association (S&L) and combine them in one giant pool. Every investor owns a small slice of the pool. When homeowners make their principal and interest payments each month, the mortgage-backed securities owners get a little bit of principal and interest paid to them. If homeowners sell their house or refinance their loan, the MBS owner gets a little more of their principal investment back that month.

A CDO is essentially the same thing as a mortgage-backed security, except Wall Street can put more than just mortgage loans in it. The specific makeup of a CDO is not limited to any type of asset. You can put anything and everything into it, and that's the beauty of it, at least from the underwriter's perspective.

In the investment world, CDOs are looked upon as purely cash flows. As long as the underlying assets are making their monthly payments, the cash keeps flowing to the bondholders. When the cash stops flowing, as it happens when one of the underlying assets defaults, there's less money to go around and someone gets paid a little less. Depending on who owns what part of the CDO—tranches are classified as senior, junior, or equity—one or more of the investor classes gets paid less money each month.

However, there's a major difference between a traditional MBS and a CDO. With a CDO, it's not which class gets its mortgage prepayments first, but rather which class gets wiped out from defaults first. In a mortgage-backed security, it's all about whether you're getting your principal back earlier or later. In a CDO, by contrast, the concern is about getting your money back at all. Clearly, with a CDO you're playing for keeps.

In the early days of CDOs, a time period that still qualifies as very recently, most of the structures were relatively simple. The first bits of collateral placed inside of them were loans that could not go into mortgage-backed securities. Those loans included things like credit card receivables, auto loans, and mobile home loans—all loans that were very common forms of consumer credit.

Then, as the size of the CDO market exploded, the underlying assets became worse. Wall Street firms were digging around for anything they could call a loan to keep cranking out new CDO deals. CDO collateral started to include things like low-quality subprime loans. Wall Street was dumping everything it could into CDOs, including home equity loans, commercial mortgage-backed securities, low-rated corporate bonds, real estate investment trust (REIT) debt, commercial real estate loans, subprime mortgage loans, and finally, when there was nothing else left, other CDOs. All of a sudden, the collateral within the CDO became anything and everything, and most of the good assets were replaced by bad assets. The assets that got more than their fair share of coverage were the subprime mortgage loans.

Merrill Lynch was one of these underwriters. Going back to the 1980s, Merrill had tried to make a name for itself in securitization, first with a failed attempt at mortgage-backed securities trading, and then in CDOs. By the early 2000s, all of its efforts were coming together. Merrill was positioning itself as the number-one underwriter of CDOs, a status it promoted like an all-star trophy on its bedroom bookshelf. However, like other Wall Street firms, Merrill was just dumping anything and everything into its CDO deals.

But what happens when the underlying assets are distressed and the coupon interest payments are just too high for the CDO to pay each month? The results, as we shall see, are disastrous for all involved. CDOs achieved their market-destroying infamy in 2008 when they helped bring down such financial giants as Bear Stearns, Merrill Lynch, Lehman Brothers, and AIG. However, these bonds of mass destruction trace their roots back to mortgage-backed securities, which in turn trace their own roots back even further to the creation of Fannie Mae, Freddie Mac, and Ginnie Mae.

*   *   *

The first seeds of asset securitization were sewn back in 1938 with the creation of the Federal National Mortgage Association, the organization commonly referred to in financial circles as Fannie Mae. For many years, small local and community banks had nowhere to sell their loans when they needed to. Whether the sale was to make room for new loans or to sell off problem loans, there was nowhere to go for secondary market liquidity. Fannie Mae's purpose was to solve this problem by purchasing mortgage loans from banks and S&Ls, but only those loans that were government guaranteed.

Before the days of giant consumer finance companies, mortgage brokers, nationwide banking, and colossal banks, things were much different when a borrower sought a loan to buy a house. The mortgage loan process involved a community bank making mortgage loans to local customers—local people who lived in the community. The person needing a loan, or perhaps the whole family, would go to their local S&L, often referred to as a thrift, and fill out the loan application. That application was reviewed by a committee made up of well-known people in the community, and oftentimes customers did their banking with an institution specifically because of the reputation of the bank's executives. Of course, whether the applicant's loan was approved also depended on the applicant's own personal reputation.

After a few weeks of deliberation, the committee would issue its decision. Assuming the application was approved, the bank would make the loan and hold it in its loan portfolio until it was paid off, a time that wouldn't come around for many years. Deposits taken in from local banking customers provided the funds to make the loans. Taking in deposits and making loans was the core business of banks, and it was a model that worked well, to some extent.

Local bankers relied on this simple process. It meant making a loan, collecting deposits, and making the spread between the two rates. It meant that the bank would borrow money at 3 percent, make mortgage loans at 6 percent, and be on the golf course by 3:00 PM. It was a description that earned thrift managers the title of Members of the 3-6-3 Club.

But there was an important drawback to local banking. It limited the economic growth of the particular community. If there was high demand for loans in a particular area, the local bank's ability to lend money was constrained by the amount of money it had in deposits. If a bank had $1 million in deposits, it could only make somewhere between $800,000 and $900,000 in loans. That was it. If the Pacific Northwest region was booming with new industries and people needed to borrow more money, there was hardly a way to channel funds into that region from elsewhere. The constraints of the local deposit base limited the availability of credit to everyone. It was a problem that hounded the banking industry until the founding of Fannie Mae.

With Fannie Mae's creation, an entirely new financial market was born, namely a nationwide secondary market for mortgage loans issued by S&Ls. Now, when an S&L needed to free up cash to make new loans, it could turn around and sell its loans to Fannie Mae. There was still one catch, however: Fannie Mae could only buy government-insured loans.

The secondary market for mortgage loans continued to grow by leaps and bounds. In 1968, the funding of government-supported housing was spun off from Fannie and rechristened Government National Mortgage Association, or Ginnie Mae. Just two years later, Federal Home Loan Mortgage Corporation was created to perform a similar function for non-government-guaranteed loans, and became simply known as Freddie Mac. Fannie and Freddie were then spun off into shareholder-owned, quasi-government corporations.

Ginnie Mae immediately began doing business a whole new way. Instead of buying loans and issuing bonds as Fannie Mae had done, Ginnie issued pass-through certificates, which were essentially the same financial instrument that CDOs would become forty years later. The pass-through certificates represented partial ownership in a bundle of mortgage loans, and the beauty of it was that they were fully guaranteed by the federal government. As such, Ginnie Mae's pass-through certificates—later to become known simply as pass-throughs—became a major hit with investors. How could anyone not like high interest rates and government-guaranteed monthly payments of principal and interest?

Throughout the 1970s, the secondary market for mortgage loans continued to grow with the help of Fannie, Freddie, and Ginnie, and that rise was dovetailing with the growing popularity of the new concept of securitization. It created an entirely new opportunity for banks of all sizes, because they could now sell their mortgage loans to a government agency, no longer constrained by the size of their balance sheet. If a customer wanted a loan, the bank could turn around and sell it quickly and easily. Banks were suddenly able to grow far beyond their local communities and pass-through investors could own pools of loans from all across the country.

These new pass-through certificates would eventually become known as mortgage-backed securities, which seemed to be the perfect investment. They offered AAA-rated credit and relatively high returns on an asset that was, for all intents and purposes, the most important bill the average consumer paid every month. What could possibly go wrong?

For starters, there are problems inherent in the mortgage-backed securities themselves. The bonds are subject to more than just the interest rate fluctuations that affect other bonds. Mortgage-backed securities have a layer of risk known as "prepayments." When interest rates fall, homeowners have the right to refinance their mortgage loans, and the bondholders end up with their investment getting paid back early. It might seem good to get back your investment money back early, but it means that just when you think you have a good investment at a high interest rate, it doesn't last for long.

Then, when interest rates rise, the homeowner enjoys a nice loan locked in at a relatively low rate, so there's little reason to pay it off. The mortgage-backed security owner gets locked in at a relatively lower interest rate too, just at a time when homeowners are paying off their loans a little slower. So no matter where interest rates go, MBS bondholders are in a lose-lose situation. It was this risk inherent in prepayments that has always dogged the MBS market.

* * *

In 1977, the bond market for mortgage-backed securities changed forever when a bond trader at Salomon Brothers came up with what was, at the time, a revolutionary idea. Robert Dall, together with his deputy Lewis Ranieri, set up the first trading desk at a major investment bank dedicated exclusively to the buying and selling of mortgage bonds. Dall realized that mortgage-backed securities—unlike many other bonds—were paying extremely good rates of return. And while owning a single mortgage loan didn't generate the kind of interest that wowed investors, owning thousands of mortgages pooled together and backed by the government was getting pretty interesting. They saw this as an idea that just could not fail. As the MBS market was growing exponentially, Salomon Brothers was going to be at the forefront of it.

That same year, Congress passed a new law that would serve as the metaphorical pebble in the pond sending massive waves through the financial system. That law was the Community Reinvestment Act (CRA), and it was optimistically expected to foster new housing opportunities for low-income Americans. Through both federal incentives and oversight, the CRA sought to encourage banks to lend money in low-income neighborhoods and allow more people to achieve the dream of homeownership. Though not requiring banks to violate what were amorphously termed "safe and sound banking procedures," the subtext of the act was that banks needed to make loans to less-qualified individuals or face restrictions placed on them by the government.

At the time, S&Ls were facing the incredible changes that gripped the country from 1979 through 1982 with Paul Volcker's inflation-fighting crusade. S&Ls across the United States were being hit hard from loans they'd made before inflation got out of control and interest rates skyrocketed. Loans made back in the early 1970s carried interest rates far lower than where banks could borrow funds, which meant that they were losing money. Representative for thrifts everywhere lobbied Congress for relief, which came in the form of two separate acts: The Depository Institutions Deregulation and Monetary Control Act of 1980 and The Garn-St. Germain Depository Institutions Act of 1982.

The new laws gave S&Ls a great deal of freedoms that had been denied to them before the law's enactment, chief amongst them the ability to charge whatever interest rate they wanted. That freedom would serve to completely deregulate the savings and loan industry, meaning that it was no longer subject to absolute government oversight and control—namely the 3 percent savings deposit rates. It also created the adjustable-rate mortgage, which is a loan that carried an interest rate that fluctuated with the bond market.

But perhaps no single congressional act played a bigger part in the explosion of the mortgage industry than the Economic Recovery Tax Act of 1981 (ERTA), also commonly referred to as the Reagan tax cuts. The tax cuts were primarily aimed at reducing the taxes for individual Americans across all tax brackets. By reducing the amount Americans of all walks of life paid in taxes, the hope was that the extra money would encourage both savings and spending. There was another provision in the law that would change the MBS market forever— thrifts could offset any losses they booked by selling mortgage loans against taxes paid as much as ten years earlier. In other words, the federal government was paying thrifts to sell their loans. What the new laws meant for the traders on the MBS desk at Salomon Brothers was that they were going to have even more mortgages to buy and sell.

Salomon, at the time, was the only game in town. It faced a tiny level of competition from the fledgling mortgage desk at First Boston, but that competition was inconsequential, at least for a while. S&Ls were desperate to off-load their old mortgage loans and buy new ones to take advantage of the changes in the tax code, so business started rolling in at Salomon Brothers. Salomon Brothers effectively became the new secondary market for mortgage loans.

Thrift managers weren't necessarily the most financially astute players in the game. They didn't even know the value of their own mortgage loans, as market prices were essentially invisible. You have to remember that this was in the time before Bloomberg terminals that told you a security's exact price at any given moment. The thrift managers had no idea what price their loans should actually be trading at.

In their view, what they got for selling their mortgage loans was inconsequential, so long as it generated a tax loss—essentially creating new revenue for the bank. And the best way to ensure the highest levels of new revenue was in numbers. Selling as many loans as possible meant higher write-offs—which created a selling frenzy with the massive unloading of mortgage loans, especially the ones that were written years earlier at lower interest rates. The tax breaks were the financial savior of the thrifts, but also created a whole new industry on Wall Street.

During that decade, the mortgage desk at Salomon Brothers was *the* place to work on Wall Street. The business was fast-paced and exciting and, most importantly for those in the business, it was the financial-industry equivalent of a gold mine. Salaries for the top traders were surpassing unheard of levels, but it wasn't all from buying and selling bonds of bonds for the sake of customers. Mortgage-backed securities were the most mathematically complicated financial products traded on Wall Street. The traders who worked on Wall Street themselves underwent a tremendous makeover. Whereas in the decades prior to the 1980s the average trader was typically smart but not brilliant, and often more street-smart than book-smart, the game changed dramatically with the birth of mortgage-backed securities.

PhD graduates who had always seen themselves as lifelong researchers suddenly saw the money their counterparts on Wall Street were making as they accepted jobs in trading. By their logic, they were smarter than the average trader, so why not get that all that easy money too? The mortgage-bond industry was a quantitative game that relied on numbers, and those who had the finesse with complex mathematical equations had an advantage. All of a sudden, if you didn't have either MBA or PhD after your name, you might as well resign yourself to life in the mailroom if you wanted to be near an investment bank's trading floor.

Salomon Brothers became the equivalent of a Wall Street nursery school, the place where every mortgage bond trader got his start and learned the craft. With the rapid expansion in the market, the need for well-trained traders was growing around the Street. All the major players on Wall Street were scrambling to get their piece of the mortgage bond pie: Shearson Lehman, Morgan Stanley, Kidder Peabody, Goldman Sachs, First Boston, and Merrill Lynch. Every major investment bank wanted to build up its own mortgage desk seemingly overnight, and traders were needed to staff those desks. Salomon alumni went on to run the mortgage desks all over New York, including Steve Baum, who would leave for Kidder Peabody to run that firm's desk, and Mike Mortara, who would leave for Goldman Sachs to do the same.

One of the more senior traders, Andy Stone, received a call from Merrill Lynch in yet another rush by the new players to get the best of the best from Salomon. Merrill was offering to double his pay—literally pay him twice the already outrageous amount he was making at Salomon Brothers—and Stone declined, citing the fact that he was happy where he was. Merrill persisted, asking what it would take to get him to leave. Stone, perhaps just to see how far he could really push it, said that Merrill would have to *quadruple* his current paycheck. The firm didn't hesitate in offering to do so. Stone, however, stayed with Salomon Brothers for the time, despite the lucrative offer.

With the frequent turnover at Salomon Brothers, as traders left for more lucrative positions or more authoritative positions, there were frequently new faces on the mortgage bond trading desk. In 1982, one of those new faces belonged to a former Las Vegas card shark-turned-investment banker by the name of Howard Rubin.

*   *   *

Howard Rubin took what might best be called a circuitous route to Wall Street. He graduated with a bachelor of science in chemical engineering from Lafayette College in 1977, though he never really put the specifics of that degree to use in his professional life. After college, according to his own recollections, he read three books on counting cards, then decided that he'd armed himself with enough knowledge to beat the house in Las Vegas. He had a keen mind for numbers, and Vegas seemed like an easy way for him to make a lot of money.

The thing about blackjack is that it's the one major table game in Las Vegas that's not independent of previous events. The roulette wheel or the craps table, for instance, offer the same statistical chance every time; the roulette wheel has an equal chance of landing on any number every time, and the dice at the craps table have the same statistical chance of coming up with every combination on every roll. But blackjack is different. Because there are a set number of cards in the dealer's shoe, the cards that appear in the first hands affect the probability of cards appearing in later hands.

For example, if the dealer is sliding cards out for the first hand and three aces appear, immediately the number of aces in the deck is reduced by three, so the chances of an ace coming up on the next hand are dramatically reduced. Of course, those odds are also influenced by the number of card decks contained in the dealer's shoe, but the idea still holds. Regardless of the number of decks, the number of specific cards—like aces, for example—is finite, and the chances of getting a particular card on a particular deal vary with every successive hand played.

It's a complicated practice to count cards, and most gamblers will employ some method to help them remember what cards have been played. But not Rubin. He didn't need gimmicks or tricks to count cards; he had a brain that could retain information over the course of a night, so he could recall what cards had already been played at any given moment. In fact, he was so good that the local casino authorities began to take notice. Even though they couldn't prove it, they were sure he was guilty of something. And even though card counting itself isn't specifically illegal, casinos do everything in their power to prevent it. Tactics can be as simple as positioning someone next to the suspected card counter to engage him in conversation and distract him, or assigning a high-speed dealer to the table as a way of confusing him. In the case of Rubin, those tactics didn't work, and casinos simply blacklisted him. Every casino in Las Vegas had a photo of Rubin, and every casino was on the lookout for him. He was barred from entering any of them, forcing Rubin to don disguises just to gain access to play blackjack.

After two years of blackjack and all the difficulties that went along with it, Rubin grew bored and put in an application to Harvard Business School. He was accepted, and graduated with his MBA in 1982. He went directly from Harvard's hallowed halls to the money tree of the mortgage desk at Salomon Brothers; one of the gems of the firm's newest class of bond traders.

Rubin's first day on the trading floor reminded him immediately of everything he'd loved about the casino floor in Vegas. This was excitement. This was money won and lost. This was where he belonged. He was a Salomon Brothers kind of guy.

Lewis Ranieri—by now known as one of the true founders of the mortgage-backed securities industry—once called Rubin "the most innately talented young trader I have ever seen." In his first year on the desk at Salomon Brothers, Rubin made over $25 million for the firm; despite that, he was paid the standard $90,000 that every other trader with his experience was paid. The following year, he banked over $30 million for Salomon Brothers; his compensation was yet again a standardized amount, this time $175,000.

Though his compensation might have seemed proportionally low, Rubin was still learning from Ranieri about the ebb and flow of mortgage bonds. Whereas most traders would bail out of a trade when the market was on a downward spiral throughout the day, Ranieri saw it as a golden opportunity to acquire more of the same bonds at a lower price. He knew that eventually the market would come back, especially if he was the one out there buying. Ranieri, being the "center of the universe" of mortgage-bond trading, had enough confidence in his strategies to hold the course, and Rubin picked up on those same ideas.

But there was more to Rubin's trading philosophy than just hanging on for the ride. Remember that Rubin was a numbers guy, and he knew that the numbers would give up the secrets that would make him rich. In studying the preexisting pricing models for mortgages, Rubin noticed a major problem. The data on prepayments was not particularly accurate for many bonds because the numbers were based on national averages. When the numbers were broken down by region, however, the prices reflected a much more accurate picture of the true state of the market.

With his revised data, Rubin scoured the market for mortgage-backed securities that were concentrated in regions of the country that typically had slower or faster prepayment speeds. While the rest of the market was still pricing bonds off of the national averages, Rubin was using the regional prepayment projections and making a killing in the market.

It was a sound strategy that, while always a little risky, made a lot of money for Salomon Brothers. However, the longer he stayed there, the more Rubin realized that he was being paid a miniscule fraction of the money he was bringing in. It struck him as profoundly unfair. And perhaps it was that feeling that was running through his brain when Merrill Lynch came calling, as a relative latecomer to the mortgage-backed securities game. Andy Stone had already rebuffed the firm's offer to quadruple his salary, Rubin, too, turned down the first offer that Merrill made. But as it turned out, Rubin wasn't quite so attached to the firm that had launched his career as Stone had been.

Of course, the fact that he was offered more than *five times* his current paycheck might have had something to do with his change of heart. When Merrill Lynch offered Rubin $1 million guaranteed annually for three years plus a percentage of his trading profits, he didn't think twice. Howard Rubin was now a Merrill Lynch kind of guy.

*   *   *

Charles Merrill was born in 1885 in the tiny town of Green Cove Springs, Florida, on the banks of the St. Johns River. His father was a physician, his mother a housewife. His father also owned a local drugstore, where young Charles worked part-time. Perhaps his greatest contribution to the family's financial well-being came in the form of increased milkshake sales that came when he manned the sales counter. Merrill's milkshakes began to grow in popularity as soon as Charles started adding grain alcohol to the concoction, and Merrill was also smart enough to raise the price to go along with the increased popularity. Merrill worked there all the while when he attended school at a college preparatory academy run by nearby John B. Stetson University, and his final year of high school was spent at the Worcester Academy, in Worcester, Massachusetts.

Following graduation, he went on to Amherst College for two years, but was forced to drop out because his family could no longer afford the school's tuition. Merrill spent two more years at the University of Michigan Law School, but never matriculated. From there, he spent a season playing semipro baseball and followed that up with a one-year stint as a writer for the *Tropical Sun*, a newspaper based in West Palm Beach. Merrill would later call his time as a reporter the "best training [he] ever had" because he "learned human nature."

Charles Merrill, despite traveling what many might have considered a rudderless course up until this point, seemed to have found stability in the person of a young woman whom he'd met while still a student at Amherst. She'd agreed to marry Merrill, and as a perk, her father offered him a job as an office boy at his textile firm in New York. He stayed on the job for two years, but quickly found out that he wasn't ready to settle down as a husband just yet. He preferred carousing with the boys around town, especially with a young man he'd met at the 23rd Street YMCA, a graduate of Johns Hopkins University by the name of Edmund Lynch.

Merrill called off his engagement and left the textiles firm, feeling it too odd working for the man who would no longer be his future father-in-law. He took a job as the only salesman in the bond department at George H. Burr & Company, and when he was authorized to hire another man to work alongside him, he called on his friend Edmund Lynch to join him. Together the pair would go on to revolutionize the way that stocks and bonds were sold on Wall Street.

By 1914, Merrill was driven to start his own firm, which he opened at 7 Wall Street in January of that year. His friend Lynch joined him in July, and Merrill, Lynch & Co. was born. The new firm staked its future on a brand new concept in retail services, the chain store. Most investors saw chains as a passing fad at best, figuring that the business of independent ownership was both the past and the future. Merrill felt differently, however. He truly believed that the chain store would be the future of American retailing. It was a prophetic feeling that proved to be both true and wildly lucrative for Merrill. He would eventually take the same concepts that made the chain store such a profitable enterprise and apply it to investing. "We must bring Wall Street to Main Street," he famously said, "And we must use the efficient, mass-merchandising methods of the chain store to do it."

Prior to 1920, Wall Street was the very closed environs for only the wealthiest Americans. Regular citizens had no role in the goings-on of the Financial District, and they had no place there. The general public typically kept its savings in a local bank. There were no 401(k) programs or IRAs, nor were there any discount brokers hawking investment services. During World War I, the federal government issued Liberty Bonds as a way of financing the war effort, and those bonds were mostly paid off by the early 1920s. Suddenly, the average American— those who had bought Liberty Bonds—had some extra money in their savings accounts, money they could then invest in the stock market.

And Merrill, Lynch & Co. was the firm that brought the stock market to the masses. The firm's brokers were on a fixed salary, with no sales commissions or bonuses whatsoever. Merrill's feeling was that such a system eliminated the impression that the firm's brokers were selling simply for the sake of generating sales commissions. By cutting out those commissions, Merrill hoped to show that his firm had the investor's individual best interests in mind at all times. And all of those individual investors received identical treatment, regardless of their status as big or small. Everyone was welcome at Merrill, Lynch & Co.

After the stock market crash of 1929, Merrill, Lynch & Co. transferred its brokerage operation to E. A. Pierce & Co., the nation's largest brokerage firm at the time. But when the retail investment business collapsed while the Great Depression gripped the country, E. A. Pierce & Co. was teetering on the edge of bankruptcy by 1939. Charles Merrill resumed his position at the head of the firm and once again took the reins of the newly formed Merrill, Lynch & Pierce in 1940. A year later, the firm merged with Fenner & Beane, a commodities broker that had also lost a substantial amount during the Great Depression, marking the beginning of Merrill's drive to truly diversify the firm's offerings.

The consumer investing business boomed following the years after World War II, and Merrill stockbrokers became known as account executives, a term that is still widely used today in the industry. Charles Merrill died in 1956, leaving control of the firm to Donald Regan, a man who would go on to be the Secretary of the Treasury under President Ronald Reagan. Under Regan's leadership, the firm with the ever-growing name of Merrill, Lynch, Pierce, Fenner & Beane sought to further expand its operations. But despite his best efforts, Regan struggled to elevate the retail-based Merrill Lynch's name to the same levels as the major New York investment banks like Morgan Stanley or Goldman Sachs.

In 1971, however, Merrill Lynch was not going to remain quiet by letting other Wall Street firms pass it by, and the company went public in June, raising the much-needed capital to expand its business. Then, in 1977, Merrill Lynch launched what *Fortune* magazine hailed as "the most important financial innovation in years," the Cash Management Account (CMA). The Merrill Lynch CMA was the first account to allow customers to sweep cash into a money market mutual fund, in addition to offering both check-writing capabilities and a credit card. Through other mergers and acquisitions, Merrill Lynch gained formidable footholds in the government and corporate bond markets, and expanded its own footprint into over forty international locations. By 1980, Merrill was one of the biggest of the big boys on Wall Street.

The Merrill Lynch business model was *the* model of the 1980s. It was a financial advisor, an investment bank, a retail brokerage, a money market fund manager, and a major trading house. And all of that was under one roof. The firm had it all. All that is, except for a major presence in the mortgage bond market, being noticeable absent from the über-lucrative market developing right before its eyes. Securitization—the financial wave of the future in investing—was not a part of Merrill's founding ideals, but the boys down the street at Salomon Brothers were making a lot of money in it. Maybe it was time to modify those founding principles and get on the mortgage-backed train before it was too late. The best way to jump-start that business was by hiring a proven winner.

The best place to poach a proven winner in the bond market was from the proving grounds at Salomon Brothers, and that's where the Merrill team started its search. When the firm couldn't lure Andy Stone away with the promise of vast riches, they ended up with Ron Dipasquale, a man described as a "third-string mortgage trader" who'd been on the bond desk at Salomon Brothers admittedly for only a short period of time. So Merrill called and offered him a two-year contract that guaranteed him $1 million a year as the new head of mortgage trading at Merrill Lynch.

And while Dipasquale would go on to become an accomplished trader years later, that time was not 1984. He was far too inexperienced to be anything approaching a head trader, but Merrill Lynch discovered that fact a little too late. Soon after arriving on Merrill's trading floor, they took Dipasquale off the trading desk and reassigned him to a back-office job. Since he'd already signed a two-year contract, as such, Dipasquale suddenly became the only back-office Wall Street employee to be banking a cool million annually. When his two years had elapsed, Merrill simply let him go and he returned to his old stomping grounds at Salomon Brothers, where upon his arrival he received a standing ovation from a group of assembled traders.

Not to be put off, Merrill went after another hotshot at Salomon Brothers, this time Howard Rubin. Rubin demurred on the first pass, saying that he "couldn't have been happier" at Salomon Brothers, where he "felt comfortable." But the money was just too much to pass up and, on the second pass, he took the bait in 1985. It was a move that everyone involved would come to regret.

* * *

As much as the concept of mortgage-backed securities became a commercially successful investment and a huge innovation in the world of high finance, derivatives on mortgage-backed securities was yet another quantum leap forward. The underlying problem with mortgage-backed securities was that investors were never sure when they were getting the principal payments paid back—the issue that dogged mortgage-backed securities for years. So Wall Street began creating new securities in an attempt to address this very issue.

One of these creations was the stripping of mortgage-backed securities into two components—the interest payments and the principal payments—and selling them as two distinct individual securities. It was pretty similar to other types of mortgage derivatives, except the whole bond was just completely split down the middle. Of course, it's the investor's choice as to which side of the coin to bet. If the investor thinks that interest rates are going up and the mortgage loans are going to pay off over a longer to period of time, it's best to go with the interest portion, or IO (interest only). Getting more interest payments over a longer period of time is better than getting fewer of them over a shorter period of time. Alternatively, if investors feel interest rates are going to fall, they'll go for the principal component, or the PO (principal only). Getting paid back quicker on your loan is better than waiting longer to get paid back.

Suddenly a new level of complexity had been added to the fledging market, making the true risks of these new inventions even harder to understand. The two halves (IOs and POs) put together somewhat balanced out the price of mortgage-backed securities in a changing market. But when investors were allowed to choose which side of the mortgage loans they wanted to own, the creations became extremely sensitive to changes in interest rates. It was uncharted territory, and traders had no way to predict how the market would react when there were big market moves.

At the same time, Wall Street firms everywhere were looking to get into this highly profitable market by hiring young and aggressive new traders. What many old-line Wall Street firms did not know yet was that it was a recipe for disaster. They were sitting in the back seat of a speeding car and didn't even know how fast they were going.

* * *

There had been a major rally in the bond market at the end of 1986 that continued into 1987, a rally that culminated with a major sell-off in April 1987. During an afternoon in late March of that year, Howard Rubin was having lunch with a major player in the mortgage bond market, Ernie Fleischer of Franklin Savings and Loan, based in Ottawa, Kansas. Fleischer was always partial to doing business with Merrill, as his son worked on the Merrill trading desk. Rubin explained the then-new concept of IOs and POs to Fleischer, and Fleischer immediately saw a valuable opportunity; feeling that the bond market was on the edge and about to decline, he said he would take $500 million of IOs from Rubin right then and there. No use waiting until they got back to their offices to finalize the deal; Rubin agreed, and the trade was done.

This was not an uncommon practice on Wall Street before the dawn of the Internet, smartphones, and instant online trading. Traders meeting at bars after work would occasionally argue over a bond's price or the state of the market. One trader would invariably agree to sell a bond to the other. Oftentimes these deals were made after more than just a single drink, and the details were inevitably fuzzy for one of the parties involved. But no matter how vague the memory of the deal, the traders always stood up to what they'd agreed to, no matter how under the influence they might have been at the time. It was part of the business; traders were only as good as their reputation. The industry had its own code that its members lived by: "My word is my bond." Of course, agreeing to buy and sell bonds in bars late at night after several rounds of drinks does not quite pass compliance procedures these days. But Rubin honored his lunchtime trade with Fleischer and found himself short $500 million IOs, the bonds he sold Fleischer, in a market on the edge of a decline.

Rubin knew that he was going to have a rough time with the bonds. When he got back to his desk, he made it a point to look around the office and get the attention of his coworkers. When he had the spotlight, he pantomimed fastening a seatbelt. As a coworker of his recalled, "Howie was clearly expecting a wild ride."

For Rubin, the next step depended on how he was going to acquire the IOs to deliver to Fleischer. Acquiring a $500 million block of regular MBS bonds was easy enough; the interdealer brokers had liquid markets, and $500 million—though a large trade at the time—could easily be obtained. It got a little more complicated getting the IO portion to deliver to Fleischer. Despite the fact that there was a market for trading IOs, getting a whole block of $500 million was slightly more difficult. The hard way was to work the markets and accumulate a $500 million block of IOs, then deliver them to Fleischer. That might take some time and move the IO market against him.

The easier way was to buy $500 million worth of MBS bonds and strip them into the separate IO and PO components, then deliver the IO portion to Fleischer. And that is exactly what Rubin did. Because he'd already presold the IO component, he wasn't worried about that part. But there was one downside to his method: it left Rubin long $500 million in POs.

The major issue associated with being so heavily invested in a single block of POs is the fact that PO prices decline very quickly when the bond market dips. As interest rates go up, it is the IO components that investors want, getting paid interest payments over a longer period of time and all. POs naturally became much harder to sell in a falling market, declining in value even faster than the mortgage-backed securities themselves.

Once he'd split the mortgage-backed securities into the IO and PO components, Rubin immediately input the PO position into Merrill's trading system, which was called MAST. However, MAST was unable to calculate the actual interest-rate sensitivity and prices of PO positions, so the newly formed Merrill Lynch MBS desk maintained a Lotus spreadsheet that tracked those positions. That spreadsheet calculated the actual interest-rate risk and the mark-to-market prices of the traders' positions, but that calculation was based on data that the traders input themselves.

And then, just after Rubin's sale in March came the massive sell-off at the beginning of April. Interest rates skyrocketed, and MBS prices plummeted. There was panic selling in the mortgage bond market; Rubin had just accumulated the largest trading position ever in his life, just when the market went into free fall.

Now Rubin was stuck. Even though he had the foresight to add a little cushion into the price of the bonds that he sold at lunch, he hadn't factored in enough to cover the kind of major sell-off that was happening. Every time he looked at his PO position, it was declining even faster than the rest of the bond market. The very terms IOs and POs had become synonymous with risk.

Rubin turned to his sales force at Merrill, urging the salesmen to unload his POs on their unsuspecting clients. He then got on Merrill's internal intercom system—what was called the "hoot and holler," or oftentimes just "the hoot"—and described the bonds that he had for sale, closing with the words that they were now "free to trade." He expected that his phone would soon be ringing nonstop with orders from the Merrill sales force, which would easily sell off the position piece by piece.

The image he cut was reminiscent of a teenage girl waiting by the phone on prom night, hoping against all odds for that last-minute date. But just like it never did for that young schoolgirl, the phone never rang for Rubin. There was no interest from the sales force.

It was a rude awakening of sorts for Rubin, as it stood in stark contrast to what he was accustomed to. During his days at Salomon Brothers, that had been standard practice. Stuck with a bad trading position? Get the salesmen to sell it to their customers and minimize your loss. The salesmen at Salomon could sell anything in the mortgage market because they had all the right connections—they spoke to the whole market. A good Salomon bond salesman could even sell a bond to a customer who didn't want it in the first place.

But, as Rubin found out, Merrill Lynch wasn't Salomon Brothers. The salesmen just didn't have the experience and connections as their brethren at other firms. Being new to the mortgage business, they just couldn't unload Rubin's POs on *their* unsuspecting customers. The bond market continued to decline, and Rubin found himself facing a loss that was now too large to admit and seemingly too large to sell and take the loss.

While it might seem completely foreign today, traders up until the 1990s typically handwrote trade tickets; individual pieces of paper served as tickets for specific orders to buy and sell, with multiple sheets of paper for each trade ticket. As the trader wrote the order on the top copy, one colored carbon copy sheet underneath went to the back office, another sheet underneath was for the settlement group, etc. In many cases, however, the tickets sat on a trader's desk for hours before being picked up. Sometimes it was because an ops clerk didn't get to the desk to pick it up; other times it was due to a trader waiting for final details of the trade before submitting the order. And in some instances it was simply a matter of trying to hide a bad trade.

In the event a trader bought some bonds only to watch the price of the bonds decline, it wasn't uncommon for him to wait until the price recovered before passing the trade ticket off to the back office. Sometimes sitting on the trade meant waiting for hours; at it could even mean waiting a couple of days. That little bit of subterfuge came to be known as sticking it in your drawer, and the phrase was a common way of describing risk management shortcomings on Wall Street at the time. And it's exactly what Howard Rubin did with his PO bonds. He figuratively stuck them in his drawer and kept his mouth shut about it.

The thing about any transaction that involves a buyer and seller, especially in the bond market, is that somebody is going to come out ahead. And when that person comes out as far ahead as Ernie Fleischer in the days following his trade, he typically likes to tell people about it. By the time Fleischer had gotten back to Kansas, he was already up $10 million on his trade, and he was crowing about it to anyone who would listen.

It didn't take long for Wall Street to figure out where those bonds had originated, because Rubin had to register the transaction with the Securities and Exchange Commission when he split off the IO portion from the PO part. From that, other traders could tell that Rubin had purchased $500 million in mortgage-backed securities, and that he'd split them into IO and PO components, but that registration would not specify which part he had kept for himself, if any. Luckily for all those watching the market, much of that information could be obtained through market chatter and rumors, so it was pretty well assumed that Fleischer had bought the IO part—especially since he was still talking about how much he had made on the trade.

That left Rubin with the POs, and the question still remained: Had he sold them in the market? Or were they tucked away somewhere at Merrill? It was just a matter of time before the market figured out that Rubin was sitting on a big pile of POs, and that those bonds were losing value rapidly.

There was an intense rivalry among the Wall Street traders who had once worked at Salomon Brothers and the traders still at the firm. Mike Mortara was at Goldman Sachs and Rubin was at Merrill, and they—together with the boys on the mortgage desk at Salomon Brothers—played a never-ending game of one-upmanship as they tried to outdo one another in trades. Rubin, in fact, wouldn't leave his desk for the night unless he knew for certain that the traders on the mortgage desk at Salomon Brothers had gone home, so as not to miss out on any trade that might occur in the market.

The boys at Salomon Brothers—still the true legends in the game—saw the SEC report and decided to have a little fun and a little gain, both at the expense of Rubin, who had once been their golden-boy protégé. They weren't above playing the same game as their former colleagues. Upon seeing the SEC report, they thought about the trade and liked it, prompting them to buy $250 million worth of MBS, which they then split into the IO and PO components, just like Rubin had done.

However, with the bond market in free fall, they kept the IO portion, which was appreciating in value very quickly, and unloaded the PO pieces on *their* unsuspecting client base. The value of good salesmen cannot be underappreciated in these situations. Conversations with clients that include comments like, "They're about to bounce, just you wait and see," are typical in such scenarios, when a salesmen are pedaling a distressed security, all the while hiding their own ulterior motives. The Salomon traders were able to quickly sell the PO securities that were falling in value, which allowed them to get into the good part of the trade, keeping the IOs for themselves.

Salomon's entry into the market accomplished a few things, none of them particularly good for Rubin. For one, the trade was making Salomon a lot of money. Interest rates continued to rise, so the market was expecting homeowners to hold on to their loans and make fewer prepayments. Salomon was holding the IO part of the bonds, so the bonds would be paying interest payments for a longer period of time. Rubin, on the other hand, had the principal payments, which were expected to get paid back slower and over a longer period of time, which is not really very appealing to anyone, especially anyone on Wall Street.

More importantly, however, at least for Rubin, it meant that there were now fewer interested buyers of POs in the marketplace. When Salomon's salesmen unloaded $250 million worth of PO bonds, Rubin still had twice that amount, and his field of unassuming customers was significantly reduced. There was just nobody left around the market to purchase what he owned. Even worse, it was common knowledge around the Street that Rubin was up a very particular creek without any sort of way to move.

It was at that time that Rubin did something completely contrary to what most traders would do. So contrary, in fact, that it could have worked. It was a strategy he'd learned from Lew Ranieri at Salomon Brothers: When the price of your bonds goes down, just buy more. The market will come back, and you'll have that much more in profit when it does. Rubin was a Ranieri disciple, and that philosophy was ingrained in him. He called up Salomon and bought more POs from the firm. That purchase upped his position to almost $900 million in the principal portion of mortgage bonds, an amount that was far beyond any trading limits imposed on him by Merrill. That massive buy helped to stabilize the mortgage market, and prices ended their free fall, at least for the time being.

Rather than sell and cut his losses, however, Rubin went for broke. He then bought another $800 million more in POs, hoping to offset the losses he'd already sustained and maybe come out of the whole mess with a nice profit. He was banking on a rally, as that was now the *only* way out of the hole he was in. But then the market resumed its fall, and Howard Rubin was finished.

*   *   *

It was, in the end, the largest single loss in Wall Street history up to that point. On Thursday, April 30, 1987, Merrill Lynch announced a trading loss of $250 million in mortgage-backed securities, trades that had resulted from what it termed "significant unauthorized activity." Rubin was said to have purchased a large amount of MBS far in excess of his trading limits without fully reporting the purchase to his bosses at Merrill. Rumors of the alleged loss had been circulating around Wall Street for weeks; those rumors were confirmed by the announcement. The Friday before, Rubin was suspended from his job. After seeing Rubin holed up in a conference room with the head trader, one trader walked by Rubin's desk and saw him packing up a big brown leather suitcase. The trader asked him, "Are you going down to D.C.?" Rubin's response was, "Not exactly."

"Not exactly" was right. Rubin was fired altogether the following Tuesday. Merrill's stock price dropped $2.625 over the course of the week. But the news got worse before it got better.

Merrill, in what is considered a major error in crisis management, continued to hold on to the losing positions. The loss, which was initially just $250 million, was compounded when Merrill decided to hold on to it. When Merrill finally unloaded every last PO it owned, the losses totaled $377 million, over $100 million more than what brought down Drysdale Securities. The total came painfully close to erasing Merrill's entire profit for the entire year before. Soon after, a second Merrill trader was fired for his failure to disclose a $10 million loss, an amount that seems like a somewhat negligible amount when compared to Rubin's financial debacle.

Merrill Lynch chose not to pursue legal action against its rogue trader, though it never gave a reason why. Merrill executives accused

Rubin of hiding his trading trades in his desk drawer, and "hiding tickets in the drawer" became a joke—and a fear—around Wall Street for years to come.

It was a charge that Rubin himself always denied. He would later say that Merrill's management didn't want to publicly admit that its trading systems couldn't properly price mortgage-backed securities, and that Rubin's supervisors didn't know what was happening in his trading account. Did Rubin actually hide the tickets for the PO trade in his drawer? The answer is no. However, for weeks after Rubin left, traders at Merrill were finding other trade tickets neatly tucked away.

What was perhaps most shocking at Merrill Lynch was the speed with which the trading losses mounted. Merrill had made its living by being slow and steady, generating sales commissions from a retail, commission-based business. High risk wasn't part of the business plan. Nor was secrecy, for that matter, and that was another issue associated with the loss that shocked the financial world. Merrill Lynch, after all, first published an annual report in 1941 purely in response to a $308,000 loss: "During the nine months of operations in 1940, we ended up with a loss of $308,000. Mr. Merrill decided that our customers were entitled to know how we had fared, so we published our First Annual Report," wrote the division director in charge of sales at the time.

The whole Rubin incident called into question how Merrill Lynch was managing its risks, especially in terms of the firm's supervision of its bond traders. The incident also highlighted the firm's lapse in judgment. One mortgage trader at another firm said of the loss Merrill sustained, "The size is incredible. It's hard to understand how management could have let it get so big." Following Rubin's firing, the firm completely overhauled its risk management systems and controls. Then it reorganized its trading operations. In the end, the firm's management realized the downside dangers inherent in allowing traders to make bets on behalf of the firm—proprietary trading. Management also learned that large positions in mortgage-backed securities could single-handedly jeopardize the well-being of its firm. Going forward, it was decided that the firm would get back to the roots established by Charles Merrill—the policy of distributing securities to its customers.

On a more global scale, the Rubin debacle illustrated very clearly to the rest of the financial world how complex and risky mortgage derivatives could be. Other banks, asset managers, and investors began to take note. Despite the lure of what seemed like easy money on the surface, mortgage-backed securities and all their variants were clearly much riskier than they appeared. But that didn't stop that market from expanding and, in more than one case, exploding.

In 1992, J. P. Morgan & Company announced a $50 million loss, all of it in MBS derivative positions. Two years after that, in 1994, Askin Capital Management collapsed altogether as a result of a $600 million loss in MBS derivatives in both IO and PO securities.

The mortgage market wasn't very kind to Ernie Fleischer during the ensuing years either. As an executive and part owner of Franklin Savings & Loan, he was hung up in the S&L crisis that swept through the country from the late 1980s into the early 1990s, a crisis that many critics blamed on banking deregulation. During that period, the Federal Deposit Insurance Corporation (FDIC) took over $400 billion worth of S&Ls that had collapsed. The FDIC subsequently liquidated its assets, costing taxpayers $341 billion in government aid. Franklin Savings collapsed in February 1990 during the peak of the crisis.

* * *

Immediately after the Rubin loss and the resulting reforms, Merrill Lynch seemed back on track and headed in the right direction. Unfortunately, however, it was a lesson that Merrill Lynch didn't learn well enough. Years later, exposure to risky CDO securities—the next stage in securitization following mortgage-backed securities—would end up sinking Merrill Lynch once and for all, and force its sale to Bank of America in September 2008.

As the first leg of the crisis hit in August 2007, word began to leak out that investment banks such as Bear Stearns and Merrill Lynch were trying to liquidate their CDO positions, but they were still stuck with incredible amounts of them on their books. In October 2007, Merrill Lynch announced an $8.4 billion charge on the revaluation of CDOs.

As it turned out, Merrill had gotten into the storage business in its attempt to place itself at the top of the CDO underwriting charts, holding on to pieces of any deals it couldn't sell. So when the subprime and CDO markets were in a rapid decline, Merrill was losing massive amounts of money. Unimaginable amounts of money. Merrill had overleveraged itself on CDO bets, and its losses were so severe that the firm was almost completely wiped out.

Several months later, in July 2008, Merrill Lynch announced that it sold $30.6 billion of CDOs to an affiliate of Lone Star Funds for $6.7 billion. Doing the math, that was the equivalent of 21.8 cents on the dollar. Merrill had ridden its losses all the way down, taking about $24 billion in losses in just the course of a couple years since the bonds were originally issued. The newspapers noted that Merrill's CDO sale was in the supersenior tranches, which were originally AAA-rated. The announcement further explained that Merrill "will significantly reduce risk exposures [and] strengthen capital positions," perhaps getting back to its founding principles once again. Merrill also issued new common shares generating about $8.5 billion in new capital.

Just like Merrill had done with Howard Rubin's PO positions during the mortgage-market sell-off twenty years earlier, Merrill had held onto its CDO losses. And just like with the PO losses, Merrill had repeated its mistake, holding on while the market collapsed around it.

Perhaps in some strange way, Merrill actually got out in the nick of time, after having taken a loss of 78 percent on its initial, overleveraged investment. When the firm leveraged up its CDO holdings, it was really playing for keeps. On the bright side, if there is one, Merrill actually saved money in the end. Many of the CDOs it had underwritten would continue to fall in value over the next couple of years. And many of them became utterly worthless. Merrill, in the end, fared better than some of its customers—those who were still holding on to worthless securities.

And of course, Merrill Lynch didn't fare well over the next few months. While Wall Street banks were meeting at the Fed during that weekend in September 2008 to discuss Lehman Brothers, Merrill was secretly discussing a deal with Bank of America to sell itself. When the news of Lehman Brother's bankruptcy hit the newswires on Monday, September 15, 2008, it was accompanied by news about Merrill Lynch. The legendary, hundred-year-old investment bank had been sold to Bank of America for $29 a share, a total of $50 billion. Merrill Lynch had finally been consumed by the securitization market. That sale, however, didn't come before Merrill executives extracted their bonuses, an amount totaling $3.6 billion. This, after reporting losses of $7.8 billion in 2007 and $27.6 billion in 2008. It's staggering to think what that bonus numbers might have been had the firm managed to turn a profit that year.

*   *   *

Howard Rubin, to his credit, ended up doing much better than Merrill in the fallout from the mortgage market. After leaving, he didn't let his bad luck at Merrill Lynch weigh him down for too long. Rumor has it that a day after Merrill announced the loss, Bear Stearns came calling. Six months later, it was announced by the head of Bear's Mortgage Securities Division that the investment bank had hired Rubin as a trader on its mortgage-backed securities desk. A pair of Bear mortgage traders supposedly nailed shut the drawers of Rubin's new desk on the day he arrived; whether or not the action was meant as a joke or as an actual risk-management technique is still unknown.

Regardless, Rubin rose to be the head of collateralized mortgage obligation trading at Bear Stearns. He eventually left Bear Stearns to go to Fortress Investment Group, one of the few publicly traded hedge funds in the world. As of this writing, Rubin is still on the board of directors at Fortress. He also holds several director positions at various financial companies. His primary occupation, however, is right where he started. He serves as a portfolio manager at Soros Fund Management, one of the most profitable hedge funds in the world.

Chapter Three

Joe Jett and Kidder Peabody, 1994

Born in 1847, he only attended school for three months—the victim of what his teacher called a "wandering mind." In fact, the young man was so often distracted that his instructor referred to his brain as being "addled." It was, to say the least, a less-than-complimentary way to describe the pupil, and that student would be saddled with it throughout his academic career. Then, to make matters worse, our young hero was stricken with a case of scarlet fever that left him partially deaf. His mother decided that the only remedy for his wayward thinking was to teach him at home, relying heavily on readings from *School of Natural Philosophy* by R. G. Parker.

His family later moved to Port Huron, Michigan, where the young man got a job working on a railroad car, selling candy and newspapers to travelers as a way of making a living. During his free time on the train, he'd perform various experiments with chemicals that were available to him—an indication that perhaps his earlier diagnosis of "addled" was misguided. It seemed that he was more curious than mentally confused.

That innate streak of curiosity—paired with an entrepreneurial instinct—led the young man to become an inventor, where he achieved a marked degree of success. By the time of his death, he held 1,093 U.S. patents, making him the fourth most prolific inventor in history. In addition to inventing the phonograph, the stock ticker, and the carbon microphone used in telephones, he is also credited with inventing the first commercially feasible incandescent lightbulb.

That student who had so much trouble paying attention was named Thomas Edison, and would go on to found fourteen different companies, including today's commercial giant called General Electric.

Just four years after Edison's death in 1931, a child was born to parents of Irish descent living in Peabody, Massachusetts. His parents named him after his father, John Welch, but they decided to call him Jack. John Sr. was a railroad conductor, his wife a homemaker. Jack attended Salem High School where, unlike Edison, he excelled. He went on to the University of Massachusetts at Amherst, from where he graduated in 1957 with a bachelor's degree in chemical engineering.

Jack Welch joined General Electric in 1960 after earning a PhD in chemical engineering from the University of Illinois at Urbana-Champaign. After twelve years at the company, Welch rose to the position of vice president in 1972, then senior vice president in 1977, and then to vice chairman in 1979. Finally, in 1981, Jack Welch was named the youngest CEO in General Electric's history at age forty-five, making him also the youngest CEO of his generation.

During his tenure, which would last until 2001, Welch led General Electric through one of the most far-reaching transformations ever experienced by a major U.S. corporation. Under Welch's guidance, the company's market value skyrocketed from $14 billion to over $410 billion, and the company became the world's most valuable company. In 1999, Welch was even named "Manager of the Century" by *Fortune*.

Getting to the ultimate zenith of managerial success, however, was not an easy road. When Welch took over the reins at GE, the company was a major provider of lightbulbs, home appliances, aircraft and locomotive engines, and countless other pieces of equipment— manufacturing products, which were quickly becoming the remnants of a bygone era. Competition from foreign companies was increasing, and that new competition was able to make higher quality products at a cheaper cost.

Since his first day at work, Welch was disturbed by how much bureaucracy there was around GE, and as CEO, he set out to change it. Within a year, he had trimmed the firm's structure, streamlining and consolidating as he went. But that was just the first step; Welch also knew that he had to change the way GE did business in general, reinventing the company from the top down in order to make it successful in the modern world.

Most of those changes were fueled by Welch's own management principles, many of which were adopted by other CEOs around the world following the success they saw at GE. His style was immortalized in a book, *Jack Welch and the GE Way*, a title that led to the phrase "the GE Way" as a way of describing his managerial strategies.

Welch's primary focus was on leadership, specifically leading more and managing less. He was known to lead by his own example, a trait he expected other leaders to embody. His feeling was that in order to spark others to perform to their fullest potential, a leader had to show the example he wanted them to follow. He surrounded himself with people who were qualified, and he trusted them to do what he had hired them to do. He believed that close supervision, control, and bureaucracy were the easiest way to destroy the competitive spirit. "Weak managers are the killers of business," he said. "They are the job killers."

Welch welcomed great ideas from anyone who might have one, no matter what the individual's status within the company. "The hero is the person with the new idea," he was fond of saying. New ideas, he argued, were the lifeblood of an organization. Change is a reality in business, and it should be welcomed as an opportunity rather than a negative. To that end, he eliminated what he saw as boundaries to the free flow of ideas that might help move the company forward.

The execution of his grand strategy manifested itself in Welch cutting out what he saw as the fat in the company. He closed factories, reduced payrolls, cut outdated units, and fired a vast number of employees that were unnecessary. His mantra was that any GE business must be either number one or two in its particular industry, otherwise it needed to be improved or cut altogether. That sort of draconian policy earned Welch the nickname of "Neutron Jack" with some in the professional world. The name was a reference to a neutron bomb, a weapon that kills nearly every living thing within the blast zone, while still leaving the structures intact. Prior to Welch's taking over GE, approximately 412,000 employees were on the payroll. During his time as CEO, that number was cut to under 229,000.

He applied the same hard-line philosophy to his management team. Every year, managers who were fortunate enough to find themselves in the top 20 percent in terms of performance were rewarded with bonuses and stock options. Those who were unfortunate enough to find themselves in the bottom 10 percent were fired.

Despite the criticism—or perhaps because of it—Welch managed to create an extremely profitable company. He successfully and relatively seamlessly transformed GE from the outdated model of a nineteenth-century manufacturing company to a modern company that was a paradigm of financial success for the twenty-first century.

One component of that evolution was his shift into financial services through acquisitions. It was one of the rockiest evolutionary roads that Welch traveled. One of those acquisitions was Kidder Peabody, a financial firm GE acquired in 1986. It would turn out to be a blemish on an otherwise nearly impeccable management record. A trading scandal that rocked the financial world would cause an implosion of Kidder Peabody in 1994, the result of the actions of a single trader. True to form, however, Welch stuck to his guns, and, when he realized that the financial firm was bound for destruction, he acted on his principles: face reality, then act decisively. It was a hard, expensive lesson to learn.

*   *   *

In 1985, another brilliant young man, cut from the same sort of cloth as both Thomas Edison and Jack Welch, graduated with a degree in chemical engineering from MIT. That young genius was named Joe Jett, and he would go on to work for Jack Welch at GE not just once, but twice.

Orlando Joseph Jett was born in 1958 near Cleveland, Ohio. As an African American man, he wasn't the prototypical Wall Street hotshot, an esteemed group that is only about 1 percent black. He wasn't a big man, yet he was an imposing figure. He had a very large personal presence. He had the drive and the brain that understood the most complex mathematical conundrums; that talent led him to the Massachusetts Institute of Technology, where he studied chemical engineering. He excelled as an undergraduate, and was accepted into MIT's master's program.

Jett graduated with his master's in science in 1984 and strode into a $36,000-a-year salary working as a research engineer at a subsidiary of General Electric in Albany, New York. For reasons that were entirely his own, Jett soon decided to accept an offer to interview for the MBA program at Harvard. He was accepted and enrolled in the fall of 1985. While at Harvard, Jett cultivated an interest in Wall Street after listening to presentations given by some of the major players, including Drexel Burnham, Salomon Brothers, and Shearson Lehman. That interest blossomed further during a summer job at Ford Motor Company in Dearborn, Michigan, where Jett assisted the company's treasury department in investing the firm's cash. The job allowed him to converse with a variety of brokers, traders, and salespeople on Wall Street, and from that moment forward, he was hooked.

He graduated from Harvard with an MBA in 1987 and accepted a position with Morgan Stanley in New York City. Joe Jett was twenty-nine years old and living on Manhattan's Upper West Side. The drug- and alcohol-soaked culture on Wall Street was a long way from Cleveland, but Jett would later admit that women "were [his] only vice." But before he could soar with the Wall Street eagles, he had to get in the door, which meant a four-month stint in Morgan Stanley's in-house training program. After successfully completed the requirement, he landed a position on the mortgage-backed securities desk, due in no small part to his superb math skills, where Jett was assigned the less-than-authoritative title of "trading assistant." The professional culture at that time was such that trading assistants were effectively the lowest of the low. They were often treated as subhuman, primarily because they had been given an opportunity that the other traders didn't yet think they had earned.

In short time, Jett proved his mettle and was promoted to the level of junior trader, which afforded him a small trading book as sort of training wheels. The kid from Cleveland was on his way, and he started to live the life of a successful and freewheeling financial wunderkind. He garnered a reputation as a partier, sleeping briefly after leaving the office and then hitting the nightclubs until four in the morning.

Then, in what was to become something of a pattern, Jett started having conflicts with other traders on the desk. He grew argumentative and confrontational, which led to his trading trade book being reduced by the senior trader. Then, as the conflicts continued, Jett found his trade book eliminated completely and his position reduced back to the rank of trading assistant. He would later say that his "critical mistake was in failing to understand how highly Morgan Stanley valued team-playing."

He was laid off from Morgan Stanley in April 1989, an action he blamed on the firm's distaste for his late-night social habits. As a bizarre form of self-flagellation, Jett removed all of the furniture from his apartment and began sleeping on the floor. He had failed and saw the need to punish himself for it. As he liked to tell himself, "Failure is not an option."

He wasn't on the rolls of the unemployed for long; in September 1989 he was hired to work on the mortgage-backed securities desk at First Boston. The firm was no longer doing anything cutting edge in the MBS field anymore and operated as a straightforward Collateralized Mortgage Obligation (CMO) packaging operation. Jett was hired as a CMO structurer, and in that capacity he was tasked with putting together the different classes and structures of the investments. Specifically, he worked to find new ways to price CMOs, especially the equity portion—that part of the CMO that was the final tranche and carried the majority of the risk, the part that traders affectionately refer to as "the nuclear waste tranche."

The term "tranche" is thrown around by those in finance, and oftentimes the concept is lost on those outside that world. The word is derived from the French word for "slice," and that is what a financial tranche is. When a mortgage-backed security is converted into a CMO, the investment bank divides it into individual pieces that can be sold off as separate securities. In the case of CMOs, those pieces—called tranches—typically range from low-risk to high-risk, with the latter offering the promise of potentially higher returns. It is the lowest tranche that carries the highest risk, and that was what Jett focused his mathematical skill on.

While at First Boston, Jett kept quiet about his social life. He'd learned that lesson the hard way at Morgan Stanley and had no interest in repeating his past mistakes. He kept his head down and didn't socialize at work, instead directing his energies toward developing a new, computer-based system that assisted in calculating CMO prices. But First Boston, despite that it had been a pioneer in the MBS industry and effectively invented the CMO, had turned conservative in the business, which sent many of its best traders to seek greener pastures. To replace them, First Boston brought in a new team from Salomon Brothers—just like many other Wall Street firms had done in the 1980s—and Jett found himself a remnant of the old guard, even though he had really just arrived. Clearly, the clock was ticking on his time at First Boston.

While still there, Jett had spent a great deal of time working with traders at Kidder Peabody, a subsidiary of General Electric—the same company where Jett's chemical engineering career was both born and died. What made Kidder exciting is that it was one of two firms—the other being Bear Stearns—to further expand and complicate the MBS market by dividing its CMOs into significantly more tranches, as many as twelve. By dividing the product into so many slices, the risk in the lowest tranches was concentrated to extreme levels, and the new structure increased both the risk, and the return, for CMO investors.

With his status rapidly diminishing at First Boston, and his connections increasing around the Street, Jett sought out a meeting with Mike Vranos, the legendary head trader of the MBS desk at Kidder Peabody. Vranos was impressed enough with Jett to offer him a job starting at $180,000 a year, and, at least according to Jett, the pair shook hands on the deal.

Vranos, however, saw it a different way. After the rounds of interviews at the MBS desk, he claims that Jett was sent to the government bond desk because he didn't understand mortgage-backed securities well enough, despite having worked in the business at Morgan Stanley and First Boston.

When Jett returned to solidify what he thought was a done deal, evidently Vranos backed off, saying that all he could offer Jett was as assistant job that carried with it a $35,000-a-year salary. Jett balked at the sudden change of heart and walked away. With still no future at First Boston, Jett slinked back in April 1990 to see if that offer was still good, and it wasn't. He was stuck.

But Jett wasn't one to take no for an answer, and he returned again the next month to interview for a different job with then-CFO Richard O'Donnell. Someone was needed to investigate and clean up what O'Donnell termed the "aged inventory" of the fixed income department. GE was nervous about Kidder's positions, and the traders' seeming inability to sell it. The "GE Way" was clearly about cleaning up old inventory positions. As senior management saw it, an outsider was needed who could come in and make the tough decisions that Kidder Peabody's traders were unwilling to. Jett saw it as a foot in the door into one of the Street's largest fixed-income trading departments at the time. Jett was hired and arrived at Kidder Peabody in July 1990 to clear out approximately $1.3 billion in old securities. He was to sell them off to the highest bidders in hopes of flipping them for a profit, or at least moving them out the door.

*   *   *

Kidder Peabody was founded in 1865 by Henry Kidder and Francis Peabody who took over the Boston-based private bank known as J. E. Thayer & Brother when that bank's founder, John Eliot Thayer, retired. The firm quickly established a reputation as a major investment banking powerhouse in the Boston area, and part of that reputation was built on the firm's close relationship with Baring Brothers, the premier merchant bank in London. Kidder Peabody quickly joined the ranks of the "Yankee Bankers," due to their northeastern U.S. concentration, numerous Harvard alumni, and white-shoe heritage.

There was more to Kidder Peabody than its Harvard connections. The firm had close ties to both the American Sugar Refining Company and American Telephone and Telegraph (AT&T), as the premier financier for those companies' bond issues. The investment bank was also a part of the consortium known as "The Money Trust"—the bankers who financed the megalithic trusts of the day, including such stalwarts as Standard Oil and U.S. Steel.

In 1905, Francis Peabody, the last of the original partners, died, and control of the firm shifted to Frank Webster and Robert Winsor. In the early 1920s, the firm's operating capital sat at about $7 million, which was enough to run its operations at the time, but the industry was changing. Robert Winsor, who had an inherent distrust of stocks because of their volatility, steered the firm on a course dedicated to bond trading and financing; that strategy, however, cost the firm heavily when they missed the bull stock market of the 1920s. Profits continued to decline, and then when the Italian government withdrew its $10 million deposit, it left the firm drastically undercapitalized and incapable of surviving the stock market crash of 1929 without outside help.

That help came in the form of a financial bailout orchestrated by J. P. Morgan. It was determined that Kidder Peabody needed a cash infusion of $15 million to survive, and several banks—many from the Boston area—agreed to help fund the bailout. In the end, the package totaled $10 million, leaving Kidder Peabody to raise $5 million on its own.

The woes associated with the lack of operating capital would continue to fester throughout the twentieth century. In 1964, due to the firm's growth in size, yet still small capital base, the partners collectively felt that the business was too large to continue as an unlimited liability partnership. The decision was made to convert the investment bank into a corporation, though it would remain privately owned and run by the partners under the articles of incorporation.

Ralph DeNunzio was the leader who emerged to guide Kidder through much of the latter half of the twentieth century. He had joined the firm immediately after graduating from Princeton in 1953 and had risen to the position of senior partner by 1969. He also held the distinction of being the chairman of the New York Stock Exchange, clearly a major figure on Wall Street for a number of years. Kidder remained a well-known name in the bond markets but still did not have much luck breaking out of that mold. Under DeNunzio's leadership, however, the firm continued to move forward and grow, expanding into new business lines, including mergers and acquisitions, and stock trading. By 1985, the capital issue once again reared its head, and Kidder was under pressure from both the Securities and Exchange Commission and the New York Stock Exchange to bring more capital into the firm, citing the fact that far too much money was tied up in its bond inventory. Both worried that a major bond market sell-off could affect Kidder's ability to meet its obligations to its customers.

DeNunzio sent his deputy, Max Chapman, to act aggressively and broker a deal with Jack Welch at General Electric. Under the arrangement, GE would buy an 80 percent stake in Kidder Peabody in exchange for $650 million, a much-needed cash infusion for the struggling investment bank. That money was a godsend and would put Kidder on the same level as Goldman Sachs and Lehman Brothers in terms of capitalization. DeNunzio and Kidder expected to retain control of the business and finally have all the capital they needed to grow. GE was expecting something else, however—to continue its financial services transformation and diversification by entering into the investment banking world through a well-known firm, then convert it to the "GE Way" of doing things. It would be a purchase that all involved would grow to regret, and it came as no surprise to the many on Wall Street who said the deal was doomed from the start.

Given Welch's experience and business esteem, it seems somewhat surprising that he would pay so much for a firm that was clearly experiencing difficulties. Perhaps he believed the GE management style would lead the company to new financial heights, a suggestion further buoyed by Welch's decision to shake up Kidder's management almost immediately. DeNunzio was out, replaced by a GE director named Silas Cathcart. Kidder Peabody was about to learn what it meant to be a GE company and to be run the "GE Way."

But before Welch could get Kidder Peabody into the GE mold, a much-publicized scandal rocked the firm to its core. A Kidder executive was publicly linked to Ivan Boesky, the man who became the public face of the 1980s scandals in insider trading. Laws had existed for a long time that made insider trading illegal, but until Boesky's prosecution in 1986, those laws were seldom enforced. As it turned out, much of Boesky's insider information had been provided by a Kidder Peabody man in the firm's mergers and acquisitions department, a banker named Martin Siegel. Siegel had originally been seeking to supplement his salary by doing freelance work for Boesky, and hoping to obtain a more lucrative job; Boesky didn't hire him, but instead paid him cash for takeover tips. The first payment was rumored to be $150,000 in cash, delivered in a briefcase that required a secret code to open. Siegel only served two months in prison, but his reputation was forever tarnished, and the public relations nightmare for General Electric had just begun.

*   *   *

By 1991, Kidder had further expanded its operations to include asset management, equity research, futures, and a major push into investment banking, but it was the fixed income department at Kidder Peabody that was the mule pulling the financial cart. Fixed income was the only profitable business in the entire firm, accounting for 110 percent of Kidder's income, and it was Mike Vranos, the head of mortgage-backed securities, who dominated the department.

Joe Jett started at Kidder Peabody—by now under the full control of General Electric—on June 24, 1991, to begin sweeping its old securities out the door. Once Jett arrived, however, the head of fixed income, Edward Cerullo, had another idea for him. By chance, Robert Dickey, who had been the head STRIPS trader, left the firm just before Jett's entrance onto the grand stage. Joe Jett was available for the job, and certainly no one in fixed-income trading wanted an outsider micromanaging its inventory positions anyway. Cerullo asked Jett if he'd be interested in that $75,000-a-year trader position, and Jett accepted. Suddenly, the former mortgage trader and CMO structurer was the head STRIPS trader at Kidder Peabody. (STRIPS, a Treasury security, is the acronym for "Separate Trading of Registered Interest and Principal of Securities.")

At the time, the STRIPS desk was staffed by three junior traders and was mostly overlooked by the other members of the fixed-income trading department. STRIPS trading was not producing the same revenue as the other desks, which meant it didn't get a great deal of respect around the trading floor. Joe Jett planned to change that immediately.

STRIPS was the name given to the divided portions of U.S. Treasury bonds after the interest payments had been separated from the principal payment, much like what many firms were doing with mortgage-backed securities. Prior to 1985, however, the practice was not supported by the U.S. Treasury, so traders who wanted to get separated coupon payments and principal payments had to do so by setting up their own private conduits. Despite the fact that it was a thinly traded market, investor demand was so strong that investment banks started pulling apart Treasury bonds with zeal, creating such conduit names as LIONs (Lehman Investment Opportunity Notes) and TIGRs (Treasury Investment Growth Receipts).

Finally, in 1985, the U.S. Treasury officially started the STRIPS program, an acronym that stands for Separate Trading of Registered

Interest and Principal Securities. Regardless of the name ascribed, the stripping process is relatively uniform across the board. Remember that a bond is a debt, and the bondholder is entitled to periodic payments of interest as well as the original principal amount when the bond matures. Every bond is essentially a series of semiannual coupon payments, with the original loan amount paid back in full on the maturity date. A $1 million bond with a five-year maturity and a 10 percent coupon means that the bondholder gets a coupon payment equal to 5 percent every six months, plus the full million dollars in principal back on the day of the bond's maturity.

In a STRIPS security, however, someone can buy the series of coupon payments or the one lump-sum principal payment (the part sometimes referred to as a zero-coupon bond). Under the new STRIPS program, when a U.S. Treasury security was stripped, a primary dealer informed the Federal Reserve Bank of New York of the intention to do so, and then sent the bond into the Fed the next day. Upon receipt, the Fed sent back both the coupon payments and the principal amount as brand new securities.

The opposite of stripping a bond is called reconstituting, or simply a recon. In a recon transaction, the primary dealer sends in the individual stripped components—both the principal and coupons—and the Fed returns the original bond. Either way, STRIPS require a single day's notice to the Federal Reserve; and this is important—there is no way to book a transaction with the Fed to strip a bond or reconstitute it with more than one day's notice.

The fact that a bond can be stripped down into components in one transaction and then put back together means there is always an arbitrage possibility between the stripped component parts and the actual underlying bond. Determining the actual STRIPS arbitrage is a complicated matter, but for those that can master it, there's some money to be made. Many investment banks assign full-time trading desks on these arbitrage opportunities. If the coupon and principal STRIPS are ever trading at abnormally high prices, the trading desk can send a bond to the Fed to be stripped, and then sell off the STRIPS pieces in the market. Alternatively, if components are trading at abnormally low prices, the same trading desk could buy them in the market and send them into the Fed to be reconstituted.

What this means for STRIPS traders is that they're constantly on the lookout for STRIPS that were trading at prices either too high or too low—then either stripping existing bonds and selling off the pieces, or buying the pieces and reconstituting the bond. The primary goal is to arbitrage both the STRIPS and underlying bonds, a task made much easier by technological advances and computer pricing models.

Kidder began its first foray into STRIPS trading in 1984, when it moved Andy Ansel into the new role of full-time trader on the newly created Zero Desk. At the time, the market was still trading LIONs and TIGRs, but the following year when the Treasury officially entered the market, STRIPS trading took off. After Ansel left, Bob Dickey, his junior trader, assumed his position, and the business escalated. The STRIPS market grew and so did the profits on the desk. Dickey made over $10 million trading STRIPS in 1988 and $15 million in 1989, making STRIPS the most profitable U.S. Treasury trading desk at Kidder Peabody.

But when bonus numbers started being discussed in 1990 for the previous year, Dickey was not happy. Despite the fact that he'd generated an additional $5 million in revenue from the previous year, Cerullo wanted to pay him the same bonus as the last year. Dickey would have stayed on for only $100,000 more, but Cerullo was adamant about the number. Cerullo's refusal to negotiate opened the exit door for Dickey, and his departure created an open seat on the trading floor just before Jett's arrival. Ironically, a dispute over $100,000 in bonus money would ultimately lead to the entire firm's destruction.

The atmosphere around Kidder Peabody prior to Jett's arrival was one of constant worry. There was talk about GE trying to sell off the firm because it never managed to fully integrate the investment bank into the GE culture. Jack Welch clearly did not like the world of investment banking, and Kidder's financial shortcomings were forcing him to spend time enmeshed in them. And that time was not being rewarded with significant gains. Welch actually did try to sell Kidder in 1992 to Primerica, but the deal fell through. When he couldn't sell it, he turned his attention to making the best of it, which meant focusing on the fixed-income trading department, the one profitable entity in the whole firm. Welch issued a mandate that the fixed-income trading department needed to be built up and strengthened.

Jett had the brains and the drive to be a leader on Kidder's trading floor, but the firm was under intense pressure to perform, so he didn't have a lot of time to show results. Kidder was considered a weak member of the primary dealer community and was perpetually in danger of having its status revoked by the Federal Reserve. The major issue was that the firm rarely bought enough new issues at the Treasury bond auctions, a requirement for maintaining primary-dealer status. That led to constant pressure to build up the government bond trading desks, which were constantly trying to compete with the mortgage-backed securities desk within the firm. That pressure was transferred to Jett, who was already putting tremendous pressure on himself. This was, after all, his third shot at a Wall Street career; if he blew this one, there probably wouldn't be another chance.

Within a month of starting at Kidder, Cerullo laid it out for him. "I expect this operation to generate a million dollars each month," he said to Jett. "I need improvement in the STRIPS ledgers, and I need it now. Or there will be changes." That thinly veiled threat was more than enough to get Jett's attention, and he set out to meet Cerullo's expectations. At first he failed miserably.

Within a month, Jett single-handedly lost $90,000 over the course of a single day. That disaster resulted in a meeting between Cerullo, Jett, and Jett's immediate boss, Mel Mullin, the head of government bond trading at Kidder. Cerullo scolded Jett for his losses, adding, "Trading STRIPS has nothing to do with accounts. It is an arbitrage market, and it's fairly simple. Does the sum of the parts equal more than the whole?" The condescension was a hit to Jett's ego to be sure, but the directive was clear: STRIPS trading had nothing to do with customer "accounts," it was all about building up a trading book. Cerullo even upped the ante when he added, "I want profits in short order."

Jett didn't need it to be repeated; he got the message the first time. Still, he had little experience with trading STRIPS, though luckily, he had a mathematical mind that made learning the specifics of the job easier. But he lacked any practical experience with buying and selling STRIPS. The status as a novice was no excuse on a trading floor, a fact that Cerullo hammered home for him when he passed by a few weeks later: "I'm expecting improvement this month," he warned Jett. "Just a reminder."

That improvement didn't show up, and by the end of December 1991, Jett's year-end bonus reflected his lack of performance. Mel Mullin broke the news in a meeting; Jett would be taking home a bonus of $5,000, an amount that was effectively a joke on Wall Street. When your bonus is $5,000, the message is pretty clear: keep your desk clean because you're not going to be around much longer.

As the calendar page flipped into January 1992, Jett was reminded yet again of the incredibly high expectations placed on him by management. "You've had six months," Mullin told him. "The training period is over. It's time to produce." This time, though, Jett would be finally able to live up to those expectations. Within just a few months, Jett would be making money, and a lot of money. His trading book was built up to $8 billion in open STRIPS positions, clearly a part of his aggressive style. His trading account showed him to be making $3 million a month for the firm—though that number would later be disputed by SEC filings—and he began commanding the respect of the other traders on the trading floor. Either Jett had finally gotten the hang of STRIPS trading and immediately become one of the best STRIPS traders on the Street, or he had found some shortcut to make it look that way.

The STRIPS desk was suddenly a big part of Kidder Peabody's fixed-income trading business, and Mullin credited Jett with raising the desk's status. He rewarded Jett with a raise, doubling Jett's salary to $150,000. The quick elevation of status and a promotion was intoxicating, as Jett would later say: "The effect of money on people at work is striking. Immediately, I became popular at work."

There's an old saying about a tiger not being able to change his stripes, and by June 1992, Jett's old stripes were shining through again. He began arguing with traders at other desks, and he clashed with his superiors in the same way he'd done at previous Wall Street stints. One source of disagreement came from the firm's government bond trading desk, the group that controlled the buying and selling of the Treasury bonds that Jett was stripping and reconstituting. The government bond traders argued that they needed to coordinate the flow of all government bond trading through a single location, specifically their desk. Naturally, it meant they made money off the internal business, which boosted their own revenue numbers.

And while it might make sense for them to feel that way, the MBS trading desk was allowed to buy and sell in the government market as it deemed necessary. It was exempt from trading through the government desk, a right acquired purely as a result of its size and profitability. The message was clear: if you made enough money, you got to call your own shots. It wasn't too different on every trading desk on Wall Street. Jett wanted the same freedom for his STRIPS desk, and breaking out led to frequent arguments with Bill Glaser, the head of the government desk.

His repeated confrontations would become something of a source of pride to Jett, who would later write about his experiences at Kidder Peabody: "I'd already thrown down the gauntlet, defying Mullin at several key junctures. I got Hugh Bush fired, I refused to deal with regional brokers, I circumvented Glaser, I balked at reducing my trading position from $8 billion to $6 billion." It says a great deal about the mindset Jett possessed at the time—that he was boasting about professional confrontation with his superiors—but apparently it didn't bother anyone at Kidder enough to cut ties with Jett. Jett was now bringing in steady money each month, money his bosses desperately needed.

Jett claimed to be making profits from three different sources: arbitrage opportunities in the STRIPS market, making markets for clients by taking advantage of the bid/offer spreads in STRIPS, and maintaining a long position in bonds while simultaneously hedging it by selling bond futures contracts. The last part is what is known as "bond basis" trading.

But the reality was quite different. Jett had noticed a flaw in the Kidder Peabody trade processing system that allowed him to book what amounted to phantom profits. He came upon this flaw when he had booked a "forward trade," and now the smart guy was flexing his mental muscles.

A forward trade is simply a trade that settles at some point in the future, generally further in the future than normal trade settlement. For example, if two Wall Street traders decide to book a forward trade, they'll decide all of the details—the security, the price, the quantity, etc.—on the trade date. That's when the details are agreed to, but not when the actual securities change hands. The securities get transferred on the day called the settlement date. Government securities typically settle on either the same day, called cash settlement, or the next day, called regular settlement.

To be clear, the Federal Reserve doesn't allow STRIPS to settle any longer than regular settlement, but as it turns out, nobody told that to the Kidder Peabody computer system. Jett discovered that he could book recon trades in Kidder's trading system with settlements as far as thirty days in the future. The best part about those forward trades: the profits generated by the trade were booked immediately in Jett's trading account. Even when no money had yet changed hands, Jett showed profits in his account, so he began booking these trades as frequently as he could. When the settlement dates neared, he simply rolled the trade forward, rebooking the settlement date of the original trade for thirty more days in the future and still retaining those imaginary profits.

Overall, 1992 was a very good year for bond traders. Prices were on a continual climb upward as the Fed had been cutting interest rates all year long. Jett was dealing with a variety of different STRIPS, and that position had paid off nicely by October. Jett had booked $17 million in profits from January 1, 1992, to October 31, 1992. Only there was one catch—all of those profits didn't really exist. When the SEC did a little checking years later, those profits were booked with forward settlement dates that had yet to be reached. Going from a trading desk expected to make several million dollars a year to $17 million was a big leap in the minds of all those around Jett at Kidder. What was even better, his whole system for booking phantom profits from forward trades was about to get even easier.

At the end of 1992, Kidder decided to upgrade its trade processing system with a new computer program called Government Trader. One of the snazzy new elements of the new system was the fact that it allowed traders to book forward trades at any future settlement date. So whereas the original system had limited traders to a thirty-day window, the new system had no such limitations. Unknowingly, by improving it trade processing system, Kidder just made Jett's trading scheme even easier.

As it turns out, there are two versions of what happened next, following the implementation of the new system. According to the SEC, Jett immediately picked up on the new loophole and began to exploit it. The first trade he booked under the new system didn't settle for 203 days in the future. Additionally, the system had a new flaw too. It didn't take into account the cost of borrowing the money to finance the trades—called the cost of carry—when calculating the profits, all of which were ignored by the system until trade settlement. So Jett was now able to book up to forty times the profit he had booked before on the same trades, thanks to the new limitless forward settlement date window. That sounds pretty cut and dried, of course, and casts Jett as acting in a clearly fraudulent manner.

Jett, however, had a different version of what happened. He claimed the new processing system at Kidder Peabody wasn't even operational until the last week of December 1992. He remembered it being the day after Christmas, in fact. The office was quiet, as most traders were on vacation. Jett, the hardworking trader, was in the office manning the fort while the other traders enjoyed their vacation. And the market was quiet too, for much the same reason. According to Jett, when he input his first recon trade on that December morning, he noticed that something was immediately odd. Whereas he'd been expecting the trade to show a $30,000 profit, the computer system credited him with a $300,000 profit.

There was clearly a computer system malfunction, and Jett claims to have brought the matter to the attention of his boss, Mel Mullin, and the computer programmer, Moishe Benatar. Benatar told him that the profits were unrealized, meaning they shouldn't be counted toward actual profits until the actual settlement day. Mullin, a PhD in mathematics, later claimed not to have understood the accounting method or the program flaw himself. One former trader who worked for Mullin even pointed out, "Mel never understood the bond market business. He had no idea." Robert Dickey, the former head STRIPS trading at Kidder, later said that the traders were all well aware of the flaws and how to exploit them.

The way Jett exploited the new system was pretty similar to the way he did it with the old system. When Jett input a forward recon trade, the system showed a bond being delivered to Kidder from the

Fed, and Kidder delivering the coupon and principal STRIPS to the Fed in return. All of this was scheduled to happen on that future date. In Kidder's system, it then showed that Jett had a long position in a bond and a short position in the STRIPS. But it wasn't a real trade with the Federal Reserve; it was just what appeared in Kidder's trade processing system: receiving a bond from the Fed and delivering the STRIPS back. Essentially, by booking a recon forward trade Jett was announcing his *intention* to execute the trade on the forward date. But no trade was done yet, and, obviously, no money had yet to change hands.

As the settlement date neared for the booked recon trade, Jett would cancel that trade, then book another one with a settlement date way off in the future. The cost of carry, or the cost to borrow money to finance those trades, wasn't factored in by the system either, so he didn't even have to pay any expenses on the "profit" he was taking. As long as he kept pushing the forward dates further into the future, he could keep on booking increasingly larger trades, showing increasingly larger profits. As long as the size of the make-believe trades kept increasing, so too did the amount of make-believe profit.

The repo desk was the part of the trading floor responsible for financing Jett's short and long positions, which also left it privy to what he was doing. Or at least privy to what was actually happening; whether or not the repo desk knew what he was doing is anybody's guess. If Jett was long a STRIPS, the repo desk would loan it into the repo market to raise the requisite cash to pay for it; if he was short, they'd borrow the security to cover the short position. The desk was quick to report to management that Jett was trading unusually large amounts of STRIPS against forward settlements that oftentimes never settled at all. The trades were being closed out just before the settlement dates with the Fed. Regardless of whether or not they understood the true nature of his trades, the repo traders noticed a pattern, specifically that Jett had very large STRIPS positions, oftentimes greater than the amount of the actual Treasury bond outstanding. That is, if you added up the size of all of the particular STRIPS that Jett was short or long on, it was more than could have possibly been stripped, because the actual bond size wasn't that large. Other STRIPS traders around the Street knew something was wrong a Kidder too. Jett's oversized positions were distorting the STRIPS market, and other firms were making a killing on it.

Regardless of who knew what, in the space of two months Jett's reported profits jumped to a total of $40.4 million—that's money he made in sixty days, mind you—which was more than double the profits he'd booked all of the previous year. It is equally surprising that neither Cerullo nor Mullin thought anything was amiss when Jett's profits suddenly skyrocketed. But again, it *was* a good year for bonds, so maybe they thought they'd just found a gold mine of a trader. So as long as the trading desk made money, they didn't quite care about the details of how it was made. Given that the other traders on the STRIPS desk had lost $10 million in 1992, the new rock star kept the STRIPS desk profitable.

Given the mechanics of Jett's trade, it's surprising that a rational trader would keep it going without restraint. It was a classic example of a snake eating its own tail. In order for the scheme to continue, his positions had to get larger and larger. At some point, Kidder, or GE, or the ability to borrow cash would prevent the business from growing any larger. If Jett ever stopped rolling his fraudulent trades and growing their size, the profits would cease, and the snake would have caught up to itself. However, at the particular point in time, Jett had no problem continuing the deception by increasing the size of his trades as forward settlement dates approached.

By the end of 1992, Jett's profits were, by all accounts, pretty impressive. Of course, they'd be a lot more impressive had they been actual profits as opposed to merely imaginary ones, but that didn't stop his superiors from taking notice and rewarding Jett for his activities. Jett was given an outstanding review for his year-end performance and was promoted to the level of senior vice president; Mullin told colleagues that "Jett has become one of the top STRIPS traders in the industry." The young trader's year-end bonus was $1.6 million, which was a far cry from the $3 million he had been expecting, but still a sizable Christmas present for a trader who'd been one hair away from begin fired just twelve months earlier.

In January 1993, Jett formalized his trading strategy, such as it was. This would become his truth, his version of what he'd been doing all along. Despite the fact that it wasn't really a viable strategy after all,

Jett would never acknowledge that he'd done anything wrong, basically because his plan hinged on the computer glitch he'd happened upon. Remember that the Kidder system treated recon and STRIPS trades with the Fed as real trades, despite the fact that there were no actual trades involved in the quasi-transaction. It was simply an internal booking for a possible future trade settlement. No more, no less.

That said, Jett needed an explanation as to why, and how, he was all of a sudden making a lot of money. Inside and outside the company, during and after his time at Kidder, he would call this his three-part arbitrage strategy or sometimes just plainly referred to it as his trading strategy. Keep in mind, the internal bookings, shown as trades with the Fed, were the cornerstone to his three-part plan. The so-called "strategy" started with the forward recon trade with the Fed; remember, that showed up as a forward purchase of a bond plus a short position in both the coupon and principal STRIPS, but those trades didn't start until sometime in the future. So step one appeared as a long position in a bond and a short position in the coupon and principal STRIPS. Next step: Jett went out into the market and purchased the same STRIPS, but settling immediately this time as a way of hedging the forward recon trade. He actually owned those STRIPS, as of the current day when he booked the trade. Finally, he would sell the bond futures contract, as he claimed, "to hedge the price of the reconstituted forward position [I] was holding in bonds."

As long as you accept the forward recon trade with the Fed as a real trade, it appears to be a sound strategy. However, when you take out the phantom trades with the Fed, the somewhat complicated STRIPS strategy isn't much of a strategy at all. Let's start with Jett buying coupon and principal STRIPS on the day of the booking. Then, he short-sells the bond futures contract, which is the equivalent of selling bonds to someone at some point in the future. For purposes of explanation, let's assume those contracts settle ninety days in the future. It's important to point out here that if a trader owns all of the coupon payments and the principal payment, in essence, it's the same as owning the actual bond itself. Now, since we know the forward recon trades with the Fed don't really exist, they're just an *intention* that exists in the Kidder Peabody trading system, we just erase those trades from the strategy. What we have left is Jett owning all the coupon and principal payments that make up a full bond and a future contract to sell bonds ninety days in the future. In other words, Jett's tried-and-true, radical new strategy for STRIPS trading was simply owning the equivalent components of a bond and selling that bond at a future settlement date.

The genius part of his plan, if you call it that, was the fact that he booked and rebooked so many trades that he was able to effectively hide that he was exploiting the flaw in Kidder's trade processing system. When the accounting team came to audit his trades—including the differences in trade and settlement dates, different bonds, recons, coupon STRIPS, principal STRIPS, and bond futures—the team was easily confused by the sheer chaos inherent in any kind of flow chart it could produce to trace his actions. In a typical recon or STRIPS trade with the Fed, there can be as many sixty-one separate components. Think of a thirty-year bond: it includes sixty semiannual coupon payments and one principal payment at the end, all trading as separate securities. Perhaps the accounting folks could be forgiven for their confusion after all.

In standard market parlance, Jett's strategy was nothing more than a "basis trade." The only real risk he assumed in his strategy was that the bonds he owned (held in the separate coupon and principal components) were not the same bonds required to be delivered as part of the bond futures contract on the delivery date. That's what they call basis risk, and it's generally very small. Regardless of risk, however, there is one important linchpin to this whole scheme. There is no mathematical way possible in which a trader can amass $150 million annually by trading the bond basis. It just can't happen that way. But nobody at Kidder Peabody seemed to pay attention to that harsh reality.

One of the reasons Jett got away with everything was in part to his skills at office politics. Obviously, it wasn't his skills with coworkers or the other desk heads, but rather, his skills with his superiors. He kept himself very close to Ed Cerullo, close enough to get invited to Cerullo's vacation home in Aspen, Colorado. Perhaps Cerullo's fatal flaw was what one of his traders pointed out: "Ed trusted everyone who worked under him to be honest." And then there were all of the astronomical profits Jett continued to bring in. All that income led to suggestions that Jett should also be running the whole government area—the Holy Grail for a trader in his position—as opposed to Mullin. Jett pushed

Cerullo to promote him and was told that the entire department would eventually be reorganized. When that time came, Jett would find himself promoted to head of all government bond trading, and Mullin would be moved to a new position as head of what was to be called Derivative Products.

The reorg came in February 1993. Jett was, as promised, promoted to head of all government bond trading, which gave him oversight of the STRIPS desk, as well as the U.S. Treasury and federal agency trading desks, the latter including such items as the securities issued by Fannie Mae and Freddie Mac. A crew of fourteen traders was now reporting to Jett. The aggressive newcomer had just taken charge, and Kidder Peabody was about to realize the magnitude of the mistake.

* * *

Right around the time when Jett assumed control of the entire group, Vranos's mortgage desk had taken a $70 million loss—a loss that completely shocked Jack Welch. The loss was large enough to wipe out Kidder's entire profits for the previous year, and Welch responded quickly by moving a new man, David Bernstein, to head up risk and compliance at Kidder. Not surprisingly, Bernstein's first assignment was to audit the fixed-income trading department. It was also a clear shift in focus for Welch. Whereas previously he'd been worried about the firm's $86 billion balance sheet, he had failed to fully understand the risks inherent in Kidder's business, which was now the center of his attention.

Welch had previously seen a limited balance sheet and asset size as a way to limit risk, but those days had changed. He was now worried that Kidder's business contained more risks than he originally thought, and of course he was right in that belief. Ironically, he chose to focus on losses that the company had booked properly on the mortgage desk instead of profits that were booked improperly on the STRIPS desk. He knew something was wrong, but he was looking in the wrong place.

Another problem was now at Cerullo's feet. Whereas before he'd been able to rely on the mortgage desk for profits to grow the firm's income statement, that avenue was now basically shut. The risk limits imposed by Bernstein would tie up the mortgage desk in terms of a source of revenue, so Cerullo had only one other option, which was the government desk. And that meant his only way of growing the firm's profits relied solely on Joe Jett.

By the middle of 1993, however, it was clear there was not going to be a problem with profits the year. The long end of the bond market had continued its spectacular rally, and the Fed had kept short-term interest rates down at historic lows. Jett was showing a staggering $66.7 million in profits for his forward STRIPS trades, though $58.5 million of that amount was imaginary. David Bernstein was now comfortable enough in his new job to challenge Jett on his profits, but Jett was prepared. Because everyone knew that Kidder's system did not properly handle trades that were booked so far in advance, Jett had kept a meticulous diary of his forward transactions in what would come to be known as the Red Book. It was, he explained, a way of helping the repo desk keep track of his forward trades. To Bernstein, that sent up a warning flare, as he expected that all trades should be accounted for in the firm's trading system in order to accurately reflect profits.

Upon further examination of the Red Book, it was discovered that as of July 1993, Jett had booked so many forward recon trades in one bond that the size of the trades was again greater than the amount of the bond being reconstituted. In other words, Jett was again projected to put back together more bonds than could possibly have been stripped—more of a certain bond than even existed in the market. The result, though, was that Bernstein simply told Jett that he could no longer book forward recon trades settling more than three months in the future because the mainframe couldn't properly handle such long periods of time. Bernstein felt he had to do something about the problem, but his action really didn't change anything.

Bernstein's opportunity for making changes would come back at the end of the third quarter in September 1993, when GE wanted to cut back on the size of Kidder's trading positions and instructed its subsidiary to reduce its balance sheet significantly. Whereas GE imagined the balance sheet was supposed to be kept below $50 billion, Kidder was routinely carrying assets in excess of $80 billion, and during the summer of 1993, with Jett's growing STRIPS positions, that figure had swelled to over $100 billion. In order to achieve the $50 billion goal and keep GE happy but not limit the revenues rolling in, Kidder needed a good plan. The result was found in a little creative accounting. Kidder first switched its accounting system to do away with recognizing unsettled trades; that meant all of Jett's forward recon trades were suddenly off the firm's balance sheet. Of the $30 billion in STRIPS positions that he was carrying at the time—three times his authorized limit—$24 billion were forward-settling trades.

To further efforts to keep GE off their backs, Cerullo wanted to cut existing assets by another $26.2 billion, an amount that included the outright elimination of $5 billion of Jett's long positions—the coupon and principal STRIPS. Jett, as was to be expected, was not happy about the move. After some back and forth with Cerullo, Jett was outright ordered to do so. As we know, Jett's scheme involved rolling his trades into larger and larger sizes, and cutting back did not figure into his game. In order to close down his STRIPS trades, he had to cancel the forward recon trades that were juicing up his profits for so long. And by cutting back the forward recon trades, he was forced to give back profits that he'd been perpetually been rolling forward.

In theory, if Jett had merely been closing out long "basis trades" by selling bonds and buying back the futures contracts, his losses would be insignificant. But there's nothing a mathematician hates more than theory. His excuse for the massive losses that suddenly appeared was that "to get the STRIPS we needed in such a short period, we paid exorbitant amounts." This neglected the fact that government securities trade with razor tight spreads, often at times with bids and offers one sixty-fourth of a point apart.

Despite Jett's claim that he was up $70 million for the year, he was forced to book an immediate $48 million loss on his positions. Truthfully, both the accounting team and the management at Kidder should have realized immediately that something was not right. When a trader can't close positions without taking a big loss, there's clearly something wrong with what he's doing. But Jett didn't let the quarter's end slow him down for long. The day the next quarter began, Jett went to work booking all of his STRIPS and recon back into the system. All of the forward recon trades and the phantom profits that had disappeared were suddenly back in his trading account. Incredibly, management ignored his sudden turnaround: trades disappeared and profits disappeared; then trades reappeared and profits reappeared.

Perhaps those above Jett truly wanted to believe their star STRIPS trader was just that good. Cerullo's bonus was partially a function of Jett's success, so maybe it was easy to turn a blind eye.

By the end of 1993, the government bond desk had overtaken the mortgage desk in terms of profits, led in no small part by Jett's imaginary revenues. The STRIPS profits rolled in at $150.7 million for the year, but there was $198.2 million in imaginary money involved. The result was that the profit for the STRIPS desk really wasn't a profit at all. In total, Jett's trading desk delivered a net loss for the year of $47 million, according to SEC documents. But Jett's star wasn't diminished at that time because no one knew about the inflated numbers. The firm even named him "Man of the Year" due to the fact that he alone had accounted for 27 percent of the entire profit generated by the fixed-income trading department, a division of seven hundred people. For his efforts, Jett took home a $9.3 million bonus and a promotion to managing director.

It seemed like everything was going well for Jett, and he was living the life he had always dreamed about; however, nothing continues forever, and all hell broke loose in the bond market in February 1994. In what's remembered as a complete surprise to the market, the Fed announced a surprise twenty-five-basis-point tightening of interest rates. The result was a massive sell-off across the entire bond market, leaving trading desks everywhere nursing huge losses. Kidder Peabody was no exception.

For months after the September quarter-end debacle and in order to win some independence from GE, Kidder was trying desperately to secure outside funding from a variety of banks, including UBS. In order to get that lifeline, however, the unequivocal message was that Kidder needed to tidy up its balance sheet by the end of the quarter, March 31. Jett saw the writing on the wall and realized a repeat of the September quarter end was in the balance. But this time he had his own strategy for subterfuge. He continued to book the forward recon trades, but also started booking the outright purchases of coupon and principal STRIPS as forward trades too. Knowing that Kidder's accounting system, as of six months prior, did not recognize the forward settling trades, it was just the next loophole to exploit. By doing this, he kept almost all of his trades off of the firm's balance sheet, with the assumption he wouldn't have to go through the fire drill of closing everything out again. The result, however, was an operations mess, with the creation of a massive number of tickets for transactions that were simultaneously being closed out, settled, and rebooked to be settled in the future.

Cerullo, despite his apparent ignorance of Jett's malfeasance the previous year, was growing suspicious. He finally took notice that once Jett sold off his positions to reduce his balance sheet in September; Jett was showing a fraction of the profit that he'd been showing before. Why this suddenly became suspicious in March 1994 but not in September 1993 is anyone's guess. Bernstein shared Cerullo's suspicions too, and when Jett was in London on a business trip, Bernstein interrogated one of Jett's traders.

It was the first opportunity that anyone ever had to speak with individuals who worked on the STRIPS desk. Up to that point, not only would Jett not allow it—he had never taken so much as one day of vacation since he'd started working at Kidder, and his physical presence prevented that type of communication. But with Jett away on business, there was finally an opportunity.

Bernstein started by asking a trader, whose name was Dave, to value the forward trades at current prices and report back to him when finished. The result, suffice it to say, wasn't encouraging. When Jett returned from London, he was told by Bernstein, "Dave here is afraid that when we allow your trades to settle, you're going to have to write a big check to the Fed."

Jett shrugged off the suggestion as he was staring down the barrel of a loaded financial gun, but Bernstein didn't give up. Bernstein next went to Cerullo and pressured him to close down all of Jett's trades, telling Cerullo, "I'm certain. I'm certain that if these trades settle, he's going to have to pay up." Bernstein's fear was palpable, and Cerullo's own anxieties fed off that fear. He authorized Bernstein to investigate Jett's trades further, but again, he was finding the right answer but looking for the wrong reason. Bernstein feared that Jett was taking too much risk, and that's what scared him. He sensed that the profits might be somehow inflated, but he assumed it was due to risk taking, not an accounting flaw in the computer system.

The financial shit hit the fan just days later when Askin Capital Management, the largest customer of Kidder's mortgage desk, declared bankruptcy as a result of losses in its mortgage-backed IO and PO trading positions. Cerullo immediately ordered Jett to unload his STRIPS trades, telling him, "This Askin Capital situation has forced us to have as simple and understandable a balance sheet as we can, so I want you to liquidate your positions." Jett's world was about to come crumbling down. He told Cerullo that they'd be taking a loss, just like he had the previous September, but it fell on deaf ears.

The trader who had once commanded hero status at Kidder Peabody knew his time was up, and he began to panic. But he reasoned that if he got out while his reputation was still intact, he had time to write his own ticket at another firm. He tried, unsuccessfully, to recruit some of the other traders under his purview to abandon Kidder Peabody with him and head to another firm.

On March 28, Jett's assets started off at $29 billion on paper, but then the liquidation began, and Cerullo was stunned at what happened. The major problem with all of Jett's STRIPS positions, from a risk standpoint, is that they weren't completely hedged. Through miscalculation or just misunderstanding, Jett was actually net long $1.5 billion worth of securities. Being long in a declining market is not the position a trader wants to be in.

As Jett kept selling his positions, cash was leaving the firm like water through a funnel. Cerullo called him on the phone directly. "Do you have any idea how much liquidating your position has cost us?" he asked incredulously. At that moment, Cerullo had determined that approximately $300 million in nonexistent profits were about to disappear, generating a massive loss, and he explained that painful fact to Jett.

Jett was backed into a corner and he knew it, but he wasn't going down without a fight. Defiant to the very end, he replied to Cerullo flatly, "Not if you return my position to me." The argument again fell on deaf ears.

A few days later Jett was called into a meeting. In attendance were some of the more powerful figures at Kidder, including CFO Richard O'Donnell, the firm's chief legal counsel, and the head of human resources. At that meeting, Jett was apprised of the situation.

"We're looking at a loss of $300 million." That loss was all Jett's, due to the fact that the profits he had booked didn't really exist. There was no hiding from that fact.

On April 17, 1994, Joe Jett received a letter at his home, delivered by a messenger service. It was a pretty straightforward message: "Your employment with Kidder Peabody is terminated." That same day, GE announced a one-time charge on its earnings of $210 million after taxes; the pretax amount had been $350 million. GE was forced to inject $200 million into Kidder's operating capital, an action that ruffled more than a few feathers at the top of the org chart. "We'd be having great numbers," Jack Welch said, "without Kidder."

During his tenure at Kidder Peabody from July 1991 to April 1994, Jett had booked a total of $338.7 million in phantom profits. His net loss to the firm turned out to be $74.7 million. And though Jett's fraud had been the metaphorical rest of the iceberg, further investigation into the firm's operations showed that there were smaller icebergs that nobody knew existed. There were two other traders holding dishonest trading positions. An options trader named Neil Margolin, it was discovered, had hidden $11 million in losses on French and Spanish government bonds. Another trader named Peter Bryant had hidden $6 million of his own losses. Both men received the same fate as Jett: they were fired from the firm.

As the truth began to come to light, Jett's confrontational side began to shine. He initially called the whole situation nothing more than "window dressing," saying it was an attempt by Kidder Peabody to disguise its balance sheet and hide the true size of its assets from GE. Ironically enough, Jett's line of attack was itself nothing more than window dressing, as he merely attempted to shift the blame for the firm's losses from his own phantom profits. And then, in a leap of logic that could only make sense to him, he claimed that because Kidder's management—the men he referred to as his "sophisticated supervisors"—had believed his strategy to be legitimate, it couldn't be considered a fraud. In other words, because he'd managed to disguise what he was doing well enough to convince his superiors that he wasn't doing anything wrong, he truly wasn't doing anything wrong.

Kidder froze all of Jett's brokerage accounts that were being held at the firm, which was expected of an employee terminated under the circumstances. The stakes got higher when his home was raided by FBI agents, and when he was called in front of an arbitration panel set up by the National Association of Securities Dealers (NASD). He received a subpoena from the SEC and was banned by the New York Stock Exchange in December 1994. It was certainly not a good way for Jett to end the year.

Jett retained two lawyers—one a specialist in securities law, the other a criminal attorney—and invoked his Fifth Amendment right against self-incrimination when questioned by the SEC. During that time, he found work with a furniture moving company in Manhattan, saying that no Wall Street firm would even talk to him. He would eventually get his day in court, however.

There were still other players who had to answer for their actions before the Jett case was ever heard; Michael Carpenter, the CEO of Kidder Peabody, had the unfortunate duty of telling Jack Welch in person during the second week of April 1994. Carpenter was forced to resign his position two months later, and was replaced by Dennis D. Dammerman, a senior vice president and the CFO of GE. Dammerman retained his GE titles, but also added that of CEO of Kidder Peabody to his resume.

Edward Cerullo was forced to resign from Kidder Peabody one month after that, in July 1994, but he didn't go without a parting gift, of sorts. He was fined a measly $5,000 for his failure to supervise Jett and was allowed to keep his bonuses, even those inflated from Jett's phantom profits. He kept a total of $35.6 million that he'd been paid in bonus money during Jett's time at Kidder, theoretically a reward for his leadership of the firm's rainmaker. He claimed absolutely no knowledge of fraudulent activity on Jett's part. He did, however, acknowledge that he had certainly "failed to supervise" Jett's activities.

Mel Mullin also contended that he knew nothing of what Jett was doing, but that ignorance didn't help him. He was fired on August 3, 1994. Charging that Mullin had failed to adequately supervise Jett, Kidder kept his deferred compensation of $2.7 million. He maintained his ignorance, but he eventually paid a $25,000 fine to the SEC and served a three-month regulatory suspension from any association with a broker-dealer.

As for Kidder Peabody itself, the firm was fined $40,000 by the SEC, and GE unloaded its albatross of an investment bank on Paine Webber in October 1994. Welch acted quickly and decisively, following another one of his famous GE philosophies: any business GE owned had to be an industry leader or else it had to be "fixed, closed, or sold." GE certainly tried everything it could to fix its problematic subsidiary but in the end, it was clearly time for GE to get out of the investment banking business.

Where GE had initially paid $650 million for Kidder Peabody in 1986, its investment ballooned to over $2 billion during the eight years that it owned the firm, pumping in approximately $1.4 billion in additional capital as it hopped from one scandal or loss to another. By the time GE finally sold Kidder, Paine Webber agreed to pay only $670 million, meaning that GE had lost just shy of a $1.5 billion on its failed experiment in investment banking. And just to add insult to injury, as part of the sale agreement, GE was forced to keep the mortgage-backed securities inventory. And it had to manage the positions without the expertise of Michael Vranos. After the Jett fiasco, Vranos resigned and moved to a hedge fund, taking approximately forty of his mortgage traders with him.

Paine Webber, for its part, mostly wanted Kidder's retail brokerage business, which employed about 1,150 brokers in fifty offices. Kidder had catered to high-net-worth individuals, and its retail broker network was extremely lucrative. Paine Webber did what it could to integrate Kidder into its existing business structure, but there were many changes. For starters, the vast majority of former Kidder employees were laid off immediately, and the Kidder Peabody name was dropped altogether. One of Wall Street's most esteemed names in investment banking ceased to exist right then and there.

As for Joe Jett, the drama did not end. The popular TV crime series *Law and Order* picked up on the Jett story, running an episode about a rogue trader who was involved in a murder. In the end, the trader was found guilty and convicted, but that was the television world; in the real world, Joe Jett's epic story would continue for years.

At the end of 1995, Jett received word from the SEC that he was "not a target" of the Justice Department, meaning there would be no criminal charges pursued against him. But then in January 1996, the

SEC officially filed civil charges against him. That same year, the National Association of Securities Dealers—the self-regulatory agency overseeing the securities industry—handed down its own ruling. The arbitration panel found Jett innocent of fraud, and ordered Kidder to return the $5 million in Jett's brokerage account. The victory, however, was bittersweet, since Jett was unable to get his legal bills covered and was forced to pay $4 million to his lawyers.

The SEC took its time with the investigation and didn't announce a ruling until March 2004. Much of that time was taken to sort out witness statements, many of which were contradictory. In several cases, witnesses gave conflicting stories over the years, which forced their removal from the witness lists. With many of the key witnesses to the SEC's case gone, the case was close to falling apart.

But the facts were the facts, witnesses or not, and the SEC eventually found that Jett "deceived the firm about his trading performance, and caused, and aided and abetted record-keeping violations." They also found that he "recognized the computer glitch that made posting profit from forward reconstitutions possible, but no one else understood the implications." In other words, Jett was guilty of being the smartest guy in the room. However, that wasn't itself a crime, and no criminal charges were ever filed against him.

In a semantic twist to this whole case, coupon STRIPS and principal STRIPS are not legally considered securities under the definition of the word, so there could be no securities fraud. The SEC was convinced that Jett "had every intention of defrauding Kidder," and he was ordered to pay a disgorgement of $8.21 million and a $200,000 fine as a civil penalty. Additionally, he was "barred from association with a broker or dealer" thereafter.

True to his character, Jett never wavered from his insistence that he had done nothing wrong. "I was desperate to argue that I wouldn't have lost a cent if Cerullo had not forced me to liquidate my inventory," he said after the dust had settled. The problem with that impassioned plea is that the whole idea is itself absurd. Worse than absurd. It's nonexistent. His defense is predicated on the false idea that the profits were real—kind of like the trader who refuses to sell a losing position because he doesn't want to take a loss. They money was already lost; refusing to sell doesn't make the loss go away.

As of this writing, Jett has moved on to become his own boss. He is the CEO of Jett Capital Management, which bills itself as performing asset management, advisory, and private equity services. The firm's website highlights the fact that "the NASD found no basis for Welch's assault against Jett and declared Jett innocent of fraud." The information conveniently leaves out any mention of the SEC's findings. The site does, however, highlight the fact that Jett "pioneered the use of off-balance sheet financing," though whether or not that is a good selling point is up for argument. He is periodically an invited guest on financial television shows, for which his appearance fee is rumored to be between $4,000 and $8,000 a show. As of 2010, he claimed to be living in the dingy basement of a former girlfriend's house, from which he filmed at least one YouTube video.

* * *

Joe Jett was never found criminally liable for his actions, so at the core of the whole case, he is in one regard innocent. But did he commit fraud in the true sense of the word? On the one hand, he didn't try to hide anything from anyone. He submitted to audits and explained exactly what he was doing, though he did so in ways that were, let's call it, less than forthcoming. He booked all of his trades in Kidder's trade processing system, had the "Red Book" for trades that were not in the system, and freely discussed everything with his superiors and auditors. So could it still be fraudulent?

The fact of the matter is that Jett found a flaw in the system at Kidder, and he exploited that flaw to the fullest extent for his own gain. Yes, his activity was in the open; he was claiming profits that he knew were not real. He was clearly and purposely taking full advantage of the flaw he discovered, plain and simple.

Being the mathematician that he always was, in an "aha" moment, Jett stressed an equation to demonstrate that what he did was completely legitimate. The equation, which he credited to Mullin, claiming that Mullin had written it on a blackboard during a meeting, reads: "c + p = bond + acc." The "c" is for the coupons, "p" is for the principal portion; "bond" is the bond's price, and "acc" is accrued interest. It's basic math and, in Jett's mind, it proves Jett was right all the time. Again, though, he is adept at using fuzzy math to justify his actions. His proof is based on a fallacy, because his equation doesn't take into account the settlement date. And remember, Jett was doing his trades as forward recons trades. The value of securities between now and ninety days from now is much different.

Jett's formula should really have the first half of the equation being today and the second half being three months from now; it was missing the cost of carry all the time. Jett's formula should read: "c(today) + p(today) + cost of carry = bond (today + ninety days) + acc (today + ninety days)." Therein lies the true secret to Jett's strategy. Remember, the coupon and principal payments are the equivalent of the bond, and Jett was able to keep ninety days' worth of accrued interest instantaneously upon booking the trade. Kidder's accounting system took all profits up front on the future settlements; it just didn't incorporate the cost to carry.

Jett was never charged by the government with losing money; after all, a trader who loses money in an honest fashion isn't guilty of a crime. If losing money on a trade were a criminal offense, there would be a lot of Wall Street traders going to jail. No, losing money is not a crime, but hiding losses and booking false profits clearly is.

Chapter Four

Nick Leeson and Baring Brothers, 1995

There is arguably not a more polarizing figure to emerge in the twentieth century than former British Prime Minister Margaret Thatcher, the so-called "Iron Lady." On the one hand, she is credited with bringing the United Kingdom out of deep recession, extremely high unemployment, and stagnation. On the other, she's vilified for the methods she employed to accomplish that difficult task. How is it that one person—the first and only female prime minister in the country's history—can be simultaneously loved and vilified? The simple answer is that it's not that simple, but at its core, the answer revolves around her unyielding views about competition.

To truly appreciate Margaret Thatcher, one has to go back to just a few years before her election as prime minister. The winter months of 1978 and 1979 are referred to as the "Winter of Discontent" in Britain. It was the coldest winter in sixteen years, strikes were rampant, and inflation had just come off its peak of 26.9 percent in 1975. Leading with the slogan "Labour Isn't Working," Thatcher was one of the loudest voices criticizing the Labour government and its policies, which culminated in her election on May 4, 1979 as prime minister.

Thatcher was a staunch disciple of a laissez-faire approach for government, meaning that she felt the government and regulations should play a minimal role in the economy. Once in power, she privatized the public sector utilities such as gas, water, and electric, including the world-famous Sheffield steelworks.

Left alone during her first term were the English financial markets, housed in the section of London that is colloquially referred to as "The City of London" or "The Square Mile." The City had been the center of the financial world throughout much of the eighteenth and nineteenth centuries, but following two world wars, New York became the new hub of the world's financial wheeling and dealing. That said, London was still a major international financial center in Europe, serving the local British economy as well as being the center of the European Eurobond markets, and the world's largest foreign exchange market.

Throughout its history, the City was run by an "old-boy network"—a system that rewarded those who went to the right English public schools (the equivalent of American private schools), and the right school crest or necktie was more important than actual hard work and intelligence. This insular structure did not end with the people who worked there. Financial firms were also relegated to one of two distinct categories: brokers and jobbers. The brokers were the sales force for the financial system, introducing buy and sell orders to the traders who made markets in the securities, called the jobbers. It was a division of labor that had existed for over two hundred years, and nobody in the City saw any good reason to change it.

Nobody, that is, except for Margaret Thatcher. When the prime minister won reelection in 1983, those who worked in the City cheered her victory. They assumed that because she'd previously ignored the City, they were safe from the Iron Lady's sweeping changes. In reality, Thatcher was opposed to any industry operating in a protected status, which included the financial services in London. Right after her reelection, she desperately set out to change everything. The brokers, jobbers, and everyone else in the City would soon be subject to reforms.

Under the old system of brokers and jobbers, the brokers were guaranteed a 1.65 percent commission, no matter what. The jobbers made their money through an exclusive right to bid and offer the securities they traded. Who traded with whom was based on relationships; one broker worked exclusively with one jobber. For example, a broker might have an order to buy shares of a particular stock, and the order would be sent to the jobber firm the broker worked with. The jobber got back with a price that made a nice profit, no matter what. Then they celebrated the trade over a leisurely lunch. Everybody won. Well, at least two of the three parties involved won; the big loser in the game was the customer.

The jobbers, meanwhile, had many shortcomings. They were, as a collective group, undercapitalized to properly make markets in the face of any kind of competition. Fortunately for them, the whole system was closed to outsiders in a number of ways. If you weren't a graduate of a distinguished British public school, you had no chance of getting in. If you were a foreign firm new to the City, you also had no chance of getting in. And if you didn't have a relationship with a good brokerage firm, you also had no way of getting in. The whole operation was rife with restrictions that afforded entry only to those with certain privileges.

For outsiders, the only sort of crumb thrown to the public was the chance to work for a bank in the position of clerk, a nice position to which a young working-class man would enthusiastically aspire. Clerk was the general name given to the support staff within a bank, including the accounting department and the back office, as well as the mail room. Most clerks would expect to hold the same job for the duration of their working lives, with a possibility of being promoted to the head of their group as the highest achievement.

The upper echelons at banks even had a term to describe the clerks; they called them barrow boys. The derogatory term originated from the boys who pushed wheelbarrows full of produce around the City markets, including the famous Smithfield meat market. The barrow boys who worked at Smithfield's pushed carts full of fresh and frozen meat up to the vendors' stalls from the subterranean trains that brought the goods to the marketplace. It was tedious, hard work that was clearly reserved for occupants of the lower rungs of the social ladder. The life of the clerk—just like that of the barrow boy—was the lowest rung for those who worked at London's banks, and the principle was the same: there was a clear and definite division that protected both the business and social structures.

Margaret Thatcher made her first swipe at reforming the City through a legal action filed against the London Stock Exchange. The lawsuit was later dropped when the London Stock Exchange "voluntarily" agreed to certain concessions, which included, among many things, opening up the financial markets to competition by the end of 1986.

On October 27, 1986, the London financial world literally exploded in what came to be known as the Big Bang. These changes were to become the most sweeping ever in a major financial center in such a short period of time. The private club atmosphere that had long been associated with the City would soon be gone. It would be replaced by what one financial reporter called "the rapacious, bonus-grabbing culture of the investment bank." It was truly the beginning of modern banking in the United Kingdom. Constraints prohibiting foreign banks and securities firms from joining the London Stock Exchange were eradicated. Suddenly the London markets were open to international players, among them a slew of Americans.

The changes were far-reaching. For starters, the Big Bang ended the exchange controls that required British investors to pay taxes to buy foreign shares. Trading floors became computerized, doing away with the open-cry system that had prevailed for centuries. A regulatory board was created to oversee the deregulation of the markets, and perhaps most importantly, it did away with the antiquated division between the brokers and the jobbers.

For all of the old traditions that were being turned upside down by the Big Bang, much like opinions of Thatcher herself, opinions were both wildly positive and negative, depending on whom you asked. Gone were the days of alcohol-infused lunches where traders swapped stories of their public school days. They were replaced with such American practices as working breakfasts, cutthroat competition, and eighty-hour workweeks. As more foreign firms moved in, even more of those American practices were to follow, such as eye-popping bonuses on top of six-figure salaries. As one reporter described it, "Britain's laxer regime brought an influx of U.S. firms, with their chinos, booze-free lunch breaks, and bumper bonuses, helping to bust open the old City cliques."

As these new changes took root in the City, the financial industry also shifted its focus from longer-term client relationships to a more short-term approach—whatever made the most money in the least amount of time. The business model became one based on competition; the broker who got the trade was the one that offered the best price at that particular time.

The changes were immense and, as it turned out, permanent. Two centuries of tradition came crashing down literally overnight. But despite the rapidly changing landscape, there were still a few longtime residents of the City who resisted the new developments. Those old stalwarts were the keepers of the banking tradition; they had ruled the

London financial world for years and weren't anxious to step into the brave new world that became the City in the late 1980s. Some of those firms continued to act as if the Big Bang never even happened. One of those tradition-steeped institutions was Baring Brothers.

* * *

Baring Brothers was known as the world's first modern-day merchant bank, and the Baring family sat high on the English social ladder, including six peerages, five of which are still active today. Earls, viscounts, and barons all graced the branches of the Baring family tree; at one point, the Princess of Wales was the great-granddaughter of a Baring. One Baring went on to head the Admiralty under Prime Minister Gladstone, and one became the controller-general, then consul general of Egypt after serving as financial advisor to the British Viceroy of India. So great was the bank's reputation that the Duc de Richelieu once said, "There are six great powers in Europe: England, France, Prussia, Austria, Russia, and Baring Brothers."

Baring Brothers was founded in 1763 by the brothers John, Francis, and Charles. Their father had moved to England in 1717, originally as an apprentice to a wool merchant. By the time of their father's death in 1748, the family was fast becoming one of the wealthiest in England, and within forty years of the bank's founding, Barings was recognized as the most important merchant bank in the world.

The secret to the family's success was good old-fashioned, steeped-in-tradition, nineteenth century–style banking. Barings had a strong presence in the New World, from financing the silver exports from Mexico to managing loans for the governments of Chili and Argentina. The family also played a big role in financing the newly formed United States: Alexander Baring presided over the loan negotiations when the country needed a $15 million for a real estate deal known as the Louisiana Purchase. Then the Barings went on to assist Cornelius Vanderbilt with the financing of vast railroad construction.

With its financial pedigree, experience, and connections, it stands to reason that the bank was always on a solid footing. But it was not the case by the late nineteenth century, when Barings' loan portfolio was dominated by loans to Argentina. At that time, as much as 50 percent of England's international investments were housed in that South American country, and Barings too found itself overexposed. In 1889, Argentina was effectively bankrupt. The country defaulted on its loans, and the country's inability to make interest payments brought Barings to the brink of collapse.

Under the direction of the Bank of England, the other City banking houses attempted to set up a financial syndicate to save Barings. At first, London's second-highest-regarded bank, N. M. Rothschild and Sons, refused to participate unless the English government joined in on the rescue fund. After repeated and increasingly forceful requests from the Bank of England, Lord Rothschild finally relented: "If capital is needed, I am here with £50 million." Barings had been saved, but a lesson had also been learned. Baring Brothers & Co. was reorganized as Baring Brothers & Co., LTD, one of the first banks to become a limited liability company. Banking was clearly not without risk, and the Baring family was not about to risk its fortune again.

By the 1980s, Baring Brothers was still under the tutelage of the Baring family, with Sir John Baring serving as chairman, Nicholas Baring as deputy chairman, Peter Baring as senior finance director, and three other Barings working at the bank. The interior was much like you'd expect in a traditional British bank: old share certificates and ventures framed on the walls, an open fire burning in the hearth, and the partners sitting at large oak desks. Modern-day Baring Brothers was clearly still run like a gentlemen's cooperative.

In the 1990s, Peter Baring succeeded his cousin John as chairman of the bank. In his fifties, Peter was known as an aloof man, which well suited the bank's reputation. Baring Brothers, however, was being confronted by the same forces of change as other City banks. The irony was that Baring Brothers represented both the old and the new City together in one institution. Nowhere in any other London bank did a contrast exist such as the contrast between Baring Brothers and its subsidiary, Baring Securities.

Baring Securities was the brokerage arm of Barings Brothers and had ridden the tide of modernism wrought by the Big Bang. Money was the name of the game at Baring Securities, and any trader or salesman who was worth the title wanted as much of it as he could make. This arm—prosthetic as it might seem—was added in the mid-1980s, the time when Wall Street operating by the slogan "greed is good."

Baring Securities broke with the Baring Brothers traditions when it came to just about everything. Whereas Baring Brothers had valued hiring people from the right schools and family ties, Baring Securities hired people who were hungry and aggressive, people who wanted to make money—lots of money. Whereas Baring Brothers had the same City address for over two hundred years, with all the style anyone would expect, Baring Securities had a shiny new office, decorated in Art Deco and located outside of the City in, ironically enough, America Square. Inside, the heart of Securities was the football field–size trading floor, with all the hustle and bustle of traders yelling and screaming across the floor to get their trades done. Baring Securities was immensely successful. Within ten years of its founding, it had grown from a twenty-man operation to one that employed over 1,400 people.

When Baring Brothers had wanted its firm to move away from the relatively safe harbor of the British markets and return to the emerging markets, it looked for the right operation to take it there. Because the wounds of its South American experience were still present even a hundred years later, the firm cast its eyes on Asia. In order to make that move, it looked to one man—the man who built Baring Securities from the ground up, the son of an Army general named Christopher Heath.

*   *   *

Christopher Heath was many things to many people, but a prototypical Barings executive he was not. Born in 1946, Heath's first career was a brief stint with Imperial Chemical Industries in the 1960s. One night at a dinner party, Heath was seated next to a City stockbroker who was working at a firm named George Henderson & Co. After speaking with the man all evening, Heath was hooked. The lure of money just waiting to be made was too much to pass up. It was surely the stockbroker's life for him. And as luck would have it, George Henderson & Co. was recruiting new salesmen; Heath quickly joined the firm in February 1969.

After a few years of learning the ropes, Heath found himself a niche business selling Japanese stocks to British investors. Up until then, it was widely assumed within the ranks of British banks that the Japanese market was pretty insignificant; there just wasn't anything going on. It was a modest point of interest at best. However, no one had counted on the Japanese economy growing as quickly as it did in the late 1970s and 1980s. By 1982, Heath was making a killing selling all kinds of great-performing Japanese securities to his customers, including a big array of Japanese equity warrants, which were completely underpriced at the time.

Heath was doing so well that he was allowed to spin off his part of the operation into what became Henderson Crosthwaite (Far East). The success he experienced didn't go unnoticed at other firms, with Baring Brothers being one of them. In 1985, Barings expressed an interest in acquiring Henderson Crosthwaite (Far East), and a deal was struck to sell Heath's business to the London financial stalwart for £5.8 million. The new acquisition would be called Baring Securities.

Heath continued under the newly branded name of Baring Securities, making what could only be called spectacular profits trading stocks in Japan. The new firm was wildly successful, even beyond the most optimistic of expectations, riding the spectacular gains of the Japanese economy. Whereas Baring Securities had been projected to turn a £3 million profit in its first year in 1986, it made £10 million. The cost of acquiring Heath's business had been covered in a single year's profits, with a few million pounds to spare.

By today's standards, the person in charge of a company that's so successful expects to be compensated handsomely. But this was Britain and this was Baring Brothers, where million-dollar bumper bonuses weren't quite as ubiquitous as they are on Wall Street today. Those expectations were just starting to drift across the Atlantic following the Big Bang, and the traders and salesmen at Baring Securities expected to be compensated well beyond their peers at Baring Brothers. Heath was reportedly making £3 million a year in salary, plus a share of the profits generated by Baring Securities. That amount alone totaled over £33 million over his first six years at Barings, making Heath not only the highest-paid executive at Barings, but also in the whole of Great Britain.

At that time and place, Heath's salary was high, scandalously high. And when word got out to the press and back to other Baring Brothers partners—some of them descendants of the actual Baring brothers—there was a less-than-generous response. The executives at Baring Brothers began to clamor for an undiluted ownership of Baring Securities. They were fine with Heath making incredible profits; they just didn't want to share so much with him.

Heath, not surprisingly, was not interested in changing anything. He had grown accustomed to his wealth. He'd purchased for himself a 391-acre home and a stable of thoroughbred racehorses. His expansive home was appointed with the finest in English antiques and fine art. And when not at home, he could often be found lounging on his 148-foot yacht. Life was certainly good for Christopher Heath. He was making a fortune and was firmly in control of Baring Securities, surrounded by a fiercely loyal group of top producers.

Baring Securities was well entrenched in Asia when the Big Bang occurred. The Big Bang meant exchange controls were lifted, and Japanese securities were wide open to British investors. British money continued to flow into Japan, and Heath's business sought out new avenues to generate more profits, expanding into derivatives trading and joining the different Asian futures exchanges, including the Singapore International Monetary Exchange (SIMEX) in 1987. The next year, the firm posted a staggering £60 million profit.

Everything was going well, and everyone was pretty happy at Baring Securities. The team in Tokyo was once described as "a loose group having a really exciting time." Another executive said that in Asia, "there was much more freedom and a lot less compliance." In other words, all of that business was being exploited by the successful traders and salesmen who worked there. Heath himself was no exception; he was constantly searching for "more money and less interference from London." In other words, he wanted the executives at Baring Brothers to leave him alone to make his fortune.

But just like any good party, this one had to come to an end. In 1992, Baring Securities posted its first monthly loss in history. It was a small loss by all standards, but the Baring Brothers executives now had an excuse to rein in the organization that they saw as out of control and playing by its own rules. Heath was running the company as his own personal fiefdom, and they wanted it stopped immediately. Though Baring Securities ended up turning a profit for the year, it was a far cry from what it made in 1988. The firm had still made £10.8 million for the year, but it had commitments to pay out £18.5 million in bonuses. The problem was that paying out more in bonus than it had made was not part of Heath's original deal with Baring Brothers.

Baring Brothers agreed to fund the year's bonus payments, but there was a catch. Changes in management were required in exchange for its financial generosity, and Heath was part of the collateral damage. He was officially asked to leave the company in 1993, and he was not the only victim of the restructuring. Many of his loyal managers and other traders were let go too. There was a full-fledged purge in the upper ranks of Baring Securities, with Peter Norris, a longtime Baring Brothers executive, moving into the role of CEO.

Unbeknownst to them, the culture at Baring Securities was completely foreign to the partners of Baring Brothers. When Peter Norris moved into the executive suite, it was just a culture he didn't understand. It was one thing to take control, but it would be another thing to manage. And trying to manage Baring Securities was, perhaps in hindsight, a grave mistake.

Heath had fostered a culture of aggressiveness at Baring Securities, a win-at-all-costs sort of attitude. "You don't understand these guys," he once told his bosses at Baring Brothers. "In our world, someone who gets £1 million just wants to make £2 million." Perhaps most importantly, he was famous for asking those he interviewed, "Are you hungry?" If the answer had anything to do with money, the candidate was a shoo-in for the job. He reasoned that a trader who was hungry would work that much harder to make even more money. But Heath didn't factor in another biological reality, namely the fact that a hungry animal—no matter if it walks on four legs or two—will take greater risks the hungrier it is. And while Heath might have been asking the question metaphorically, in reality he was asking recruits if they were willing to take whatever risks were required to make the most money. If they said they were, they got the job.

As it turns out, Nicholas Leeson was one of those recruits; he was very hungry.

* * *

Nicholas William Leeson was born on February 25, 1967, in the London suburb of Watford, a town consistently ranked well below the national average in terms of income. He was the first of four children; his father Harry was a plasterer and his mother Anne a nurse. Though they were far from living on the brink of starvation, the family was nevertheless working class, and the combined income of his parents did not allow the family to own a home. All six of them lived in a small flat. It was a place that bred a kind of hunger, the kind of hunger to get out of Watford and make something of yourself.

Leeson attended Parmiter's School, where he was better known for his soccer playing than his academics. His performance in school—coupled with his parents' meager income—meant that college was certainly not in his future. As Leeson set his sights on working in the City, his basic education and lack of family connections meant he was only a candidate for the job of clerk, and he was lucky if he got such an opportunity.

As luck would have it, Leeson did just that after he graduated from high school in 1985. He was offered a position as a junior clerk with Coutts & Co., one of the City's oldest and best-known financial institutions. He worked hard, but also played hard. He was only 18 years old, so perhaps he should be forgiven for some of his well-known social transgressions. At night after work he found himself overindulging at local pubs and involved in fights, and there was sometimes police involvement.

His temperament was indicative of his aggressive nature, and when the Big Bang hit in 1986, that personality would serve him well. A friend told him of a job opening at the newly formed office of Morgan Stanley. They were looking for a settlement clerk, a small step up from his junior clerk status, so he applied for the job and was hired in 1987. There, he found himself in the right place at exactly the right time.

Morgan Stanley had offered Leeson one of two positions: he could choose to work in either foreign exchange settlements or in futures and options settlements. He opted for the latter, working in the back office, processing trades as well as confirming contracts and money movements with other companies. The money was good for Leeson; a £20,000 base salary plus a £20,000 bonus was a huge sum compared to what his friends were making back home in Watford.

Leeson was able to build a strong reputation for being hardworking and extremely detail-oriented. Though he had bigger dreams for himself, he was well known for a variety of boasts around the office. One was a claim that he had played semiprofessional soccer for an English team named Hayes, which was part of the Isthmian League. While it is true he was an exceptional athlete in high school, there was no record of him playing for Hayes or any other semipro team. His story hit a snag when a coworker attended a Hayes game and noticed quite obviously that Leeson was nowhere to be seen.

The boasts hinted at the bigger picture of Leeson's aggressive nature and his desire for more. Soon after, he turned in his resignation to Morgan Stanley, giving the firm a month's notice of his intention to leave even though he did not have a new job.

Luckily, his unemployment didn't last long, as he started at Baring Securities in July 1989. During the interview process, Leeson was asked about his career ambitions, and he replied quite frankly that he wanted to go into trading, despite the fact that he was not one of the City's educated and connected elites. "I have a low boredom threshold," he told the interviewer. His hunger propelled him forward, and he joined the settlements division at Baring Securities, again in futures and options. There, he quickly established himself again as someone who worked hard, and he proved he was more than capable. His superiors took notice; the working-class kid was clearly head and shoulders above his social peers.

* * *

The Jakarta Stock Exchange in Indonesia has something of a turbulent history. It was first opened in 1912 by the Dutch colonial government, but faced closures during World War I and World War II. It was finally reopened in 1977, and Baring Securities was one of the first European banks on the scene. The move, however, was not without logistical difficulties. For starters, Barings had no office in Jakarta. Instead, the employees there worked out of a room at the Hotel Borobudur. The lack of a traditional office was only a minor setback compared to the backlog of approximately £100 million in unsettled East Asian stock certificates the firm had accumulated by 1989.

At that time in Asia, stock certificates were mostly issued in physical form, unlike today, where securities are electronic and transferred from one account to another via computer. Such a backlog was symptomatic of problems that plagued Baring Brothers collectively. On one hand, Baring Brothers was entrenched in its past traditions; on the other, Baring Securities rushed into new markets without much thought as to supporting the new businesses. Regardless, Barings needed someone to sort things out, and that someone was Nick Leeson.

At the end of 1989, Leeson traveled to Indonesia to sort out the Jakarta mess. The certificates were housed in a windowless, airless room that more closely resembled a medieval dungeon than a world-class clearing depository. Papers were scattered everywhere, many of them damaged. The certificates were oftentimes in different denominations, with the purchases not matching up with the sales. Leeson had to match up all of the shares with the clients' accounts and sort it all out. It was a Herculean task.

He labored for three months on his own before Barings sent reinforcements to assist him. One of those reinforcements was a woman named Lisa Sims, who would later become Mrs. Nick Leeson. After a year's work, the team managed to whittle the amount of outstanding certificates down to a mere £10 million, an amount that was acceptable to Baring Brothers, at least for the time being.

The executives who assigned Leeson to the Jakarta cleanup were very impressed with his work and dedication, and as a reward, Leeson was tapped to run the firm's new operation in Singapore. Barings had acquired a seat on the SIMEX exchange back in 1987 but had yet to make it operational. The firm needed someone to set up the office, hire the staff, serve as the general manager, and make the whole thing profitable. That is, it needed someone with the kind of dedication and drive that Leeson had exhibited in Jakarta. At the age of twenty-seven, Nick Leeson was offered the opportunity of a lifetime for a kid from working-class Watford.

*   *   *

SIMEX was a futures exchange modeled after the old-school style of open-outcry trading—characterized by traders wearing oddly colored jackets, shouting at the top of their lungs while making various hand gestures. It was throwback to the old trading pits of its earliest days, before modern technology began to creep in. Despite the fact that it was a relatively small marketplace, many customers preferred to trade on the SIMEX because it had less rigid rules than other exchanges, including lower margin requirements.

Margin deposits are a fail-safe for exchanges, as they provide a cash cushion to offset potential losses if members are unable to pay their bills. At the end of the trading day, the exchange tallies up each broker's open contracts and sends the broker a margin call—a request to pledge either cash or securities to the exchange. The exact amount depends on a number of factors, including the rules of the exchange, the volatility of the market, and the underlying instruments.

After receiving the margin call, the futures broker will then collect the requisite margin amount from his own customers to cover the payment. The one caveat is that brokers are allowed to calculate their clients' collective positions as a net amount. In the event that one client is long a contract and another client is short the same contract, the broker is not required to deposit any margin at the exchange. However, the broker still collects margin from both of the individual clients. Additionally, because customers often don't want to be bothered with margin deposits every day, they will typically leave "excess margin" on deposit to cover the day-to-day margin calls. The end result is that the futures broker often has a lot of excess margin sitting around in the account—funds that can be invested at a profit.

The futures market is also what's called listed derivatives, or sometimes exchange-traded derivatives. In basic terms, a derivative is a contract whose price is determined (or derived) from the price of another instrument—like a commodity or a stock index. It's the equivalent of a bet at an athletic event. For example, if two men are sitting at a football game and they want to bet on the outcome, they're betting who wins and who loses that particular game. They have no stake in the ownership of the team, the TV rights, which players are in the lineup, or what plays the coach calls. Rather, they're simply betting on the outcome of that game.

The value of the S&P 500 stock index is a good example of a financial instrument used for futures contracts. Contracts are traded based on the price of that index at some month in the future, say December. If the price of the S&P 500 drops twenty points today, that decline will be reflected in the value of the December S&P 500 futures contact.

One important thing about exchange-traded derivatives is that they are regulated and standardized. Futures contracts trade on exchanges like the Chicago Mercantile Exchange (CME) or the London International Financial Futures Exchange (LIFFE), and they have predetermined delivery months and a strict delivery requirement for the underlying instrument, such as a specific type of wheat. And standing between the two parties in the transaction is the futures exchange's clearinghouse, which guarantees the payment of the contracts.

One of the most important stock indices in Asia is the Nikkei 225, which is much like the S&P 500 or Dow Jones Industrial Average in the United States, but it's a basket of 225 Japanese stocks. Nikkei stock index futures happen to trade on both the SIMEX and the Osaka futures exchanges. In the case of the SIMEX exchange, the market is smaller and less liquid, meaning that large orders can have major effects on the market, pushing prices one way or another. By contrast, the Osaka exchange is larger and more liquid; being the main futures exchange in Japan, it gets much of the domestic trading volume. And just as London evolved from open-outcry exchanges before the Big Bang to electronic trading, so too were similar changes happening in Asia. Osaka was an all-electronic marketplace, whereas SIMEX was still open-outcry. The differences in geography, open-outcry versus electronic, and market depth between the SIMEX and Osaka all created opportunities between the two markets.

Trading methods weren't the only difference between the two exchanges. Whereas the SIMEX had minimal margin requirements, the Osaka exchange initially required a 9 percent margin deposit. Then in the summer of 1992 the Japanese government imposed tighter restrictions on the exchange, and the Nikkei 225 futures contract margin was ramped up to 15 percent. The new rule also required that no interest could be paid on those deposits. It created a much higher cost of doing business on the Osaka exchange, and many customers fled for the friendlier environment at the SIMEX. The result was a huge influx of new customers to the market where Baring Securities was by now a fixture.

And the main fixture at the Baring Securities Singapore office was Nick Leeson, its hard-working and hard-partying manager. He worked long hours—usually coming into the office at dawn and staying long into the evening. But after work, he was drinking just as hard as he worked. As one colleague said of the newly married Leeson, "His behavior was more like that of a bachelor."

Despite his status as the office manager, there were two immediate supervisors who Leeson reported to: Ron Baker, a hard-working Australian, and Simon Jones, the regional operations manager of Barings South Asia, who everyone knew cared little for futures and options. Jones was officially in charge of the office and was Leeson's direct boss, even though everyone on the trading floor knew that Leeson was really running the show.

Leeson and the other Barings floor traders had no authority to trade for themselves; they were strictly there to fill orders on behalf of clients. The Singapore operation was off to a good start, as Leeson was providing excellent service filling futures orders and bringing in new revenues to the firm. His trading floor skills were so immediately apparent that the Baring Securities' traders in the Tokyo office even gave him the authority to hedge their positions at his own discretion.

* * *

One of the many reasons why exchanges worldwide moved away from open-outcry to computer-based trading was to minimize trading errors. Amidst the confusion of a crowded trading pit, with traders yelling and gesturing at one another, it was easy for an order to be misunderstood by one party or the other. It wasn't uncommon for pit traders to make errors such as booking the wrong amount or booking a trade the wrong way. For example, an order might be understood to be five contracts when it was supposed to be fifty. The trader simply heard the word "five" as opposed to the word that had actually been said, namely "fifty." Worst-case scenario, an order yelled over to the pit trader was intended to be a buy order and understood as a sale. Any trade that doesn't match what the other counterparty knows is called an out trade.

In cases of small discrepancies in the execution of futures orders, brokers typically rely on the firm's error account. This is a cash reserve that serves the exact purpose its name suggests—covering trading errors. Generally such an account is reserved for small errors, problems that are less than $1,000.

Baring Securities maintained its own error account for futures out trades in its London office in an account numbered 99905. But as the volume of transactions in Singapore grew, so too did the number of minor trading errors the office was forced to account for. It became a quite the tedious and time-consuming process to maintain the error account in London, so the home office authorized Leeson to open his own error account in Singapore.

On July 3, 1992, Leeson was told to open an account and instructed to hold any minor execution errors there, sending only margin call requests back to London. He set up an account numbered 88888, or the "five eights account," as it was called, to serve as the number on the account. Singaporeans are very superstitious as a population, a characteristic passed down from their Chinese origins, and the number eight was thought to be a lucky number. Because more eights meant greater luck, it was assumed that five eights would be a very lucky account number indeed. It would not turn out to be quite so lucky for Leeson, however.

The new error account got its first use just a couple of weeks later, on Friday, July 17. That Friday, a new clerk on the trading floor made what can be called a grave mistake—she sold twenty March Nikkei futures contracts instead of buying them. The problem was intensified when the error wasn't discovered until the end of the day; by that time, the Nikkei was up four hundred points, and the loss realized by her gaffe was up to £20,000.

In the young clerk's defense, she was new to the profession. Barings management had cut costs by hiring young and inexperienced personnel, as they were only paying clerks £4,000 a year in salary. But more importantly, her error opened the door for Leeson, making him realize he could easily hide losses as he saw fit. His plan was to temporarily hide the loss in the five eights account, giving him time to work his way out of the problem.

In order to do so, Leeson booked a fictitious trade with a customer, Fuji Bank, for the twenty contracts mistakenly sold. After "buying" the contracts back from Fuji Bank internally, he booked the trade in the 88888 account, leaving a £20,000 loss. It was a temporary fix, he reasoned. It would be there just long enough to avoid showing the loss over the weekend. He naturally planned to cover back the loss when the market opened again on the following Monday.

That Monday morning, Leeson studied the market conditions in the trading pit before the opening bell. The rally on that previous Friday was a big one, and he reasoned that investors would be pulling back at the start of the day, selling off to book some profits. His instincts were wrong, however, and the market continued to surge ahead. Rather than admit the error, he continued to hold on staying short the contracts. By the end of the day the loss was up to £60,000, an amount he couldn't possibly admit to Simon Jones.

Since he couldn't go to the London office to cover the shortfall in the 88888 account without the error being discovered, Leeson searched for another way to cover the funds. The easiest source of immediate cash was the excess funds in the customers' margin accounts. Of course, that was supposed to be sacred money; the funds were only supposed to cover margin calls. But Leeson told himself he could use it temporarily as a short-term loan and pay it back before anyone knew it was gone. There could be no harm done, really.

Baring Securities kept its clients' margin deposits in an account at Citibank in Singapore. With all of the clients that Baring represented, there was plenty of money in the account, so it was an easy source of cash. But Leeson had to get access to it first. He had no specific authority to withdraw funds from the account, but he was allowed to channel excess funds from one account to another. All he had to do was redirect money into the 88888 account. And because he was in charge of the back office, there was no one to challenge his money transfers that were now covering the losses. Problem solved.

The excess customer funds were sufficient for a while, but they began to run out as the losses mounted. Soon after the first trading error, Leeson made one himself when he incorrectly sold twenty Nikkei futures contracts instead of buying them on behalf of a client named Mitsuko. By the time Leeson figured out his mistake, the market had jumped up two hundred points, and he lost £18,000. Of course, the new loss went straight into the 88888 account.

By the end of 1992, an additional thirty errors had sapped up the resources of the 88888 account and the excess margin—a fact that should have been a stark embarrassment for Leeson, though he was still determined to make it all back. Before he could do that, he had to juggle more accounts to hide the losses for the month-end reports, which were being checked by the accounting department. Fortunately for Leeson, the Citibank margin account held a good chunk of money in it; at one point, he was siphoning £3 million out of it *daily*. When that wasn't enough, he was also able to deduct some of the losses from its futures trading commissions, yet somehow nobody seemed to notice. Leeson would later say of his use of margin funds, "My dabble in error account 88888 had been a useful way to buy time."

His secret was safe for time being, but the 88888 account was becoming something of an addiction for Leeson. By having a fallback to cover any trading errors, he garnered a reputation for giving clients fantastic executions in the futures pits, though many of those orders really resulted in losses for Barings. It wasn't a problem for Leeson, though; any bad fills were just dumped into the 88888 account. In reality, had it not been for the 88888 account, he would have been just another run-of-the-mill floor trader. But because he had a method to cover bad fills so easily and not have to account for them, he seemed to have a Midas touch in the pit. His vanity grew by leaps and bounds, and he did everything he could to enjoy his rock-star reputation.

As the losses accumulated further, it became increasingly difficult to hide them. After a while, he was at his limit with the client margin and with using the futures commissions. One more titanic blunder on an order and the difficulty was about to go up exponentially. The inevitable trade happened when the wrong direction was executed on a particular sell order. The intent was to sell one hundred Nikkei futures contracts, but the floor trader had bought them instead. The market was moving fast and the immediate loss was up to £150,000; Leeson knew "[w]e were in trouble," as he later said of the incident.

The amount was too large to charge against the commissions or the margin account; there just wasn't enough there to cover the loss. Of course, the easiest option would have been to ask the London office to wire in the money after admitting a mistake, but that thought ran against every grain of Leeson's ego. He couldn't do that. He had to come up with a new way to raise money, and the only thing he could think of was to sell some options.

Options are financial contracts that give one party the option to buy a stock or a financial instrument from another party. The option contract is only good for a specific period of time and at a specific price; the date is called the expiration date, and the price is called the strike price. Options come in two varieties, calls and puts.

A call option is the option to buy a financial instrument, whereas a put option is the option to sell it. For example, if a trader thinks a stock is undervalued and expects the price to go up, a call option allows the trader to purchase the stock at a specified price if the stock's price indeed moves higher. Assuming the trader bets correctly, he doesn't have to actually own the stock to participate in the stock price appreciation.

On the reverse side, if the stock price falls, the trader is only out the money he paid to buy the option. And that's the important point here. When traders want the right but not the obligation to buy something, they have to pay a price for that right. That's the price of the option, or the premium. Say a trader paid $1 for the right to buy a stock at $10 a share. Someone else was willing to sell the trader that option, and was paid $1 a share. If there were one hundred thousand shares involved, the buyer is paying $100,000 for the option to buy, and the seller received a $100,000 premium by selling the option. The seller just made a lot of money, but also took a lot of risk, sometimes a huge amount of risk. If the stock price moves higher, the seller must deliver those shares at a price of $10, no matter where the stock is trading. The stock's price could reach $15 a share, or even $30. Selling options can be very risky, and options traders have been known to take significant losses.

The upside for traders who sell options is that they keep the premium if the price of the security remains the same or goes down. In both of these cases, the option expires worthless with no further money changing hands. That's the scenario that Leeson was banking on when he first walked into the Nikkei futures options pit to sell options. Let's just say he was hanging his future on it.

Leeson reasoned that if he sold two options at the same time, puts and calls, he could collect premiums and be partially hedged against the market moving slightly in one direction or the other. On the last day of the month, right before the London office reviewed his reports, he sold the two options simultaneously, which is the practice known as selling a straddle. In the straddle, Leeson collected the premiums from the options buyers and prayed the market didn't move suddenly before he bought back them back. On the first day of the next month, he bought back the options, giving back the options premiums to the traders in the options pit. It was an easy way to dig up some quick cash. Again, the risk was large, but it was only for one day, just enough to cover up his hole, at least as far as Barings in London was concerned.

When the dust had settled on his first straddle trade, Leeson had successfully raised £3.7 million in funds for that one-day period. What's best, he had found a new source of cash to cover his burgeoning losses. There was, however, one problem with his straddle strategy, Leeson knew futures contracts really well, but options were a whole different world; he didn't fully understand the intricacies of pricing them. When he walked into the options trading pit on the last day of the month, he was flying blind by all standards—overpaying every time he bought and sold. Options traders use sophisticated pricing models to determine where they buy and sell, whereas Leeson only knew that he needed money right then and there, and he didn't have any other way of getting it. He had to take whatever prices they were offering.

None of the options traders had an inkling that Leeson was trading for his own account; they simply assumed he was trading for a client—a misinformed, misguided, and just naïve client. But despite his success is raising funds, Leeson was also losing as much as 10 percent of the cash he was generating just by paying the bid/offer spread by getting into the trade one day and getting out the next day. Over the course of a year—twelve months—it meant paying 120 percent of whatever amount he was borrowing, a fact that clearly made the options traders very happy. He actually became pretty popular in that area of the exchange too, and his activity in both futures and options around the SIMEX didn't go unnoticed. After a while, he caught the attention of a man named Ang Swee Tian, the president of the exchange, who then introduced Leeson to a "valued client of the SIMEX," a man named Philippe Bonnefoy.

* * *

Bonnefoy was what a Las Vegas casino would refer to as a whale. He traded upwards of five thousand Nikkei futures and options contracts daily, a number that put him second to only the legendary George Soros in terms of trading volume. His company was the Bahamas-based European Trust and Banking Company, and he wanted Leeson to handle the execution of his trades. In other words, just the buying and selling component—the clearing was handled by FIMAT, the futures broker owned by the French bank Société Générale. Bonnefoy also valued his privacy; his name was not supposed to become public, even within Barings. Around the firm, he would only be known only as "the mystery client" or "client X."

Just days after their initial meeting in February 1994, Bonnefoy gave Leeson an order to buy four thousand futures contracts. It was a sizable order, and generated a commission of approximately £8,000. Bonnefoy immediately liked the futures prices Leeson got for him, so perhaps Leeson's reputation as being able to execute the best prices was true; he therefore sent his new trader more and more of his business. The increase in orders added to Leeson's status around the pits as well as in the halls of Baring Securities. From all angles, Leeson appeared to be a rising star.

As time passed, Leeson continued to afford Bonnefoy the same privileges he extended to his other clients—filling orders at extremely good prices and booking any losses in the 88888 account. Any mistakes or bad fills just ended up in the error account. One thing to remember: more volume meant more mistakes, which also meant the losses in the five eights account were growing. They culminated when Leeson mis-executed a straddle options trade on behalf of Bonnefoy that resulted in a loss of £650,000.

Speculation as to the identity of this mystery client ran rampant around the Barings offices. Most people assumed it was a hedge fund, but nobody was sure. The partners at Barings, however, just knew that Leeson was making a lot of money executing trades for the client, whoever it was. Peter Baring, speaking to the Bank of England about the surge in Barings Securities' profitability, described it as "amazing."

The mood at Baring's Singapore office was equally jovial. This new client was helping Leeson dig himself out of the financial quagmire he'd created with the 88888 account. Other traders on the trading floor were in awe of the size of Leeson's trades. At one point in July of 1993, Leeson actually managed to erase all of the losses in the 88888 account. He was once again on top of the world. As one trader put it, "He began to believe his own press clippings." But just as Icarus flew too close to the sun and the wax on his wings began to melt, Leeson fell back to Earth; Nick Leeson was destined for collapse.

As Bonnefoy was pushing larger and larger trades Leeson's way, the execution errors magnified. Given the young and inexperienced staff at Baring's Singapore office, the chances of an error on any transaction were better than average. Most firms would have looked at the situation and realized there could be problems, then incorporated changes to limit the risks. But Leeson was young and wanted to prove himself. Rather than admit he needed additional help, he just continued to hide the losses the same way he'd done in the past.

The losses, however, began to pile up again. In the late summer of 1993, a loss totaling £70,000 ended up in the 88888 error account. Then, in September, a computer shutdown on the Osaka exchange sent orders scrambling into the SIMEX. On the first day, Leeson finished with a £75,000 loss and obviously expected to make it back the next day. Once again, the financial gods weren't smiling down on him, and when the market turned against him, he found himself down a staggering £1.7 million.

Had these losses been discovered when they were still small, something could have been done to prevent them, or at least minimize them. Just having the error account located in London would have made all the difference. By now Leeson was convinced that he could trade his way out of anything, much like a gambler who doubles down after losing. Casinos stay in business for a reason: the gamblers keep coming back.

Losses aside, within Barings Leeson appeared to have all the markings of a major success, and in October 1993 he was promoted; with the title of assistant director, he was officially given charge of both trading and settlements. At the same time as his promotion, his losses added up to £32 million, all of them sitting in the 88888 account. At the end of the calendar year, he was able to scrape together £6.5 million from the customer margin account at Citibank, plus a last-minute £25 million from selling options. He was safe for the moment, but he was clearly at the end of his rope. He must have known, on some level, that neither of his cash sources was going to hold out forever. But he was able to close out 1993 on a positive note, taking home a £135,000 bonus from Barings.

Within a month, however, nothing was going his way. His losses had grown once again, this time up to £50 million, and the end of the month was rapidly approaching. He needed to find some money fast, or it would be clear that something was amiss in Singapore. Leeson's ego—or perhaps his naïveté—wouldn't allow him to admit the losses. He still needed to prove himself. At this point, he was in dire need of a major cash windfall if he was going to successfully navigate his way out of his mess. The losses had grown so large that even selling options straddles wasn't enough; raiding the customer excess margin wasn't either. In a last-ditch effort to save himself, Leeson opted for a radical plan. He invented a new business strategy for the Singapore office that he called "switching."

His new business was modeled on the art of arbitrage. In financial terminology, arbitrage is the exploitation of price differences between two different markets. In the futures world in Asia, a trader could theoretically make money buying and selling the same futures contracts on two different exchanges. Think of how many exchanges around the world trade wheat or metals. For Leeson, the main futures contract on the SIMEX exchange was the Nikkei 225 stock index, which was also traded on the Osaka exchange. Given that Nikkei futures often moved more quickly on the SIMEX than they did on the Osaka exchange, there was an opportunity to profit by arbitraging the prices between the two exchanges. And because Baring Securities was one of the few brokers who had seats on both exchanges, Leeson was in the position to do exactly that.

The only thing standing in his way was his lack of funds, but that was easy enough to overcome. Leeson managed to convince those in London that he was uniquely positioned to spot tiny differences in the prices of Nikkei futures contracts between the SIMEX and Osaka exchanges, and he could make massive profits exploiting them. He just needed the London office to wire him funds to post as margin for his trades at the exchanges.

Leeson had the perfect explanation for needing additional cash, money that was really using to cover losses in the 88888 account. On the surface, his request made perfect sense. If he owned Nikkei futures contracts on the Osaka exchange and was short on the SIMEX exchange, he needed money to post as margin at both exchanges. Exchange rules dictate that margin deposits are required, so there'd be nothing suspicious about Leeson's need for additional funds. However, a fact unbeknownst to the executives in London was that SIMEX margin rules specifically allowed them to net their margin payments if they had an offsetting position at the Osaka exchange.

Leeson sold his strategy in basic terms. He told them he was simply long futures on one exchange and short on the other. One early arbitrage trade he had done made some decent profits, netting him £16,000. Given that the trade took approximately two and a half seconds to execute, Leeson promoted the trading strategy heavily, and the London office saw it as easy money. Leeson was, at least temporarily, a financial genius in its eyes. He had an easy way to double dip on margin fund requests and had access to more cash. In layman's terms, he created a massive lie to his bosses.

Financial reporters, taking note of his trading, asked Leeson what he was doing. He replied that he was "buying Nikkei futures here and selling them there." It sounded so simple, and plenty of other traders tried to employ the same strategy. Not surprisingly, they found they couldn't make enough money to make it worth the risk and the effort. One Japanese executive said of Leeson's methods, "We figured that it is such a sophisticated operation that they probably had a hedge going in another market that we didn't know about."

Leeson's business was about to take a turn for the worse. Philippe Bonnefoy—the mysterious "client X"—had ceased using Leeson to execute trades on June 27, 1994. That meant Leeson had to work even harder to create the appearance that he still had some big client making gargantuan trades. Between needing money to cover margin payments for this now-nonexistent mystery client and the equally nonexistent need to post margin deposits for arbitrage, Leeson was pressed to explain away his continuing need for more cash from London.

The subterfuge and spiraling losses were driving Leeson to the brink of insanity. "I may have looked calm to everyone else on the floor," he said, "but I felt that my obsession for sweets was a giveaway. At least they kept me off my nails. I didn't like the look of my nails anymore. They were chewed and beginning to go red at the rims."

Throughout the summer of 1994, the Nikkei continued to fall. Leeson was still executing some trades on behalf of his clients, but by now, he was mostly making speculative trades on his own behalf. At this moment, he transformed himself from the office manager to an outright speculator. His trading strategy was pure and simple: stay long the Nikkei futures contracts. Leeson contended it was "the only way to make back the losses." He was holding out hope that the market would go higher, enough to bring him back in the black. "A bounce had to be coming soon," he said.

Other floor traders didn't quite share his optimism, and they even warned SIMEX officials that Leeson was something of a gunslinger who needed to be watched. Leeson camouflaged himself well with the façade that he was trading for the big mystery client. He even started to support the Nikkei futures price by buying more contracts every time the price fell. Naturally, he explained to the Baring Securities trader in Tokyo that it was an order on behalf of his mystery client.

Leeson then started to branch out into other futures contracts, which included JGB futures. JGB stands for Japanese Government Bond, and the SIMEX exchange trades futures contracts on JGBs, just like the CME trades futures contracts on U.S. Treasury bonds. Leeson reasoned that if Japanese stock prices were going up, then bond prices would fall. That is, after all, a well-established correlation in the financial markets—that the bond and the stock markets tend to move in opposing directions. So before Leeson's position got too large in

Nikkei futures contracts, he added a short position in JGB futures contracts to essentially bet the market in the same direction. That is, by staying short JGB futures, he could benefit similarly from a rise in the Nikkei stock index. Leeson, once again, found that fate was still not in his favor. At year end, the 88888 account loss was up to £80 million.

The situation had worsened so much that the only thing he could do was buy more futures contracts in order to support the market and prevent it from moving lower. Leeson had moved from using customer funds to selling options straddles to inventing a strategy called switching to outright trading. And being long in a declining market meant only one thing: he needed more money from London. That left him entirely dependent on a woman named Brenda Granger, the head of futures and options settlements in London, for that money. And the home office was growing increasingly inquisitive as to why Leeson needed a seemingly unrelenting cash infusion.

The entire time he was propping up the Nikkei futures market, he was also selling options straddles valued at around £150 million. The risk was tremendous, and if the market moved significantly in either direction, he'd be dead in the water. He had to do whatever he could to keep the market stable, he reasoned, which meant increasing his position in the Nikkei futures even further. By February 1995, he owned 50 percent of the open interest in Nikkei futures and was short an unbelievable 85 percent of the JGB futures traded on the SIMEX exchange.

His trading positions made for quite the public image for this young trader. He could literally move the markets at his whim, despite the fact that he was still considered a novice, just by stepping into the pits and buying. Swiss Bank went so far as to produce a research paper offering five different potential explanations as to why Baring Securities was holding such massive Nikkei futures positions. Word was getting around everywhere too, and he was approached by a collection of news organizations that included the Nihon Keizai Shimbun newspaper, Bloomberg, the Associated Press, Dow Jones, and Reuters, all asking about the size of his positions, to which Leeson replied, "We're fine. I don't know which way the client's going to play it."

The game was very close to being over for Nick Leeson. "Everyone knew that I was long, and they were looking for me to sell my position and cane the market. The locals were scared of me; they were on to a good selling run, but I could single-handedly turn the market and push it back way above their selling." But what those locals didn't know was that Leeson's hands were tied by a rope he'd woven for himself. If he sold even a little bit, he'd drive down the price on his remaining position. He couldn't win.

*   *   *

By this point, Leeson was quite adept at moving money around and fooling the London office. However, he still had auditors to worry about, and there was a huge hole in the balance sheet that had ballooned to over £170 million by the end of 1994. Anyone who looked even somewhat closely at the accounting reports could discover that a substantial sum of money was not in Baring's coffers. As Leeson himself said, "This was getting absurd, but obviously nobody was looking at the accounting packages we were sending them." But rather than acknowledge his problems and come clean, he chose to stick his head in the metaphorical sand: "I stopped looking at the 88888 account balance. I knew that it was large, but I was just intent on surviving each day."

In fact, the amount that would be missing on the accounting statement on December 31, 1994 totaled ¥7.78 billion (Japanese Yen). It was the same amount it would take to bring the 88888 account back to zero, and it was the same amount that was sitting at the SIMEX exchange for margin deposits on his futures positions. Falling back on the mantra about desperate times calling for desperate measures, Leeson needed to show in the internal records that Baring Securities had not only pledged the requisite ¥7.78 billion, but also that someone owed that money back to Barings. If an internal auditor happened to check the records, an account receivable equal to ¥7.78 billion would probably pass the scrutiny. On the Baring Securities' books, Leeson booked a ¥7.78 billion OTC trade between his firm and Spear, Leeds & Kellogg, a broker-dealer based in New York.

Questions were still piling up in London, and Brenda Granger called Leeson directly. "We need to talk," she told him. "Nobody in Singapore can answer any questions without you there." Leeson would blame that on inexperience, citing the fact that his staff was very young, but also fiercely loyal.

Baring Brothers management was growing increasingly suspicious of the apparent reconciliation errors, but nobody investigated the matter too thoroughly. The truth of the matter was executives didn't really understand what they were looking for, or for that matter, what they were looking at. James Bax, who was in charge of Baring Securities' Singapore operations, told Ron Baker that it was just a misunderstanding. "It's just a nontransaction," he said. "It's an error. It is a back-office glitch. Don't worry about it."

Simon Jones, however, wasn't quite so easily convinced, and he confronted Leeson directly about the inconsistencies. Leeson backpedaled a little, saying, "They're just banging on about an intra-day funding limit." He left it at that, and apparently Jones was pacified for the time being.

On January 17, 1995, things went from bad to worse at precisely 5:46 AM. Leeson started out the day in the hole £200 million, and he had a large gamble in the form of a March Nikkei options straddle. It was a major bet that the Nikkei index would not drop below 19,000 before March 10 of that year. It was, at least in his mind, a pretty safe bet. Such a precipitous drop would require something akin to an act of God himself. And that's exactly what Leeson got.

The earth began to shake at 5:46 AM on that January morning, and the ensuing earthquake that registered a whopping 7.2 on the Richter scale was centered near Kobe, Japan. In its wake, it left three thousand people dead and twenty-five thousand buildings completely destroyed. It was the worst earthquake to strike Japan since the great Kyoto earthquake of 1923. And it sent the Japanese financial markets into a free fall.

Leeson knew he had to do something to keep the index from falling below 19,000 and preserve his long position in Nikkei futures, his short position in JGB futures, and his short options straddle in Nikkei futures. He stepped into the trading pits and began buying contracts at a feverish pace. His efforts worked, as the Nikkei index came slowly crawling back again. He was suddenly even making money from the contracts that he bought when it hit rock bottom. But then, news of the massive earthquake had reached across the globe. Friends and relatives began frantically calling Japan, desperate for news of their loved ones. The phone lines were down, and chaos once again took over. Another wave of panicked selling hit the market, and the Nikkei dropped over 1,175 points. "I'd never seen it move so fast," Leeson recalled. "Every five minutes I was waiting for a bounce which never happened."

By the close of trading that day, he was down ¥7 billion, or £50 million. It was a product of both the drop in the Nikkei and the rally in JGB futures. He was losing on both ends of his bets simultaneously. Leeson got a call from one of the Baring Securities traders in Tokyo who demanded to know, in no uncertain terms, what in the hell was going on. Leeson fell back on his imaginary mystery client and said, "I don't know what's happening. This guy is crazy."

At home that evening, Leeson floated the idea to his wife that he should resign from his job, and that they should move out of Singapore. He wanted to get out while he knew he could, but he didn't mention that part to her. In her blissful ignorance, Lisa replied that they would be better off waiting until he got his bonus check, because that money would "set us up for life."

Meanwhile, in London the auditors were still poring over Leeson's records. A woman named Pang Mui Mui was the accountant from Coopers & Lybrand who had been assigned the task of going through Singapore's records. One of her main questions centered on the ¥7.78 billion OTC trade between Baring Securities and Spear, Leeds & Kellogg booked by Leeson that previous December. Leeson told her that it had been a SIMEX mistake—that Barings had paid the money out, and it was still owed back to them. "I'm getting the money back," he assured her.

Coopers & Lybrand wanted a more thorough explanation, citing a need for documentation for the supposed trade, and Leeson received an e-mail from the Barings group treasurer, Tony Hawes, asking about the transaction. Leeson was then supposed to speak with Simon about it, but his boss postponed the meeting. "Put it off until tomorrow, will you?" Simon told the young trader. "I've got to go and play squash." It was a quintessential moment of pre-Big Bang banking, and one that gave Leeson a window of opportunity to save his own hide.

Leeson spent the rest of the day rifling through his desk drawers, searching for any correspondence from Spear, Leeds & Kellogg. He stumbled upon an original letter that had been signed by Richard Hogan, a managing director there. He had a signature. Now he just needed a confirmation letter.

He typed up a confirmation letter regarding the OTC trade on plain paper, then cut the Spear, Leeds & Kellogg letterhead and Hogan's signature off the original letter, putting them on the plain-paper letter he'd typed. When he went off to make a realistic-looking copy, "I stood at the photocopier for over an hour, trying to get the letters to look normal."

The confirmation letter itself wasn't the only piece of the documentation he needed; he also needed an approval letter from Ron Baker authorizing the trade. That was easily accomplished by writing it out on Baring letterhead and closing it with a forged signature. He'd seen Ron's signature enough times to know more or less what it looked like.

There was still one more component he needed, and that was the trickiest of all. He needed a money wire confirmation from Citibank indicating that ¥7.78 billion had been transferred from the Citibank account to the Baring account. He left the office and called a junior clerk on his cell phone, asking the clerk to book a money transfer in the amount of ¥7.78 billion from the Citibank account to the Baring house account. After checking the balance, the clerk told him that it wouldn't go through because there wasn't enough money in the account to cover it. He told her that was fine, just go ahead and request the transfer, then reverse it immediately after. What Leeson knew was that the moment the transfer was requested, Citibank would send a fax confirmation of the transfer, and it wouldn't show that it had been canceled. So he waited patiently next to the fax machine for the confirmation to come through. When it did, he had all of the documentation he needed to show the auditors.

Leeson returned home and faxed the fake documentation to Coopers & Lybrand. Interestingly enough, nobody paid any attention to the fact that the fax header read "From Nick and Lisa," indicating that it was sent from his home fax and not from the Spear, Leeds & Kellogg offices in New York, but again, nobody seemed to notice. Or if they did, nobody seemed to care. They had the documents they needed, and the case was closed. The auditors accepted the documentation as valid, and on February 3, 1995, Coopers & Lybrand issued its report for Baring Securities' 1994 audit. Everything was above board and clear as far as they were concerned. But the matter was far from closed in London.

Tony Hawes still had doubts about the trade. "What's bothering me is where you got all the money to actually pay Spear, Leeds & Kellogg. I mean, it's the equivalent of seventy-eight-million pounds. It just doesn't add up, you know?" he said to Leeson. Leeson was in no mood to further defend himself, so he dodged the question altogether. "I've got to dash," he told Hawes. "I'm running late, and we've got company for dinner." He would later admit that he had masterfully played on Hawes's traditionalist sentiments. "I knew Tony would understand an excuse like company for dinner in a way in which he'd never understand having to dash off and do some work."

But the questions persisted, with meetings galore in London about the suspicious trade. All of Leeson's superiors were asking about it, desperate for clarification as to where the money had come from. "The SLK matter continued to rumble on in London after it'd been cleared in Singapore," Leeson recalled. Time was running out.

By February 1995, it was clear that there wasn't much sand left in the hourglass of Leeson's career. He had taken approximately £850 million from the Baring Brothers' treasury to cover both his margin deposits and his accumulated losses. On February 15, his wife called a moving company, telling them that they needed storage space. Leeson had sold his Rover sports car and was leasing a Mercedes so as to keep up appearances and keep down costs.

The next day, February 16, the London office received a call from a senior director at Schroders, another London merchant bank. The caller was curious about a rumor that had begun circulating regarding Barings' imminent default in Singapore. Soon after, another call arrived from the Jardine Fleming investment bank in Hong Kong; the caller was asking about the same rumor.

There was a moment when the rumors looked like they might be nothing more than just that. Leeson had built up a long position of about thirty thousand March Nikkei futures contracts, and the tide was momentarily in his favor. After he sold out of 1,100 of those contracts, he was able to book a profit of £15 million. "Suddenly it looked like I had a chance," he recalled later. But his total loss still stood at over £200 million. It was going to take a lot more luck with his other futures contracts to cover that mountain.

Leeson's phone was ringing constantly. One caller was an Associated Press reporter, asking him about his very large position in March Nikkei futures, to which he replied, "I don't know what the client is going to do." Other calls were coming in from the London office, expressing concern over the size of his positions. Leeson continued to bob and weave, like a fighter refusing to give up despite blood pouring out.

Despite the financial avalanche he'd wrought, Leeson was still anticipating a bonus from his employer. He had in his mind a number around £450,000; Baring Brothers was actually planning to pay him £700,000. But there was a large string attached to that bonus promise: Leeson would have to reduce his holdings. That was essentially an order from the powers in London, who were still under the impression that the mystery client was carrying the outrageous positions, which was requiring Baring Brothers to put up all of the margin.

Back in London, the investigation into the odd Spear, Leeds & Kellogg trade was ongoing, and the truth of what had really happened—in addition to Leeson's unauthorized and illegal funds transfers—was getting closer and closer to being brought to light. Leeson needed another £45 million for a new margin call from the SIMEX. When he requested the funds, he told the office he'd explain why he needed it later. He never did.

By now, Leeson was completely unreachable; nobody could contact him. Worries began to grow about what he was doing and what happened to him. A fax arrived in London requesting that £45 million in funds, despite the fact that Leeson had been ordered to reduce his position size.

Back in Singapore, the market was dropping even further, and Leeson's losses were continuing to mount. The Nikkei index hovered just above 18,000 and threatened to head lower. Leeson bought another fifteen thousand contracts to stave off another drop. He felt that the index would have gone down as low as 17,500 had he not bought the contracts.

On Wednesday, February 22, the Nikkei was still at 18,000, and Leeson had another £30 million margin call to meet. The next day on the trading floor, everyone was shouting directly at Leeson, who had bought every Nikkei futures contract that anyone on the floor had to sell. It was another attempt to prop up the sagging market, but it was a futile attempt. The index closed down 330 points at the end of the trading day.

The London office was still fixated on what it called "the hole in the balance sheet" created by the ¥7.78 billion transfer, and began to take notice of what other traders on the floor already knew. Leeson was so deep into his position that there was no way out of it. The time had come, as Leeson said, to run.

On Friday, February 24, Leeson was long 61,039 Nikkei 225 contracts valued at approximately £11 billion, in addition to his short position of 28,034 JGB futures contracts. In total, he owned 49 percent of the entire March 1995 Nikkei futures contracts and 24 percent of the June 1995 contracts. There was no way to sustain his holdings and unwind the positions with any kind of profit. The Nikkei closed that day at 17,885. He gathered his things and walked off the trading floor. He went to his desk and penned a short note, addressed to nobody in particular.

The note read simply, "I'm sorry."

By 11:30 PM that night, Nick and Lisa Leeson were gone from Singapore. They checked into a hotel in the Malaysian capital of Kuala Lumpur, Leeson instructing his wife to pay for everything in cash and to not sign anything. Around the world, the news began to surface that Barings had lost more than £600 million, and the firm's employees were in stunned shock. Leeson and his wife were holed up in the Malaysian resort town of Kota Kinabalu for a week, staying mostly in their room and living off room service. After being on the run for a week, they were ready to try their luck and return to London.

They left for the airport at 7:00 AM, buying economy-class plane tickets to Frankfurt and paying with cash. When they landed in Germany, the police were waiting for Leeson. He was detained in Frankfurt, where he awaited extradition. Singapore authorities requested that he be returned to them to face trial, but Leeson held out hope that his home country of England would fight to keep him. He felt he stood a better chance of leniency in an English court.

Once the news about Leeson broke, the Nikkei futures market crashed. Everyone knew that Leeson had massive futures holdings, and they all knew too that Baring Securities would have to dispose of the position quickly. The market opened down 880 points on the following Monday, closing the trading day at 16,960. And because traders also knew Baring Securities was short JGB futures, those contracts went up fifty points. Employees of Baring Securities were officially banned from the SIMEX trading floor.

At Leeson's office, Singapore authorities were busy searching his desk, confiscating everything, including stationery with fake letterheads and a fraudulent ticket listing an £80 million deposit at Citibank in the name of Baring Securities.

* * *

While Leeson was fleeing to Kuala Lumpur, Peter Baring received a phone call at his home in Notting Hill, notifying him of the situation. It was 7:15 PM, and Baring, unlike his American counterparts, had long since called it a day at the office. Alarmed by a call at such an hour, he said, "It must be serious if you're calling me at this hour." The Baring executive on the other end lamented that it appeared "one of our barrow-boys has gone AWOL."

At 8:30 PM that same evening, the Baring Brothers' directors met at their London headquarters and immediately informed the Bank of England of what had happened. The mood in the room was incredulous. "We're a bank with a crest, not a trademark," one executive exclaimed. But that crest couldn't alter the reality that the losses stood at £385 million at the time. The firm had £308 million in equity, plus debt capital of £101 million. It was enough to survive, assuming it received a capital injection. But it was still susceptible to any decline in the Nikkei average. If that number dropped, the losses would be magnified.

There were two major issues that required immediate attention. First, the firm needed to raise capital in the form of a bailout. Secondly, it would need to find a buyer for its futures positions. The former, it was hoped, would come from the London banking community as a whole, much like the 1890 bailout. The latter issue was slightly more difficult, though it was hoped a hedge fund would emerge to buy the futures positions—a hedge fund that was willing to bet heavily on a rise in the Nikkei.

With the support of the Bank of England, Baring executives estimated they needed a bailout fund amounting to £400 million, and began canvassing the City to get commitments from the other banks. After knocking on the doors of N. M. Rothschild & Sons, Schroders, Barclays, National Westminster, Morgan Grenfell, Deutsche Bank, among others, they soon had the commitments to meet their immediate financial need. Then came the call from Baring Futures in Singapore. As it turned out, there was also a massive short options position that was just discovered. It meant the deficit was £200 million higher. The bank now needed £600 million to stay afloat.

Other City banks, however, were discovering things about Baring Brothers that made them uneasy. After reviewing Barings' books, it was discovered that Barings was still planning to pay out bonuses for 1994, an amount that was approximately £84 million. That money, the other banks were horrified to learn, would be coming from the bailout money they were providing. They were basically bailing out the bank and lining the pockets of some of the people who had been responsible for this mess in the first place.

That distaste added to the fact that the other City banks—including the Bank of England—were having a difficult time coming up with the money to cover the required £600 million in the first place. The £400 million had been hard enough; £600 million was proving next to impossible.

The more the other bank executives contemplated the situation, the harder it was to believe how any financial institution could get itself into such a mess. Questions swirled about how Barings' managers could be so incompetent as to allow losses to accumulate as they did, not to mention depositing over £700 million in margin at their Singapore office. That amount alone was more than the bank was worth in the first place. How did the bank's executives allow a massive sum to be sent to a small subsidiary on the other side of the world to finance positions they didn't even know existed?

All of the questions surrounding the Baring Securities fiasco caused the interest in a Barings bailout to collapse as quickly as it had grown. Support evaporated, and the bank collapsed after it was unable to find a buyer for the futures and options positions. In the end, the bank that had financed such projects as the Louisiana Purchase and the Panama Canal, a bank that had been around since 1762—making it older than the United States—ceased to exist. It was sold for £1 to the Dutch bank International Netherlands Group (ING).

* * *

When the dust had settled, Singapore authorities filed twelve charges against Nick Leeson: four charges of forgery, two of amending prices, and six of implementing cross-trades in order to reduce his margin. Those charges were less than what he faced in London—where his character had already suffered an irrecoverable assassination—but he still wanted to return to his home country, telling authorities he wanted to be closer to his family.

In reality, Leeson knew he would face a hostile crowd in Singapore, where he was assured of being found guilty, just as he would be in London. He feared that he would be "thrown to the wolves" in Singapore, a country well known for harsh punishments that included the act of caning for even minor infractions. He literally begged for a trial in London. But the British Serious Fraud Office, after investigating the case to determine whether or not it would seek extradition to London, declined to pursue it. "The SFO does not have evidence which warrants an extradition application being made for Mr. Leeson," the office announced. Leeson's worst fears were realized. He was going to stand trial in Singapore.

Rather than face a circus-style trial, Leeson pleaded guilty in Singapore District Court to one charge of cheating the Singapore International Monetary Exchange and one charge of cheating the accounting firm of Coopers & Lybrand. He was sentenced to six-and-a-half years in prison, a sentence he began serving in November of 1995.

To some, Leeson was a victim, a working-class lad who became a whiz kid and was forced to take the fall for the failings of the upper-class Barings bank. But to many more, he was the face of all that was wrong with the Big Bang. He had grown greedy, putting his own interests above everything else. His ego did not allow for him to admit mistakes, which eventually led to the destruction of one of the country's oldest and most well-respected financial institutions.

Leeson served four and a half years of his sentence in the Singapore Tanah Merah prison. He was granted early release on July 3, 1999. He wrote a book about his experiences at Baring Securities entitled *Rogue Trader*, which was later made into a movie.

In 2005, he got a job as a bookkeeper for Galway United Football Club, a small soccer team in western Ireland. He's also spent the ensuing years as a speaker at conferences and other gatherings, and has a website that promotes his services. In 2013, he joined an Irish debt-restructuring firm called GDP Partnership. The company works with indebted people who find themselves underwater to help renegotiate their mortgage debts. When asked why the company would hire someone like Mr. Leeson, the answer was quite simple.

"He does have a wealth of business experience with distress based on his personal difficulties."

Chapter Five

Brian Hunter and Amaranth, 2006

It's surprising to know that the father of the hedge fund was not an American; in fact, he was born in Melbourne, Australia, in September 1900. At the age of four, Alfred Winslow Jones immigrated with his family to the United States and immersed himself in the land of opportunity. A superb student, Jones graduated from Harvard in 1923, after which he traveled the world for ten years as a purser on a passenger liner. It was, to be sure, a far cry from where this journeyman's brains would take him.

In 1930, Jones joined the elite American Foreign Service, and was appointed the vice consul of the American embassy in Berlin, Germany. From there, he went on to Spain, working as a reporter during the Spanish Civil War. He was married during that time, honeymooning with his bride on the front lines of the war and drinking cocktails with the likes of Ernest Hemingway and Dorothy Parker. After the war, he returned to the United States and enrolled in a graduate program in sociology at Columbia University. There, he earned his PhD after successfully defending his dissertation entitled "Life, Liberty, and Property," which was a survey of attitudes toward property in Akron, Ohio.

With his doctorate in hand, Jones took his brains to *Fortune* magazine. It was 1948, and the seeds were being sewn for what would come to make Jones one of the most legendary investors of all times. He was researching an article entitled "Fashions in Forecasting," which was essentially a look at predicting trends in the stock market. Buying and selling stocks is something of a gamble, and any money manager who can claim a over a 50 percent winning percentage would be the one you want to leave your money with. Jones felt there had to be a way to consistently earn profits on more than half his investments, and he was determined to prove it. Everyone he interviewed told him it was impossible to forecast the fluctuations of the stock market to achieve that lofty goal, but Jones was not to be put off.

Rather than listen to conventional wisdom, he began to try the stock-picking business himself. At the age of forty-eight—bordering on ancient in today's financial world—Jones established an investment partnership and raised approximately $100,000. Jones combined that money with $40,000 of his own personal savings, and he was suddenly in the money management business.

Jones studied the stock market, especially its fluctuations, and was absolutely determined to find a way to earn profits in the market while, at the same time, eliminating many of the risks inherent in trading. That might mean predicting the direction of the market on any given day—or at any given minute—and investing accordingly. If it was impossible to predict the direction of the market with any kind of certainty, then investors were collectively beholden to the overall direction of the stock market over the course of time. That idea is what's called market directional risk today.

Alfred Jones wasn't satisfied with faith alone, however, and he proposed a portfolio that he called fully balanced. A combination of undervalued stocks, which he would buy, and overvalued stocks, which he would short-sell. The end result was the creation of a stock portfolio that was fully hedged, meaning it was what we call today market neutral. The idea, although simple once explained, was revolutionary. The stocks he was buying were, by all accounts, undervalued, so their price per share was expected to go up. Meanwhile, he was short-selling stocks that were overvalued, which meant that when the overvalued prices had sunk to more reasonable levels, he'd buy them back. Either way, he was making a profit.

Short sales have been a common stock-trading technique since the dawn of stock trading itself. Under a short sale, a person is selling a security—in this case, a stock—which the person does not own, betting that the stock is overvalued, and that the stock price is going to fall. When that time comes, the person can buy it back for considerably less money. Of course, when you sell something to someone the buyer expects to receive it, so the short seller must borrow the stock in order to deliver it to the buyer. It amounts to a loan of the security, and it's what is called a stock loan in the financial industry. When it comes time to buy back the stock, hopefully for less than it sold for, the trader is able to return the borrowed stock to the lender. Assuming the stock was bought back at the right time, the investor can make quite a tidy profit in a short sale.

One problem with short selling is that the trader is often betting against the overall direction of the stock market. As the stock market tends, on average, to go up from year to year, even if someone did all the research and sold a completely overvalued stock, the weight of the overall market might push that stock's price higher anyway. In order to avoid fighting the overall trend of the stock market, it's best to have another component of the trade to offset losses from the stock market rising from year to year. That's where those long positions came into play. Assuming Jones had done his homework on those stocks, the odds of losing on both the shorts (overvalued stocks) and the longs (undervalued stocks) were slim.

Clearly, the foundation of his approach—the linchpin of its success or failure—was riding on his research, and that was the work he had to do. If Jones studied the markets intensely and identified both the over- and undervalued stocks that were going to make him money, he was making a pretty safe bet. In essence, Jones was simply betting that other investors were not doing the same research he was doing. It turned out that he bet right. In his first year of investing, he was up an enviable 17.3 percent.

Jones continued to make money—lots of it, in fact—using a pretty basic investment strategy. But unlike in today's world, where über-successful traders crow from the rooftops about their gains, Jones preferred to keep quiet. He had the equivalent of the golden egg–laying goose, and he didn't want to share his secret. After many years when your strategy beats out the second-place stock fund in terms of performance by 87 percent—that's *eighty-seven percent*—it's hard to keep it quiet for too long.

In April 1966, Carol Loomis wrote an article for *Fortune* in which she explained the specifics of Jones's trading strategy. He'd had it all to himself for seventeen years and had already made plenty of money by that time. The article was entitled "The Jones Nobody Keeps Up With," and it gave away most of the blueprint for how Jones was beating the stock market. Now the cat was out of the bag, and Jones's secret formula was no longer quite so secret. In addition to explaining the strategy, Loomis also coined a phrase to describe it. She called it a hedge fund.

It was a revolutionary time in the financial industry because investors had just been introduced to quite possibly the greatest money-making technique in history. Following the publication of the *Fortune* article, 130 hedge funds sprang up in the course of three years; George Soros' legendary Quantum Fund was among them. The bear markets that characterized much of the 1970s further fueled interest in hedge funds, because those investors could make money despite the falling market conditions. Clearly Jones's model was as close to perfect as investors could have hoped.

Another aspect that was unique to the Jones structure was a 20 percent incentive fee that he charged his investors. If he didn't make a profit, he didn't charge a fee—and all of the expenses associated with fund management were paid out of his fee, so his investors felt Jones's interests were pretty closely tied with theirs. At the time, it was a very cutting-edge way of getting paid.

As other hedge funds developed, the pressure for them to turn a profit grew that much larger, especially as the field grew more competitive. The easiest way to ratchet up the profits in an investment portfolio is to use leverage. By borrowing money to own more of the same investments, even a small return can become much larger. And, of course, the fees for the hedge fund manager would become larger too.

Like so many things in the financial world, using leverage sounds much simpler than it really is. As we have already seen—and as we shall see again very soon—leverage is a double-edged sword. On the one hand, it can multiply the profits if you bet right. But if you bet wrong, you also magnify your losses. Consider this example: A ten-dollar stock you thought was going to hit twenty bucks just went down to five dollars. If you paid the full ten dollars out of your own pocket, you just lost five dollars. However, if you put up five dollars of your own money and borrowed the other five, you have to pay back the money you borrowed and your entire investment was completely wiped out. What was just a loss of your cash on hand before is now a loss of everything.

Hedge funds—at the time of their invention and today—are organized very much like a corporation, with a single general partner and several limited partners. The general partner is the fund manager (Albert Jones was the general partner in his fund, for instance), and the investors are named limited partners in the corporate structure. And the number of investors is strictly limited by the Investment Company Act of 1940. That act dictates that an unregulated fund can have no more than ninety-nine investors, all of whom must be considered qualified investors. In other words, if you have to ask how much the minimum investment is, you probably can't afford the investment.

By following the rules dictated by the act, hedge funds were afforded exemptions from many U.S. securities laws, exemptions that included having to register with the Securities and Exchange Commission. Recent legislation has changed that slightly, but for many years, hedge funds were literally able to operate in whatever manner they saw fit. They didn't have to report their trades to any regulator, and they could leverage themselves as much as they wanted. Their investors were supposed to understand the risks they were undertaking, and the assumption was that they didn't need a babysitter looking over their shoulders.

Albert Jones stayed in the financial game for quite a long time after his strategy went public. Eventually, his investment fund was solely made up of his own personal investment portfolio. His fund became what is now known as a fund of funds in 1984, meaning he invested only in other hedge funds. The father of the hedge fund died on June 2, 1989, after a thirty-four-year run as a hedge fund manager. In that time, he had only three years in which he suffered a loss.

Though the style of the game has changed considerably since Jones's entry into the financial markets, the basic principles he established in 1948 still guide hedge fund operations around the world. Throughout the hedge fund industry, many fund managers still use Jones's original strategy of balancing long and short positions. The strategy had evolved into many forms, and market lingo now calls it a spread trading strategy, in which an investor seeks to take advantage of the price difference in two securities, typically with the trader long one security and short the other. Whereas Jones was originally betting on the prices of specific stocks, spread traders are betting on the narrowing or widening of the spread between the prices.

Today's hedge fund managers haven't stayed in the relatively safe waters of the stock market that Jones had pioneered. Instead, they go after any and all markets, so long as there's a spread to be exploited. Although the stock market is still a central part—fund managers are often long one stock and short another—the list of potential opportunities is nearly endless. A hedge fund trader might be long a bond and short the bond futures contract or perhaps long the front-month futures contract and short the back-month contract. It all gets down to where the spreads are.

A common characteristic of hedge funds is that they are typically headquartered in countries with generous tax considerations. Places like the Cayman Islands, Bermuda, the British Virgin Islands, and the Bahamas are the typical locations where hedge funds register. Those offshore locations also assist hedge funds in further avoiding securities laws.

Despite their offshore registration, many of these funds have trading floors in Connecticut, a geographic placement that creates something of a commuter oddity every morning. Many of the more affluent executives at the investment banks that populate Manhattan's Financial District actually reside in southern Connecticut, and their morning commute consisted of traveling south on Metro North out of Greenwich. These men and women had put in their time as analysts and traders living in the city, and when it came time to settle down and start a family, they preferred to return to the relative calm and pastoral setting of Connecticut each evening.

At about the same time that these older executives are boarding a train heading south, an entirely different group is boarding a train in Manhattan. This group tends to be younger, the sort of brilliant minds that will eventually rise to those executive positions, the corner office, and eventually the home in Connecticut. But they'll have time for that later. These folks are living it up in the city, as they say. Early in the morning, they're doing what amounts to a reverse-commute. They board in Manhattan and ride up to Greenwich, to the offices of many of the world's most successful hedge funds. As their train passes the southbound one, it creates an interesting tableau of personalities. On the one side of the train tracks is the group that feels that living in Connecticut is a reward for long years spent in the trenches; on the other side is the group looking for best rewards by working at a hedge fund in Connecticut.

One of those Greenwich-based hedge funds was founded in 2000 by Nicholas Maounis. Maounis, a native of Stamford, Connecticut, spent ten years in the financial markets in New York City before moving back up to Connecticut and founding his own hedge fund, Amaranth Partners. His professional background was that of a convertible arbitrage bond trader. A convertible bond is one that can be exchanged for a specific number of the company's shares of stock at some predetermined point in the future. Convertible bonds are typically issued by companies with low credit ratings and higher growth potentials. The convertible part is to give investors a little more incentive to own the bonds—what's referred to as an equity kicker.

Maounis employed traders who were experienced in a variety of trading strategies, including credit and statistical arbitrage, merger arbitrage, and plain old stock trading. Merger arbitrage was his original business strategy for Amaranth, however, and Maounis dedicated over half the firm's capital to it.

Then in 2001 the merger arbitrage market almost came to a complete standstill, and Maounis refocused the firm's energies on convertible bond arbitrage. That decision paid off, and Amaranth posted a 22 percent return that year, but that market seemed limited going forward. Maounis was determined to establish himself as a major player, and the only way to grow the fund even larger was to be even more aggressive.

In 2002, Maounis shifted gears again, this time pointing the firm's strategic arrow toward the wide-open market of energy trading when he hired several traders who had worked for the collapsed energy trading giant known as Enron. Despite the addition of the high-powered energy traders, the firm returned an acceptable—yet not exciting by hedge fund standards—11 percent return for the year. Things began paying off the following year, when profits jumped up to 17 percent. Amaranth was doing well, but Maounis was still struggling to find the right mix of instruments that would make the big numbers and attract the big investors. Hand in hand with the search for the right strategies was the need to find proven traders.

As the world of energy trading seemed to be a significantly growing market, Maounis realized that he wanted to expand the firm's energy-trading business even more. Word had gotten around about an all-star young trader currently pedaling his skills at Deutsche Bank in New York City. He was only thirty years old at the time, but he'd been promoted to the head of Deutsche Bank's natural gas desk in just two years. During that time, this up-and-coming hotshot made the bank in excess of $69 million in one year. His name was Brian Hunter.

*   *   *

Born in 1974 in Calgary, Canada, Brian Hunter always had a head for numbers. He stands six feet five inches tall and speaks with a soft-spoken and calm demeanor. Curly dirty blonde hair and blue eyes complete the picture of the charming, all-American boy, excepting the fact that he's actually Canadian. A crooked front tooth is the only imperfection you might notice in his smile. He is an exceptionally smart man too. He majored in physics at the University of Alberta then stayed on to earn a master's in applied mathematics there.

When it comes to clothing, Hunter prefers the uniform favored by most hedge fund traders commuting north from New York: jeans and a button-down shirt. That said, he's also known to wear a jersey from his favorite National Hockey League team, the Calgary Flames. He's a self-described numbers guy who loves his family, never missing an opportunity to talk about his two sons. But if someone rings his doorbell and asks to speak to Brian Hunter, Brian himself will tell the caller that he isn't home. And he's adamantly opposed to having his photograph taken.

After graduating with his master's in 1998, Brian went to work for his father laying concrete at a large sports complex in Calgary. A worker on the jobsite told Hunter that the TransCanada Corporation, a large pipeline corporation, was looking to hire energy traders. Knowing Brian's background, the fellow laborer thought Hunter might be a little more suited for that job than for pouring concrete. He applied for a position and was hired as a junior analyst, charged with developing a way to profit from anomalies in energy prices.

In 2001, a rival energy-trading outfit at Deutsche Bank offered him a position trading natural gas; he accepted and moved to New York. Hunter was immediately off to a strong start. During his first year on the desk he made $17 million, an amount that no doubt would have been much higher had the country's financial markets not plummeted in the days following the attacks on the World Trade Center. His returns for the following year were even better, as he made $52 million for the bank in 2002.

His numbers for 2003 remained solid, as his desk was up $76 million on the year in December, with Hunter alone accounting for $40 million of that. But then, in a single week in December, the group lost $51.2 million in what Hunter called "an unprecedented and unforeseeable run-up in gas prices." Despite his claims that he was still net positive for the year, the bank refused to pay him a bonus. Hunter sued, and the case took four years to be resolved in favor of Deutsche Bank. Outcomes aside, it was, at the time, a telling moment for Hunter's career trajectory. He and his wife weren't in love with New York in the first place: "We didn't like the culture," he said of life in Manhattan. "I hated my job and hated New York."

So when Amaranth came calling and offered Hunter a position on its energy-trading desk in early 2004, it was appealing on many levels. For one, it gave the Hunter family the chance to get out of New York and into the more family-friendly setting of Connecticut. But the deal was really struck when Nick Maounis hinted that, if things worked out, Hunter would even be able to move back to Calgary. And as it turned out, 20 percent of the world's natural gas came out of Calgary anyway, so it was actually a win-win for Amaranth to have a trader on the ground out there. It was a chance to start over in a place a lot more appealing to Hunter than New York.

Hunter joined Amaranth and got up and running trading the natural gas markets fairly quickly. Most of his trades involved exploiting the differences in natural gas futures contract prices at various times during the year. He would buy and sell the different seasons in the natural gas market that he believed were mispriced; if he was right, the payoffs were huge. His strategy was always designed to minimize risk and maximize reward, staying long one natural gas contract and short another—the same mantra Alfred Jones had built a financial movement on. Brian Hunter found his way into the hedge fund world quite easily, and within six months of joining, he was up an astounding $200 million. Not too shabby for the new guy on the desk.

By the spring of 2005, Maounis realized he had found his calling, and Amaranth was trading almost exclusively in energy. Convertible arbitrage trading was essentially dead in the water, and statistical arbitrage had been flat for more than a year. But energy trading was in demand, and the market was growing. Derivatives, futures, options, swaps. It didn't matter. If it had to do with energy, Maounis wanted a piece of the action. His firm didn't trade any physical natural gas, of course; there were plenty of suppliers and distributers who were better at that. There was one guy making most of the money, and Brian Hunter was the guy making it at Amaranth.

That same year, Maounis got wind of the fact that another hedge fund—SAC Capital, based one town over in Stamford, Connecticut and managed by Steve Cohen—had come calling after Amaranth's golden boy. Cohen wanted Hunter so badly that he dangled a million-dollar signing bonus just to switch offices. Maounis acted quickly and decisively to head off any sort of poaching. He immediately promoted Hunter to cohead of the energy desk at Amaranth, gave him authority to trade his own book, and changed his allocation of capital to an unbelievable 30 percent. In an instant, Maounis had transferred much of the firm's risk taking to a single man. And that man was all of thirty-two years old, with only one exceptional year trading at his firm. It was a gamble you'd be hard-pressed to find someone in Las Vegas to take.

But Maounis bet right. In 2005, Brian Hunter placed an enormous bullish bet on natural gas prices. Had he been wrong, this story might be drastically different, but Hunter knew what he was doing, and when the dust had settled at the end of December, Hunter had made in excess of a billion dollars for Amaranth. Hunter reportedly took home between $75 and $125 million for himself for the year. *Traders* magazine listed him as one of the top thirty highest paid traders. Life was good for Brain Hunter.

And then life got even better when Maounis allowed him to move back to his native Calgary. It was an interesting move; despite the fact that the area was such a major natural gas producer, Maounis was quick to boast that his firm had world-class risk management systems. A major component of his risk management was that all trading activities were kept at the Greenwich office, where he could monitor everything as it happened. But Maounis made an exception for Hunter, and Hunter didn't give him any reason to doubt the move. By the end of April 2006, Amaranth's assets under management had swelled from $6 billion to $8.7 billion. By the end of the year, that number would grow to $9.2 billion. And that growth was entirely due to the success of Brian Hunter.

A Greenwich, Connecticut, office, a billion-dollar-a-year trader, a hedge fund moving into the big leagues; Maounis himself had a shot at becoming one of the legendary hedge fund titans. But there was more to some of Hunter's phenomenal returns than just good old-fashioned hard work. There was a component of his strategy that was not quite legal. Had Hunter been in the Greenwich office, he most likely would never have been able to utilize it, but because he was 2,400 miles away in Calgary, it was much easier for him. That strategy was what traders refer to as banging the close.

* * *

Natural gas is a commodity that, not surprisingly, has its seasonal ups and downs. About 25 percent of its uses are industrial and another 25 percent are for power generation. Because the remaining roughly 50 percent is used for heating, natural gas is most often used in the winter. But that's from the consumer's perspective, not the supplier's. Suppliers want to have as much natural gas on hand before the winter season hits as possible, so they stockpile what they can during what's called injection season, which usually runs from April through late October or early November. Wholesale demand is at its peak during this time, though end users are still enjoying warmer months. Then draw season begins in November, when consumer demand begins to increase as the colder weather creeps in, and as the weather gets colder, consumer demand for natural gas continues to increase.

From an energy trader's perspective, however, wholesale demand is entirely secondary. It's the consumer demand—and the price that wholesalers are willing to pay to meet that demand—which is the trader's primary concern. That's the part of buying and selling natural gas that really moves the markets.

Natural gas contracts are traded on multiple futures exchanges, but the contracts hedge funds follow the most are on the New York Mercantile Exchange (NYMEX). Those contracts are naturally tied to the wholesale price, and not the retail price. Energy prices are all related, to be sure; they're all dependent on the weather. If wholesale buyers think it's going to be a cold winter and that retail demand for natural gas will be high, they're going to stockpile more of it. That, in turn, drives up the wholesale price. A good gas trader has to be a step ahead of the wholesale buyer, however, because he has to know what the wholesale buyer is doing before the wholesale buyer knows himself. It's all about weather and temperature, predicting heat waves and cold spells that the rest of the market doesn't expect.

There's demand for natural gas throughout the whole country, so the gas has to physically get there. That is accomplished by a network of pipelines crisscrossing the country. The pipelines are fixed; that is, there's no way to take a side road to get there any faster or move past a blockage. That means it's difficult to modify supply routes when a particular area of the country is extremely hard hit by the winter cold or the pipelines are disrupted. These are many of the variables all coming together in natural gas prices, so prices can be volatile, and trading natural gas contracts is certainly not for the faint of heart.

There are four distinctly different ways to trade natural gas. The first, and perhaps the most simple, is buying and selling the actual gas. Those who do that will buy it, store it, sell it, and ship it. The logistics involved in this kind of trading mean that there are comparatively few major players who do so; suffice it to say, you won't find one in any Greenwich hedge fund office.

The second and most common method of trading natural gas is through futures contracts. These contracts trade on the NYMEX, and each single contract represents an agreement to deliver 10,000 British Thermal Units (BTUs) of natural gas to the "Henry Hub" in Louisiana. Again, though, the traders aren't interested in the gas itself; it's just the contracts that they're trading. They're betting on the price of natural gas at some future date.

Outside of those two methods, there are two other ways that are a little more exotic and involve what is called over-the-counter (OTC) trading. OTC trading is done directly between the buyer and seller; there is no exchange serving as a go-between or an overseer in the transaction. That means, among other things, there is another degree of risk associated with the trade—what's called "counterparty risk." When there's no exchange to verify the creditworthiness of a counterparty on the opposite side of the trade, make margin calls, or maintain rules, it's all up to the two parties involved.

In the world of OTC, sometimes called natural gas derivatives, there are two types of contracts. One is traded on the Intercontinental Exchange (ICE), which is not an exchange in the typical sense of the word. Rather, it's simply a facility that brings together buyers and sellers who are interested in trading OTC contracts between themselves. It is purely an electronic marketplace, though they do have one enhanced feature. The ICE exchange itself can serve as the counterparty, so the contracts that are traded on the ICE exchange are then called ICE OTC cleared contracts.

The final method of trading OTC gas derivatives is though swaps contracts, and it's about as simple a transaction as you can find. A buyer meets up with a seller, and the two come to terms on a price for the contract. There's no exchange or execution facility involved, just two traders talking on the phone or through a broker.

Regardless of the type of contract—NYMEX, OTC, ICE, or swap—and whether or not they're traded on an exchange, most fixed-rate natural gas contracts settle based on the NYMEX futures contract closing price. That number is the gospel for these traders, and even though the terms of some contracts might vary, the NYMEX price is sacrosanct. Every trade on every exchange or between two counterparties closes at whatever price the NYMEX futures contract settles at.

Brian Hunter was trading natural gas in every way, including NYMEX futures, ICE cleared contracts, and OTC swaps. That is, all except physical natural gas, which needs to be preapproved by the NYMEX powers that be, and a hedge fund was not going to be on that list. Nor did Hunter have any interest in moving gas around the country, for that matter. They were traders for a hedge fund—pure natural gas speculators, after all, not natural gas suppliers or distributers. But here's one catch: because Amaranth could not take physical delivery of the gas, it had to be completely out of its contracts by the end of every contract month. In other words, all the contracts its traders were long or short had to be closed out before the end of each month. More exactly, they had to be closed before the last second of the last minute of the last trading day. Otherwise, they'd be on the hook for delivering or receiving the gas at the Henry Hub, something they didn't want to do, nor were capable of doing.

When it came to Amaranth's natural gas trading strategy, the public line the company advertised was that it sought "to hold winter month positions and short summer month positions." In just a few quick lines, it summed up the entire strategy that Hunter employed with great results. The logic behind it is pretty straightforward. Barring some sort of cataclysmic weather pattern, the winter natural gas price would never dip below the summer price. In the long winter–short summer strategy, the potential losses are limited. Assuming you accept that proposition, then the greatest possible loss that one could take is the spread between the two prices. The term traders give to this strategy is called a calendar spread, because you're betting on the spread between the prices of two different calendar months.

The reason Hunter liked this strategy so much—aside from the fact that it worked so well for him—was that, to his mind, it was a pretty safe bet. The typically narrow spread between the winter and summer prices would widen considerably if winter prices for natural gas suddenly increased. If there was some type of weather event, even if it occurred in the summer, the winter natural gas price would generally spike higher than the summer price. This was Hunter's basic trading strategy.

Hunter did have another trading strategy that worked pretty well too. It involved the theory that given enough volume and trading size, one trader could push around the market for a short period of time. It might sound far-fetched, to be sure. There are thousands and thousands of futures contracts that exchange hands in an average day; how can one trader's actions have any kind of effect on that kind of volume? Remember that we're talking about hedge funds here, sometimes using unlimited amounts of leverage and risk. By using enough position size and savvy trading techniques, an experienced trader can, in fact, move the markets one way, albeit for a short period of time. And then profit handsomely once it's done.

Suppose there was a massive trading sell-off in a specific futures contract at the end of the day. Now, suppose that sell-off happened on the last trading day of the NYMEX natural gas futures contract. The bigger the sell-off during the last few minutes of trading, the bigger the price drop. Keep in mind, a price drop in the NYMEX futures settlement price is reflected in the ICE swaps contracts closing price too.

Consider the following scenario: A trader establishes a huge long position in the front natural gas futures contracts on the NYMEX. At the same time, he hedges his long futures position by going short the equivalent number of natural gas swaps contracts on the ICE. Remember, they're both essentially the same thing, except one is a future contract and the other one is an exchange cleared swap.

Right before the market closes for that contract—say the last eight minutes—that trader sells his entire long NYMEX futures position, which drives the price of the futures contracts down at the close, and thus, the settlement prices for both the NYMEX and the ICE. The trader sells all of the long position on the way down and cashes in on the short position settling at a lower price. The only window of risk is the period in which he's selling off his long position, during which time he has no hedge to counteract a potential price run-up. Given that it's a window of only eight minutes, it's highly unlikely there's going to be any kind of sudden natural disaster during that time to drive up the price. Hunter was pretty safe in knowing that the selling was going to push down both the NYMEX futures contract and the ICE swaps contract. And when it did, he walked away with a real tidy profit.

There's actually a technical name for this trading strategy (well let's say manipulation strategy)—it's called banging the close. Technically, it's illegal. A trader is willfully manipulating market prices so that he can profit not once, but twice. The catch is that it's sometimes hard to prove. There's a fine line between allowing traders to execute trades that are in their best interests and calling them criminals. Those who get away with it can typically hide their intentions very well and disguise their trades. Brian Hunter, despite his intelligence and experience—or perhaps *because* of his intelligence and experience—

didn't feel the need to disguise what he was doing when he banged the close.

On February 23, 2006, Hunter sent a message to another Amaranth trader. "Make sure we have lots of futures to sell MoC [Market on Close] tomorrow," he told him. The futures he was referring to were the March 2006 natural gas contracts, and they would be expiring the following day, February 24. When that next day came, Amaranth opened with a net short position of seventeen hundred natural gas futures contracts on the NYMEX, plus short twelve thousand of the same contracts on ICE. As the day progressed, Hunter steadily switched his NYMEX short position to a long position of three thousand contracts. He remarked to a colleague in an electronic communication, "I just need H [the designation for March contracts] to get smashed on settle, then day is done." In other words, he needed the price for March futures to get pushed down. He needed to bang the close.

During the last thirty minutes of trading on that day, Hunter placed an order to sell his three thousand futures contracts, but gave explicit instructions to the pit broker that the order was not to be executed until the last eight minutes of the trading day. As it turned out, during the last four minutes Hunter unloaded 99 percent of the long position he was holding, which included 78 percent of those contracts in the last sixty seconds of the trading day.

Hunter's hubris was such that he would brag about it to other traders—traders at other firms, no less. "We have 4000 to sell MoC. Shhhh." The trader asked him why he would do that, unless he was "huge bearish" in his view of the natural gas market. Hunter replied nonchalantly that it was "a bit of an expirment [sic]."

While his "expirment" worked, it didn't go unnoticed by Amaranth's management. On March 10, 2006, Amaranth issued an internal compliance memo outlining the firm's position on trading techniques like banging the close. In no uncertain terms, the memo stated that the firm prohibited any sort of fraudulent and manipulative practices, including engaging in "trading or apparent trading activity for the purpose of artificially causing the price of a commodity to move up or down." In other words, management knew exactly what Brian Hunter was doing, and even though the managers were going to pay him handsomely for all the money he was making, they wanted to cover their asses in case anybody noticed what he was doing.

Hunter, though, didn't take the new memo to heart, assuming he read it at all. When April rolled around, he was right back at it again. Throughout the month, Hunter built up a trading position in May 2006 natural gas futures contracts and swaps. By April 26, 2006, he held a position of long three thousand NYMEX futures contracts and a short position consisting of a staggering nineteen thousand swaps contracts. Hunter was setting up another round and getting ready to bang the close, except for one little sticking point. Hunter was concerned that another natural gas trader named John D. Arnold, whom he feared, was a buyer.

You see, Hunter and Arnold were energy-trading rivals, and both men were so competitive that they liked to win on every trade. A Senate investigative report would later comment that "many traders were reluctant to take positions opposite Amaranth, regardless of their view on market fundamentals." But John Arnold wasn't one of those traders. He welcomed the chance to go head-to-head with Brian Hunter. Arnold was widely considered the best natural gas trader in the business.

John Arnold started his trading career at the ill-fated Enron, a company that was deeply involved with natural gas, including the physical delivery of it. Those days gave Arnold a huge trading advantage, especially because he knew the actual physical flows of supply and demand.

Following Enron's collapse in 2002, Arnold set up his own hedge fund, Centaurus Energy, where he brought with him a selection of Enron's best energy traders. And in what turned out to be the perfect moment in energy trading, he started Centaurus just as the hedge fund boom arrived in energy. Before Enron collapsed, there were only a very few companies trading energy outside of a select few firms. In 2001, the capital devoted to energy trading stood at approximately $5 billion; by 2006, that amount had exploded to over $100 billion. The field for energy trading was getting crowded, and everybody wanted a piece of the action.

Hunter expressed his concern to David Chasman, Amaranth's head of energy risk management: "Arnold is getting scary short into the number tomorrow. I am worried that Arnold has taken the other side of everything." In other words, Hunter was nervous that his rival was going to screw up his plan to bang the close by buying up futures contracts just as Hunter was selling them. In that case, Hunter could end up short the ICE swaps contracts just as Arnold was pushing prices higher, which was definitely not the manipulative effect he was looking for.

Chasman asked him point-blank about whether or not Arnold was aware of what Hunter planned to do: "Does he know [what you] are up [to] [with respect to] rolling off short?"

"Probably," Hunter acknowledged. "Arnold is the master of moving the close."

But Hunter went ahead with his plan anyway. He placed orders to sell five hundred futures contracts, then 544, and finally two thousand. All the orders had the same explicit instruction: do not execute the sale until eight minutes before the close.

The thing about selling something is that the sale only works if you've got somebody who wants to buy what you're selling, especially when your selling window only amounts to the last eight minutes of the day. Natural gas futures are a large and liquid market, but the sheer volume Hunter had for sale was too big for the market at that particular moment in time. In the end, only 1,675 of the over three thousand sell orders got sold. Hunter still got what he wanted. The price of NYMEX natural gas contracts dropped, and his epic short position in the ICE made good money, but not the gold mine he was expecting, had the balance of the contracts been sold.

This time, Hunter's actions didn't go unnoticed. On August 2, 2006, the Compliance Department of the NYMEX exchange sent a letter to Amaranth inquiring about the firm's trading activities in the May 2006 natural gas contract. More specifically, its trading activity on April 26 had raised suspicions of some, let's say, unorthodox trading activity.

Amaranth took its time with a response, and wrote back on August 15. The hedge fund brushed off the NYMEX accusations, saying, "If any of Amaranth's orders were executed in the post-close session, that was not due to Amaranth's instructions to do so." The response went on to suggest that the delayed orders "perhaps occurred because a floor broker erroneously failed to comply with Amaranth's directive." In other words, the firm was saying that it hadn't directed anyone to push orders through during the last few minutes before the close. If it did happen, it was somebody else's fault, not the firm's.

It was a flimsy excuse. It was the equivalent of saying, "It wasn't me. Honest. It must have been someone else." Despite the lack of an actual defense, however, the NYMEX accepted Amaranth's explanation, and the issue passed, at least insofar as NYMEX was concerned. The U.S. Commodities Futures Trading Commission would eventually have a few questions it wanted answered, but that would come later.

* * *

Ironically enough, what brought down Amaranth wasn't illegal. There was no insider trading, no stealing from clients, and no hidden flaws in the accounting system. The collapse didn't even involve market manipulation by Hunter. No, what brought down Amaranth was, of all things, nice weather.

That said, it could be argued that Hunter was employing the same strategy he used to bang the close; he wanted to amass a large-enough position so as to push the market in his direction. He was hoping to combine his knowledge and expertise with natural forces and really drive up the price of natural gas. The seeds for this plan were actually sewn back in 2004, before he was allowed to move back to Canada, and before he started his overly public banging the close operations.

The year 2004, from a weather perspective, was a major year; there were a record number of hurricanes and storms in the Atlantic and Caribbean. When disasters such as hurricanes hit, the price of natural gas skyrockets, and so too do the futures contracts. Hunter, true to form, was firmly entrenched in his standard long winter and short summer trading position, and in 2004 he cashed in when the price of natural gas jumped 80 percent higher than its summer low. The profits were huge and really caught the attention of Amaranth's management. One fellow trader described Hunter: "He was incredibly intelligent. Just incredibly intelligent. Brilliant in terms of his analysis."

The next year, he pushed his luck again, taking on the same strategy as he did the year before. He was long winter and short summer, praying for a massive hurricane to make his financial gamble pay off.

His prayers were answered on Tuesday, August 25, when what had been previously called Tropical Depression 12 formed into a Category 1 hurricane off the coast of the Bahamas. The hurricane was somewhat unique in that it was actually the blending of two depressions—Tropical Depression 10 had basically sputtered out, but enough of it remained that when Tropical Depression 12 intersected with it, a hurricane was born. It was the eleventh named storm of the Atlantic season. Her name was Katrina.

By Friday, August 26, all indications were that Hurricane Katrina was going to make landfall in Louisiana, approximately sixty miles from the city of New Orleans. New Orleans, like the hurricane that was about to lash it, is unique in its formation. It is a city built, literally, below sea level. Much of the city sits an average of one or two feet below sea level; ten feet below is the maximum that any building sits. This just happens to be one reason for the popularity of mausoleums in New Orleans cemeteries. If you try to bury a body in the city, you'll hit water before you're six feet down.

In addition to the above-ground burial crypts, the city is also home to a massive levee system constructed by the Army Corps of Engineers, a system designed to keep water from flooding into the city. The levees were thought to be capable of withstanding whatever Mother Nature might throw at them. By Sunday, August 28, Hurricane Katrina had become a Category 5 storm, with maximum sustained winds topping 175 miles per hour. New Orleans mayor Ray Nagin told residents it was "the storm most of us have feared," and the National Weather Service issued a warning that New Orleans residents should expect "devastating damage" when the storm hit.

That damage came early the next morning, when the hurricane made landfall sixty miles away in the town of Buras-Triumph. Within five hours, water levels were estimated to be as high as ten feet on some New Orleans streets, and by two o'clock that afternoon, officials were confirming that the levees had failed. When the water finally receded, over eleven hundred people were confirmed killed by the storm's wrath. It was a disaster that will forever be etched in the minds of those who lived through it.

If there is a silver lining to be found in such a catastrophe, it is surely to be a subjective silver lining that only benefits a certain small segment of the population. In the case of Hurricane Katrina, that segment was natural gas traders. The hurricane severely damaged natural gas pipelines and production facilities throughout the Gulf of Mexico, knocking out approximately 70 percent of the region's production capabilities. And prices for natural gas futures contracts jumped accordingly.

And then, just to add insult to injury, Hurricane Rita appeared on the radar, again threatening to hit New Orleans. Experts predicted that even a near miss would result in the complete and utter destruction of the city. But there was nothing anybody could do but pray that the storm turned in a different direction. The storm, thankfully for both New Orleans and natural gas traders, turned west, making landfall at Sabine Pass, Texas.

Sabine Pass is technically part of Port Arthur, Texas, the town that annexed Sabine Pass in the 1970s. In addition to being the birthplace of legendary singer Janis Joplin and football coaching legend Jimmy Johnson, Port Arthur is a part of the massive Texas petroleum industry, which includes natural gas production. As a result of the destruction wrought by Hurricane Rita—destruction wrought throughout the already battered Gulf Coast region yet again—the natural gas industry was looking at unfathomable damages to its infrastructure. The price of natural gas went through the roof. Brian Hunter's prayers had been answered in spades.

After being down about 1 percent overall for the first half of 2005, Amaranth was looking at a very, very profitable end to it. Hunter's fund—itself a major beneficiary of the meteorological unpleasantness of the summer—had made the firm over $1.26 billion, and Amaranth's income statement at year end showed a 21 percent profit. For his efforts, Hunter was paid a bonus rumored to be $100 million in cash, though others claimed it was actually $75 million in cash and $50 million in deferred compensation that would vest over a period of several years.

Hunter was suddenly the golden boy who could do no wrong at Amaranth, and Maounis became completely enamored of the young trader. News of his success had made its way through the financial news grapevines, and investors were flocking to Amaranth. By the end of 2005, the hedge fund had $8 billion under management, making it the world's thirty-ninth-largest hedge fund. Hunter was now allowed to move his family back to Calgary, despite the fact that all the traders who reported to him were located in Greenwich, Connecticut. But with this kid's brains and insights, it didn't matter if he was on the moon. In Maounis's mind, Brian Hunter could make billions in his sleep.

* * *

For much of the latter half of 2005 and the beginning of 2006, weather prognosticators were talking about something they call La Niña, a period during which sea temperatures are lower, on average, by three to five degrees Celsius. What it means for the Atlantic and Gulf Coast regions of the United States is that there is an increased probability of high-intensity storms, including hurricanes. Paired with the dire reports about increased storm activity associated with global warming, anybody who expressed an opinion on the subject was sure that 2006 was going to be a devastating hurricane season. That was music to the ears of Brian Hunter. He was betting heavily that 2006 would mirror the previous two years in terms of destruction, and, as a result, there would be the same spike in natural gas prices.

Hunter once again opted for the standard trading strategy, going long the winter contracts and shorting the summer, working under the assumption that winter prices would go up following the disastrous storms of the summer. The summer contract would not get hit so hard, since it was still at the very beginning of injection season. It was the same way he made over $2 billion over the past two years. And if a trade is working, keep doing it until it stops.

The problem was, though, that other traders had figured out what Hunter was doing; long positions in natural gas were making a lot of money, so many of them opted for similar strategies. And what's more, the natural gas producers were doing everything they could to build up their own reserve supplies of physical gas so that they'd be ready for a disruption in supply. After all, when everybody is talking about how bad a year's hurricane season is going to be, people started getting prepared. From the traders' collective perspective, they knew Hunter was betting on it and making a killing to boot, so many other traders and hedge funds got in on the action, buying up as many natural gas contracts as they could.

The year 2006 started out well enough for Hunter. The spread between summer and winter contracts was around $1.40 in February, meaning that winter gas was trading about $1.40 higher than summer gas. Hunter placed his bet on the calendar spread, buying winter gas and selling summer gas. In late April, when that spread moved out to as high as $2.20, Hunter was piling even more on his already gargantuan positions. It looked like Hunter was once again going to make a killing in natural gas that year. But there was a hint of potential disaster. His positions became so large that they might have become too much for the market.

Before 2002, hedge funds had been relatively unimportant in the world of energy trading. It was the producers and suppliers who actually drove the derivatives markets, because they were the ones buying and selling the physical product. Few people in the energy markets cared about what hedge funds were doing, or where they were putting their money. But by 2006, funds like Amaranth had become major participants, controlling so much trading volume that suddenly it was the derivatives traders who were moving the market. The tail was wagging the dog.

By April 2006, Hunter was up nearly $2 billion, single-handedly accounting for nearly all of the fund's profits for the year. Amaranth publicly announced that it was up 12 percent for the year, a gain attributed singularly to energy trading. But by the beginning of May, things started to get a little crazy. Many other traders were buying natural gas derivatives through the June and July contract months, and at the same time natural gas producers were generating as much of the product as they possibly could. It was the single largest buildup of prewinter natural gas inventory in history.

Hunter continued betting on a repeat of the previous year's destructive weather, and his position reflected his confidence. He had extended his short summer–long winter position out over several years, expanding the scope of his bet years into the future. In the event of any weather disaster, he'd make a fortune. It was what some investors began to call a simple hurricane play.

At this particular point in time, the markets had completely accounted for the possibility—even the probability—of a severe hurricane striking the natural gas production and distribution infrastructure of the United States. However, by the spring of 2006, the industry had fully recovered from the previous year's destruction, and had learned from its mistakes. The year 2006 saw reserve storage holdings at levels more than 40 percent higher than they'd averaged the previous five years. The market was preparing for natural disasters unlike it had ever done in the past. This was something new, and it was something Hunter did not anticipate. The natural gas market had been adjusting for a disaster *before* Hunter had built up his trading position to such a huge size.

The market finally turned in May, and natural gas prices dropped down to about $6.00, even going as low as $5.88 at one point. Amaranth was now down 10 percent for the entire year, and Maounis sent out a letter to investors explaining that the firm was cutting back on its leveraged trading positions. Brian Hunter wasn't worried, though. Or if he was, he didn't show it. He was still positioned for the year, holding fast in his bet that summer prices would fall and winter prices would soar. He held over one hundred thousand NYMEX contracts, a number that constituted nearly 40 percent of the total outstanding natural gas futures contracts on the exchange. "He thinks he's bigger than the market," one natural gas trader said of Hunter.

Size was the key ingredient to Hunter's strategy, as he felt that large positions could drive the market. In other words, if he owned enough contracts, he could dictate the price himself. His position was concentrated too; at one point, Amaranth controlled 75 percent of the outstanding contracts for November 2006. The NYMEX imposes limits on position sizes as a way of preventing a single person or group from acquiring the ability to literally corner the market. As a way around that, when Amaranth hit its limit on a particular contract, it just went to the ICE exchange and kept right on buying. It was reported that at one point in 2006, Amaranth controlled between 60 and 70 percent of the natural gas futures contracts for the 2006-2007 winter season. And that included every exchange.

One downside with moving from NYMEX futures into ICE contracts was that the size of Hunter's position was beginning to filter out into the market. Whereas trading futures contracts is anonymous, Hunter's OTC contracts on the ICE exchange required a counterparty on the other side of the trade. The more ICE contracts he bought, the more people who knew that he was behind all of the trades.

Hunter's positions had gotten so large that it was quite possible that any attempt to reduce his positions would result in a major price decline. Plummeting prices would then cause him to lose considerably more amounts of money, more losses then he'd already booked in May. The problem was that there were just too few buyers out there to pay for the contracts he owned. Maounis finally realized that Hunter had overextended himself. "They counseled Brian to get out," one Amaranth trader recalled. "He needed to be ordered."

In May of 2006, Amaranth showed that its fund was down over $1 billion, a staggering figure that management thought was impossible to hit—especially given that the investment strategy had relied so heavily on calendar spread trades. It was, at least according to Amaranth's calculations, over four times more than it was supposed to be able to lose. It was the sheer size of its position that was killing the firm, which was crumbling beneath the weight of its own holdings.

Amaranth owned the calendar spread of short summer/long winter, so even though it was both long and short at the same time, any attempt to sell one and buy the other would just result in the calendar spread itself literally inverting. Given the amount of contracts the hedge fund still owned, any more selling on its part would have made the existing billion-dollar deficit look relatively small in comparison. A rival trader said of the situation, "It was naïve to think that they could get out of the market with a size of one hundred thousand positions."

The traders were stuck in their trade, and all they could do was hope for a miracle in the form of an über-destructive hurricane that would send gas prices through the roof. It had worked for two years in a row, and there's an old saying about bad things coming in threes. So it might make sense that this year would be a repeat of the last two. There was still reason to hope.

That optimism dissipated, however, as the season wore on and no major hurricane was even beginning to organize itself. Hunter was told to cut back his position, but he couldn't. Everyone in the industry knew exactly what he was doing, and the position he was in. He was stuck. So he did what many gamblers do; he started to double-down on his bets. The logic was that if he added to his position at lower prices,

his average purchase price moved lower. If he lost, he lost less; if he
won, he won more. By purchasing contracts, he was also helping to
support the market and keep it from sinking even lower. It certainly
wasn't the first time a trader felt he had to keep buying to defend his
position. But it wasn't a sustainable strategy. One rival trader said after
the fact, "I knew Amaranth would eventually implode. It was just a
matter of when."

On paper, Hunter showed some inconsequential gains since
May; the losses were not as devastating now. But making money on
paper is like kissing your sister. It's just not real. So he kept on buying,
moving the calendar spread out even more. That spread moved so
much, in fact, that it triggered the collapse of one of Amaranth's rivals,
MotherRock LP, who had been betting the other side of Hunter. When
you take out a rival in a game, it's a good thing. Reports even surfaced
that Amaranth actually acquired MotherRock's positions while closing
it out.

By a stroke of good fortune, Hunter had finally managed to move
the natural gas market into the range of profitability, with gas futures
contracts trading as high as $8.30. Remember, the price was down to a
low of $5.88 just a couple months prior. A $2.40 price swing is a pretty
big movement in gas prices. But because of the limitations due to
Amaranth's inability to actually own physical natural gas, it was going
to be faced with the obligation to close out its contracts before the
delivery date. And as any good art collector knows, a piece of artwork
only appreciates in value if someone is willing to pay more than you
originally paid yourself. The size of Hunter's position made that reality
logistically impossible.

In August 2006, Maounis gave an interview to the *Wall Street
Journal* in which he defended his trader and their strategy. "What Brian
is really, really good at," he told the paper, "is taking controlled and
measured risk." Perhaps he was trying to convince himself as much as
the readers of the newspaper. There was nothing controlled or measured
about the risk Brian Hunter was taking.

November 30 is the official end of the Atlantic hurricane
season, though that doesn't mean storms cannot hit the region after
that date. By September, the 2006 hurricane season was considered a
nonevent. To most people, it was a blessing. It meant less destruction

and loss of life. But to the traders hitching their financial wagons to it, like Hunter, it was a financial disaster.

On top of that, the summer of that year was relatively cool nationally, which meant a lower demand for electricity. Lower electricity demand nationally meant less demand for natural gas, as it is used in many electricity generators. Speculators continued unloading their long gas positions, further driving down the price of the contracts Hunter was holding. Hunter, however, did not stop in his pursuit to acquire more contracts. When you factor in the storage glut that producers amassed in anticipation of another disastrous hurricane season, the price for natural gas was in free fall. There was even talk of an extremely small injection season that year, and Amaranth started receiving margin calls to cover its declining positions. At the time, the hedge fund already had $3 billion out to the exchanges and counterparties covering its margin calls.

The price for natural gas had sunk to its lowest level in four years, and Amaranth had run out of money to pledge as margin. The only choice was to begin unloading some of its positions. Hunter was in a huge hole of his own digging; he had hoped for an unprecedented rebound in the price of natural gas. But the more Amaranth unloaded, the lower the price sunk. On the fourteenth of September, Amaranth posted its single worst day ever, losing in excess of $560 million as the price of natural gas dipped below $5.50, and the summer/winter spread collapsed.

Closing out the remaining positions would only drive prices lower and further the already crippling losses. The only hope was for a blisteringly cold winter—some type of surprise storm, anything—but all reports indicated there was nothing in the forecast.

There was, at the time, a widely held belief by those in the inner-circle energy traders that Hunter's old nemesis John Arnold was working against him to drive prices lower. Maounis realized he needed to liquidate, and his sales pitch told potential buyers that there was a single person working against them, so a savvy buyer could easily realize a billion-dollar profit. He gave that pitch first to Goldman Sachs on Friday, September 15, while other Amaranth traders called a host of other banks looking for a buyer. In after-hours trading that night, natural gas prices continued to fall, indicating that the word continued to spread about what was happening with Amaranth.

On September 16, a swarm of investment bankers descended on Amaranth's office in Greenwich. Both Goldman and Merrill Lynch made offers that day, and by Monday morning, Amaranth was putting the final touches on a deal with Goldman. Maounis knew he had to get the deal done by Monday, because after that day, it would be common knowledge that the firm was in serious trouble with its massive holdings. That news would inevitably result in yet another precipitous drop in prices. And any further price drop would be the death knell for Amaranth. Maounis wanted to calm his investors, and he sent out a letter detailing the losses they'd sustained, but assuring clients that a deal was being finalized that would save the firm.

There was a conference call that Monday morning that included Amaranth, Goldman, NYMEX, and J. P. Morgan, who had served as the source of financing for Amaranth's margin deposits. J. P. Morgan had loaned Amaranth money so that it could acquire even larger futures positions. It's a common practice in the futures industry, and it is known as margin financing. Like any loan, a margin finance loan requires collateral, and in this case that collateral was the futures contracts themselves. The law provided J. P. Morgan the option of either buying the contracts in bankruptcy court or taking control of the assets itself in the event that Amaranth defaulted. Goldman balked at the situation, and Amaranth urged J. P. Morgan to pledge that it wouldn't seek recourse in the event of ba   lined, and Goldman backed out of the de   ncertainty in the waters.

Soon after, Maounis received a call from Ken Griffin, the head of Citadel, a Chicago-based hedge fund. Maounis laid out the situation for Griffin: "It's real simple. We need a bridge loan and a couple hundred million to stay in business." Griffin immediately assigned forty Citadel employees to work on putting together a deal and sent two of his senior managers on Citadel's private jet to Connecticut right away as well. Those two lieutenants joined the other investment bankers digging through the Amaranth offices.

The next day, Tuesday, September 19, the future appeared even bleaker for Amaranth. Natural gas prices continued to fall, and the prospect of getting a bridge loan and staying in business was looking impossible. The firm had lost so much money that it needed to liquidate its entire portfolio. The natural gas market continued its downward spiral in free fall, with prices hitting a new low of $4.35. As a result, Amaranth's net assets were down to $3.5 billion, only thirty percent of the $9.2 billion it had boasted of just a few months earlier.

With gas prices so low, those around the situation sensed blood in the water and chose to pounce. J. P. Morgan called Maounis, offering a compromise deal. J. P. Morgan would agree not to seek recourse in bankruptcy court if Amaranth would allow it to purchase 50 percent of Amaranth's natural gas assets along with Citadel. Seeing no other option, Maounis had to agree to the terms, and the deal was struck.

Immediately after news of the sale became public, natural gas prices rallied. Traders knew that the contracts Hunter had been holding were no longer about to be dumped on the market. The new owners were in strong financial shape and didn't need to sell any more in order to stay liquid.

The media would later report that both J. P. Morgan and Citadel "made a fortune on Hunter's positions." Amaranth posted a $6.6 billion loss, with $6.5 billion of that coming in the space of a single month. It was, at the time, the largest single trading loss in history. It was reported that Citadel made a profit of $1 billion from the transaction. Assuming that J. P. Morgan made a similar profit, given that it was holding an equal number of contracts as Citadel, the collective gain for those two entities alone resulted in a $2 billion profit. That estimate implies that approximately $4.5 billion was made collectively by other energy traders, and it has to be assumed that Centaurus Energy—the firm led by John Arnold—was one of them. Given that Centaurus posted a 150 percent gain over the previous year, Arnold truly won the title of the best energy trader out there.

*   *   *

Following the Amaranth collapse, Brian Hunter was immediately accused of violating antimanipulation rules by the Federal Energy Regulatory Commission (FERC) stemming from his banging the close trading in February and April of 2006. He immediately flew to his lawyer's office in New York City to voluntarily provide testimony as to what had happened. He claimed that there was no intent on his part to deceive anyone, nor did he attempt to cover up his trades from his bosses at Amaranth. But when Hunter's attorneys noticed that a FERC lawyer was setting up a video camera, they asked him what he was doing. "Oh, this provides superior impeachment material," the lawyer replied, and Hunter's lawyers immediately ended the interview.

That story doesn't quite mesh with the version told by Joseph Kelliher, the chairman of FERC, who told to reporters that Hunter simply left the room and never came back. "Hunter was in the middle of an interview and there was a lunch break," he explained, "and he never came back."

While Hunter may or may not have been dodging the FERC's investigation, the U.S. Senate Permanent Subcommittee on Investigations issued a report in June 2007 in which it claimed that excessive speculation by Amaranth had caused the price of natural gas to fluctuate dramatically, and the end result was that Amaranth caused the price of natural gas to go up for end users. Ironically, Hunter's trading had sent the price of natural gas down in the end, directly opposite of what the report claimed, but the end users are really voters, and that's who really mattered to the senators.

The U.S. Commodities Futures Trading Commission (CFTC) disputed the Senate subcommittee's reports, citing the fact that natural gas prices were already unusually high due to the commonly held belief that the upcoming hurricane season would be bad long before Amaranth was involved. They concluded that "Amaranth trading was responsible for the spread price level observed during 2006," but that it was essentially the result of a bad bet that came back to bite it.

It didn't mean the CFTC wasn't after both Hunter and Amaranth. The commission focused intently on the alleged market manipulation perpetrated by Hunter, much like the FERC lawyer was investigating. But after Hunter filed a suit against the FERC, the case was thrown out because the futures market was not under the FERC's umbrella to investigate. That duty fell to the CFTC.

So the CFTC filed a complaint in which it claimed that Amaranth attempted to manipulate the natural gas futures contracts prices on the NYMEX on both February 24 and April 26, 2006. The complaint did not explicitly say that Hunter *did* manipulate market prices, only that he attempted to do so. Additionally, the complaint accused Amaranth of trying to cover up the trader's actions by issuing "false and misleading statements" in its letter dated August 15, 2006 to the NYMEX. In the end, Amaranth agreed to pay a $7.5 million fine levied against it jointly by the FERC and the CFTC. That payment came after Amaranth settled a class action lawsuit brought by other industry traders for $77.1 million in April of that year. Despite the payouts, many felt that justice was not served, because nobody seemed to be held responsible for Hunter's actions.

The whole investigation of Amaranth and Brian Hunter revealed a host of problems with the process in general. Taken together, many of the missteps resulted in the appearance of a turf war between the Senate and government regulators. Rather than putting together a stronger case, critics said, different government entities were more concerned with establishing their own position in the pecking order. Throughout the investigation, there also seemed to be a lack of communication between the various agencies, which were often claiming that Amaranth and Hunter had committed different crimes; sometimes one agency claimed the opposite of what another one was claiming. For example, whereas the Senate found that Hunter had driven prices up, the CFTC study showed that he'd actually driven prices down. But at its core, the fight became one of who had jurisdiction over what and whom.

* * *

Immediately following the Amaranth collapse, the question flying around the energy markets was, "Where is Brian Hunter?" Rumors were rampant about where he was and what he was doing. One commonly circulated story held that he'd fled to Canada to avoid prosecution. Of course, he'd been living there for over a year at the time, so that one didn't hold much weight.

The truth is that in 2007, he tried to organize a new hedge fund called Solengo Capital Partners. Solengo is a Tuscan word meaning, appropriately enough, "lone wild boar," and is also the name of a high-end Tuscan wine. Hunter started it with four of his former colleagues from Amaranth and had $800 million in funds pledged from twenty-five new investors. Eventually that money disappeared, and the directors resigned; Hunter claimed the market manipulation charges were preventing him from moving forward. The lone wild boar was on his own, however, and he sold Solengo's minimal assets to Peak Ridge Capital Group, where he was then hired as an advisor.

As of the last report, he is still living in Calgary, where he keeps an office that is virtually empty. He continues to be employed by Peak Ridge Capital Group, devising trading models and strategies for the firm's own energy trading. "I never enjoyed trading," he said of his life with Peak Ridge. "I like design. This allows me to do what I like to do. I don't have to deal with investors or risk management."

But if you really want to find Brian Hunter, he's honestly not that hard to spot. The man who avoids having his picture taken is actually quite easy to find when you know what car he drives. And when you live in Calgary—where the average median income is around $30,500, in Canadian dollars—anybody who drives a Bentley Arnage with a list price of over $200,000 U.S. dollars is fairly easy to spot. In fact, he's the only person in Calgary who drives around in a Bentley at all. So the next time you're at a Starbucks in Calgary and you see a Bentley Arnage drive up, you can bet it's Brian Hunter.

Chapter Six

Jérôme Kerviel and Société Générale, 2008

The life of a monk is supposed to be one of religious devotion, marked by vows of poverty, celibacy, and silence; of devotion to the study of religion and a peaceful way of life. While that image is mostly true today, such was not the case throughout history. Back in the eleventh century, the Catholic Church was literally fighting to spread its faith throughout the world, battling for control of the holy lands in the Middle East. Under the authority of the Pope himself, Christian soldiers were sent on a series of religious crusades to take back the holy lands, spreading their message along the way.

During the First Crusade, Jerusalem was captured by the Christians, who secured the town that would become a popular religious pilgrimage throughout the next century. Opening up this route meant a steady parade of devotees making their way along rugged terrain. It was a hard and long trek, especially in those days. It also meant an abundance of thieves along the way who were eager to rob the unarmed and unassuming pilgrims.

After a scandalous number of robberies were reported, a French knight named Hugues de Payens proposed the formation of a monastic order dedicated to the protection of the pilgrims headed to Jerusalem. And thus was born the Knights Templar.

Members of the Knights Templar lived under a very strict code of conduct, which included eating in silence, avoiding women, and adhering to a specific dress code. The dress code included the well-known white mantle that featured a large red cross emblazoned across it. Collectively, members became known as "*Les Moines-Soldats*," or "the soldier monks."

The Knights were fanatically devoted to both spreading the word of God and destroying all those who opposed his word. Their dedication was both admirable and contemptible. As the Knights' ranks and reputation swelled, so too did their reach. They entered into financial arrangements with the pilgrims, providing letters of credit and overseeing the business affairs for those off fighting in the Crusades. Money began pouring in at the various headquarters of the Knights Templar, which led to various European monarchs worrying about the group's power and influence. Accusations of financial impropriety—as well as various crimes against the church—began to surface, and the Knights Templar were outlawed. Many historians have argued that the Knights were merely scapegoats, and their dissolution was arranged by the king of France—a move he made to avoid repaying his debts. The Order of the Knights of Templar was disbanded, semiofficially, in 1312, and *les moines-soldats* were relegated to the history books; at least for the time being.

The soldier monks ceased to exist for many centuries, until the idea was resurrected by a new group of French devotees in the late twentieth century. In its new manifestation, *les moines-soldats* weren't interested in spreading religious beliefs, nor did they take up arms for their cause. They did, however, immerse themselves in the financial world, and they carried with them the same level of dedication as their predecessors, though in a slightly different way. The new soldier monks were blindly dedicated to their cause and were followers of a Frenchman named Antoine Paille.

He was born in the ancient French town of Le Mans, a place best known for its twenty-four-hour endurance car races; his parents owned an apple orchard, scratching out a living as best they could picking and selling fruit. He was ambitious from birth and gifted with an innate ability in mathematics. He attended college at the elite École Nationale de la Statistique et de l'Administration Economique, France's top statistical school. During his time at ENSAE, as the university is colloquially known, he was initially drawn, ironically enough, to the teachings of Karl Marx.

Paille was so drawn to socialist thinking that he came close to joining the Communist Union while still a student. He had begun attending regular meetings of the group and asking many questions. When a group leader responded to one of his questions by merely quoting a passage in Marx's *Das Kapital*, Paille changed his mind about joining. To him, in their minds there was no possible answer except that which was prescribed by the book. Paille realized he was too much of a freethinker to subscribe to their way of life—a way that was dictated by another's words. That personal stance would become the lifelong pursuit of the brilliant mathematician.

Paille graduated from ENSAE in 1977 and applied for admission to the École Nationale d'Administration (ENA), the graduate school that trains students for senior positions within the French government. He was denied admission, however, and opted instead for a position with a computer software company, where he spent his days developing computer programs for the French banking industry.

As the age of the personal computer dawned, Paille began to imagine the potential for these new, widely accessible machines. With his professional background in banking and finance and expertise in math, he saw a future where computers played a greater role in the world of finance. It was what he called the "triptych detonation," a reference to the three-panel art displays favored by many painters and photographers. The three components—computers, math, and finance—were going to combine to revolutionize the investment world. And Paille was about to find out how correct he would be. In 1984, at the age of twenty-nine, he left his computer programming job, intent on realizing this dream of a triptych detonation in finance, and joined Société Générale.

*   *   *

Société Générale was the creation of Emperor Napoleon III, the nephew of the more famous French emperor, and formed by imperial decree on May 4, 1864. The newly formed bank—whose name literally translates into "general company"—was charged with the task of developing both the industrial and commercial sectors for the nation. It was founded by a group of industrialists and financiers led by Eugène Schneider. Société Générale—or SocGen, as it's commonly known in the banking world—grew rapidly and soon afterwards was able to boast a network of fifteen branches in Paris and thirty-two branches across the country.

From its inception, the bank was dedicated to financing the major domestic industrial manufacturers, but in 1901, executives began to look abroad and opened a subsidiary in Saint Petersburg, Russia. That experience gave SocGen the ability to open other new branches in both India and China, which in turn, allowed the bank to enter the lucrative business of currency exchange.

SocGen was nationalized following World War II, which meant that the government of France became its sole shareholder. The years following the end of the war were marked by severe inflation throughout France, a condition that remained constant through 1958. Then, in 1963, a new piece of legislation passed that opened the door for a new type of open-ended investment product, the Société d'Investissement à Capital Variable, or SICAV. It is essentially the French form of a money market fund, wherein the risks and returns of investing in stocks and bonds are shared by the shareholders. Société Générale was one of the first banks to offer this new product to clients.

Beginning in 1986 with a new government in France, a wave of privatizations swept the country, and Société Générale's chance came one year later. The bank was held up as an example to its competitors, with enviable risk ratios, equity capital, and overall productivity. On June 27, 1987, the entire company's equity—17.2 billion francs worth—was floated on the Paris stock exchange, and the bank's privatization was complete. SocGen was no longer government-owned; however, years of being state-run had left its mark, and the bank continued to reflect the culture of the French government. Most noticeably, bank executives were exclusively graduates of the "*grandes écoles*." Anyone with any chance of succeeding at SocGen clearly had to be a member of this prestigious club.

By 2008, the bank was one of the three largest in France and had grown to over 162,000 employees, with its headquarters in La Défense, the epicenter of the French financial world situated on the outskirts of Paris. In its investment banking group, SocGen had developed a large proprietary trading operation, which mainly focused on European equities. In fact, most of the bank's capital and risk on the trading floor were dedicated to equity derivatives, whether trading for its own account or making markets for clients. By 2008, SocGen was the European leader in this business.

* * *

Equity derivatives are mostly based on the pricing of options, which goes back to the original brainchild of Antoine Paille in 1985. Société Générale's options traders were known throughout the industry as "the soldier monks." Recruits were among the best and the brightest the country had to offer, especially in the field of mathematics. Selecting those with only the best academic skills was characteristically French. According to Alexandre Fleury, the former deputy head of global exotic trading at Société Générale, "The French have distinguished themselves in equity derivatives because of their love of complicated math."

Paille put it much more bluntly: "Our strategy was to be a world leader."

As a Frenchman, Paille saw it as a moral obligation to hire only those from the top schools in the country—France's *grandes écoles*. In addition to being French, they also needed to be brilliant. This elite club had advanced degrees in brain-frazzling subjects such as partial differential equations, probability concepts, stochastic calculus, and Brownian motion.

Their brilliance was necessary for trading of equity derivatives, though Paille had even grander ambitions for his squad of geniuses. Recalling his days writing software, Paille knew he needed custom-designed computer programs to achieve financial domination, and in order to create these complicated programs, it required the smartest people he could assemble. Together they formed an exclusive club, and if you hadn't graduated from one of France's *grandes écoles*, you need not apply. They were the modern day *moines-soldats*.

But at Société Générale, the soldier monks were characterized by more than just their intelligence. They were, like the group they were named after, fanatic in their devotion to their work. They were known throughout the company as being possessed by their jobs, going far beyond the generic classification of workaholics. "We considered it a mission," Paille said of his group. And of course, they were intellectual beyond compare, reveling in complex theories and pricing models. A favorite saying amongst *les moines-soldats* was, "It may not work in practice, but it does in theory."

That dedication and drive earned them quite a reputation throughout the industry. And, as their reputation grew, so, too, did their confidence. Working in fourteen-hour shifts from 8:00 AM until 10:00 PM, the soldier monks designed, programmed, bought, sold, and traded some of the most complex financial instruments ever to be assembled into equity derivatives. The instruments obviously carried substantial risk, but the soldier monks knew their superior intellect had enabled them to manage that risk, primarily through their complex computer models and risk management systems.

As the business grew and technology advanced, the group added computer systems fast enough to process these complex risk models in real time. That, combined with the brainpower they had accumulated, allowed it to make more money in equity derivatives than any other bank in the world. Whereas other banks sometimes had down years, the soldier monks at Société Générale only had down months. Two of them, to be exact, in the span of fifteen years. These *soldats* wore their success like the cross of the Knights Templar, and they dominated the trading floor.

Despite its apparent successes later on, the options trading group was a somewhat obscure team up until the late 1980s; at least until the traders got their first big break. France's equivalent of the U.S. Export-Import Bank, Compagnie Française d'Assurance pour le Commerce Extérieur, wanted to buy some currency options to hedge its risk, so it sought out prices from all of the French banks. SocGen easily won the trades, which put its business on the global map.

More recognition came when the bank added interest rate and equity options, which in turn, continued to grow the profits at the bank. An industry-leading business was great for the bank, but it also resulted in a flurry of job offers for the soldier monks, and Paille started to see his team slowly diminishing. Though the team's dedication to the job was legendary, members' loyalty to their employer was most definitely for sale. In an effort to stem the exodus, Paille approached Société Générale's top executives and proposed a profit-sharing plan that would have rewarded the top traders, effectively giving them an equity stake in the business. The executives, however, rejected the proposal.

Frustrated by the steady loss of traders and his inability to tie their long-term interests to that of the business, Paille departed Société Générale and went over to Frankfurt, Germany, where he set up the derivatives unit at Commerzbank AG. The leaders at Société Générale, in turn, reorganized the importance of the derivatives unit and created an entirely new division—this time headed by Jean-Pierre Mustier, one of Paille's earliest disciples on the soldier monk team.

Mustier's takeover preserved the exclusivity of *les moines-soldats*, a designation that was still not open to outsiders. They were doing, after all, supremely complex work, so naturally only those who came from the right background and studied at the finest of schools were still allowed in. Surprisingly though, it would take a middle-class kid from a small fishing village in Brittany to crack the glass wall surrounding the soldier monks. That young man from the provinces would prove that brains were no match for cunning. His name was Jérôme Kerviel.

* * *

Jérôme Kerviel was born in Pont l'Abbé in Brittany, France, a small coastal town with a full-time population of about eight thousand. The source of the town's income came from fishing and tourism, neither of which appealed to Jérôme. His father was a blacksmith who also taught a metal shop course at the local school, and his mother was a hairdresser. Again, neither profession beckoned. The bright lights of Paris and the money to be made in its financial district were quite the lure for his young mind. But that required an education.

Kerviel earned his undergraduate degree from the Université de Nantes and his master's from the Université Lumière in Lyons. Neither of them could ever be considered *grandes écoles*, and both schools were somewhat looked down on by those from the superior schools. His education would do nothing to improve the image of a country bumpkin from Brittany around the halls of SocGen; it only solidified that he was not part of the French elite.

But Kerviel still managed to land himself a position in the middle office at Société Générale in 2000. He did what he could to improve his image by dressing well and was known to be polite and helpful around the office, two characteristics not typical of top traders

who moved both Heaven and Earth. The middle office wasn't the
trading floor to be sure, but those coveted spots were reserved for the
hypereducated, a group Kerviel would never be a member of.

Working in the middle office was tedious, as its name suggests.
The position itself is stuck in the middle, between the trading floor and
the back office. He was essentially a liaison between those who executed
the trades and those who processed them. He and his middle-office
colleagues were the primary point of contact for anyone with questions
about the traders' activities. His days consisted of generating reports,
calculating profits and losses, inputting trades, reconciling errors, and
performing other relatively mundane, menial tasks.

In 2002 things started looking up for Kerviel when he was
offered the position of assistant trader. It was a significant a step up from
the middle office, because now he was doing work related to securities
trading. His main responsibility was entering the traders' orders into the
computer processing system, but it was more engaging than merely
typing in trades. Most importantly, he had a seat on the trading floor.
That also afforded him access to the proprietary trade processing system
that SocGen had developed called "Eliot." He learned firsthand about
risk management and the trading monitors that the bank employed,
and in future years, he would put all that learning to his own personal
use.

In 2004 fate once again smiled on Jérôme; he was promoted to
junior trader and assigned to the Delta One trading desk in the equity
derivatives division, a trading desk that was rapidly rising in importance
at SocGen. Though he still wasn't part of the elite *moines-soldats* club—
not yet, anyway—he was at least rubbing elbows.

The word delta means change, and in investing terminology a
security's delta is the change in the price of an option relative to a
change in the price of the underlying security. In other words, given a
move in the price of a security, it's how much of a nearly identical move
will result in the price of the option. A delta of one means the options
price moves one for one with the price of the underlying security. These
were options that were considered the most plain vanilla—that is, with
the least risk associated with them—and they were the primary products
that the Delta One desk at Société Générale traded.

Remember, options give the investor the right—not the obligation—to buy or sell a security or an index at a given price by a given future date. Typical options are "calls," which give the investor the right to buy a security, and "puts," which give the investor the right to sell a security. Equity derivatives, too, are typically made up of options. Antoine Paille, the father of les moines-soldats, loved trading these kinds of options, as they "seemed to unite math, statistics, and computers." In other words, they embodied everything he loved about finance, all in one convenient package.

Delta One trading desks are frequently defined as trading financial products that have no optionality. The delta of one. Their products often incorporate baskets of securities wrapped up into a single instrument. Examples might include things like swaps based on a group of stocks, stock index futures, and exchange traded funds (ETFs). Most Delta One desks have a trading business in equity index arbitrage—exploiting the difference between the prices of the individual stocks within an index and the stock index futures; this tends to be their main source of revenues.

A "typical" Delta One trading desk can be difficult to define, however, simply because there is no real definition. The desks often encompass a broad range of trading activities that vary from bank to bank, and their position on the trading floor varies along with their activities. They're either situated as part of the equity finance division or the equity derivatives division within major banks. At SocGen, the group was part of the equity derivatives division.

The primary products traded on Kerviel's Delta One desk were warrants. They are basically long-term options on stock indexes or baskets of stocks, and just like an option gives the owner the right to buy or sell a particular security, the warrants give the same right, except it lasts for many years or sometimes never expires at all. In the overall scheme of things, regular warrants are notoriously unsexy when it comes to financial derivative trading groups, like SocGen's. They were still plain vanilla and predictable, just like regular options, and what a mathematician might call linear. Given that, they were not very intellectually challenging for the soldier monks at Société Générale, who preferred to flex their mental muscles and demonstrate their intellectual superiority in more complicated areas of derivatives. At

SocGen, parts of the Delta One trading d these plain-vanilla options into increasi ic instruments called "turbo warrants."

Turbo warrants were the SocGen Delta One desk's preferred instrument because they're what are classified as "barrier options." A barrier option is a form of an option that becomes active or inactive when a specific price "barrier" is reached. For example, if a customer owned a large amount of German stocks and wanted to be protected from a large drop in the DAX, the customer might buy a turbo put warrant from Société Générale. That option only became active— meaning exercisable, or sellable—if the DAX's value dropped below a particular price. The turbo warrant doesn't really exist until a certain price is broken by the index.

On top of all of that, turbo warrants come in a variety of permutations, which made them even more attractive to the intellectually elite *moines-soldats*. For starters, they come in both longs and shorts. A long turbo—nicknamed a "down-and-out call"—is a contract to buy the financial instrument, which might only become active after the index has moved 10 percent higher or 10 percent lower. Alternatively, a short turbo—also known as a "down-and-out put"— allows the customer to bet on the price of a security falling, but only once the barrier price is hit. Yet another subset of turbo warrants are called "knock-out options." If the preset price barrier is reached, the option expires worthless; it gets "knocked out."

For sophisticated buyers, all of these types of turbo warrants allowed them to bet on a change in the price without having to pay as much premium for it. Customers will often purchase long or short turbos because they're cheaper than regular options. Given that the options are not active until the stock price rises or falls substantially, a customer can find a way to hedge large moves in the market without paying that much for it. They can serve to protect an investor from some calamitous event that sends stock prices plummeting, or alternatively, skyrocketing.

Buying and selling of options is complicated enough on its own. With turbo warrants, the equity derivatives group at Société Générale began bundling all kinds of different options into single instruments. There were options to buy or sell based on whether the market trades at certain levels. That means there are many layers of options built into one financial instrument. On top of that, *les moines-soldats* were putting these turbos together for a whole variety of underlying instruments, including baskets of stocks, ETFs, stock index futures, and indices like the DAX and the Euro STOXX 50. It took an incredible amount of mathematical equations to price a single transaction.

It takes a keen understanding of advanced mathematical concepts to adequately map out the intricacies of these sorts of instruments—it's no wonder that the soldier monks at Société Générale loved their work. Calculating an option's price is itself a mathematical exercise, and a complex one at that. But calculating the price of an option conditional on another price level or that became active or inactive based on certain events is even more complicated.

One thing that's more or less standard for a typical Delta One desk is that it's typically a low-risk operation, meaning there's less price volatility that arises from large moves in the markets the desk trades. When they did have risky trading positions, those trades were always hedged in one way or another. For that reason, the Société Générale Delta One desk seemed like the perfect place for a newly anointed trader, such as Jérôme Kerviel, to cut his teeth.

The DAX and the Euro STOXX 50 were the two main stock indexes traded on the SocGen Delta One desk—they're what Kerviel focused on. DAX, an abbreviation for Deutscher Aktienindex, is a blue-chip German stock index composed of thirty major German companies traded on the Frankfurt Stock Exchange. Included in that index are such world-renowned companies as Adidas, BASF, BMW, and Deutsche Bank. The DAX is essentially the German equivalent of the American Dow Jones Industrial Average.

The Euro STOXX 50 index is much the same thing, except a little different. It encompasses fifty stocks from eighteen European countries, and includes some of the same stocks under the DAX umbrella. Just as the DAX is the blue-chip stock average for Germany, the Euro STOXX 50 is the equivalent average for all of Europe.

Kerviel's assistant's job eventually progressed to that of turbo warrant trading. In that role, his primary job was to buy turbo warrants that were issued by other banks, a process known as "turbo warrant arbitrage." Because the traders at SocGen knew they had the best pricing models in the world, the soldier monks liked to buy turbo warrants issued by their competitors, just knowing that the other banks often mispriced all the complexities involved. It was a lucrative business, to be sure—yet also another way for *les moines-soldats* to demonstrate their intellectual superiority.

Then in 2005 something that had previously been unthinkable happened: Kerviel was promoted to the full position of trader. He had longed for the chance to join in on the more complex trades, but now he was officially in the world of *les moines-soldats*—the trading position that was once reserved for only those with the best upbringing and education. In short, Kerviel entered the world reserved for the graduates of the *grandes écoles*.

He had beaten the odds and received the promotion, which also came with a first-year salary and bonus of €100,000. Though that amount was still considered low for an experienced derivatives trader, he knew he was fortunate to get the position at all. Kerviel said of his newfound status: "I was aware, starting from my first meeting in 2005, that I was less well considered than the others, [regarding] my university degree and my professional and personal background. I had passed through the middle office, and I was the only [trader] to have done that."

Though he still wasn't truly one of them, Jérôme Kerviel was determined to be accepted into the ranks of *les moines-soldats*. In the space of the next couple of years, they'd do much more than just notice him. They'd come to revile his very existence.

*   *   *

Beginning in July 2005, Kerviel began his initial foray into unauthorized trading. He started by buying shares in Allianz, a German firm focused on insurance and asset management, which amounted to approximately ten million euros worth of the stock. As the month progressed, he switched his long into a short on July 21, and the trading position was discovered. Kerviel was verbally reprimanded by his boss for having an unhedged position, and he promised to rectify the situation, selling out all of the shares altogether.

The main problem with his trading position, at least from the company's perspective, was that it was completely unhedged. Kerviel was allowed to have trading positions—that's what you're supposed to do on a trading desk—but SocGen didn't want them to take market-directional risk. If the Allianz stock price started to tank, Kerviel could easily book a large loss, and that wasn't the company's business. Taking a large trading position was OK, as long as it was hedged with another position. In the future, Kerviel needed to have a safety net when he was getting long or short in the market.

The lesson he learned from the slap on the wrist wasn't necessarily what his boss had in mind. It was the risk management group that had caught Kerviel's imbalance and alerted management. Kerviel now knew that as long as he booked unhedged trades, the risk-monitoring system was going to send up red flags. But because Kerviel had an insider's knowledge of the software, he knew exactly how to beat it.

The real lesson Kerviel learned from his boss was that he needed to hide his activities a little better. Of course, the best way to avoid the warnings was to have positions that looked like they were hedged. Kerviel had ideas of what to do. The best way to show the intellectual snobs that he was their equal was by banking huge profits, something he couldn't quite do with low-risk hedged trades. So he faked it. He just booked false trades that showed a hedge for something like his Allianz stock in the risk management system, thereby pacifying the system into thinking that he was doing what he was supposed to.

Right after he was reprimanded, a tragic event took place in London that happened to make him a lot of money. On July 7, 2005, suicide bombers had detonated a coordinated series of explosions throughout the London mass-transit system during the morning rush hour. Fifty-two civilians were killed in the attacks, and several hundred more were injured.

In addition to the loss of life, the event sent huge shockwaves rippling through the financial markets, including a drop of more than 200 points on the FTSE 100, the stock market index for the London Stock Exchange. Kerviel, however, was one of the few people smiling following the sell-off, because his short position was suddenly in the money. The profits the new trader booked so pleased his bosses at Société Générale that they rewarded him with larger trading limits.

With the power to trade more and take on more risk, Kerviel continued trading the stock markets over the course of the next year. However, these larger trading limits didn't satisfy his need to increase his trading position even more. If his trading position was getting a little too large, Kerviel would just pass an offsetting trade to hedge it. Anytime he needed a hedge to offset some risk, all he did was book a false hedge in SocGen's system. By August 2006, his trading positions were up to approximately €140 million worth of DAX futures contracts, with fake trades posted in the system to hide the true risk.

It was a pattern that would repeat itself many times over the next three years. From 2005 until 2008, Kerviel booked phantom hedges for his trading positions more than 947 times, all for the sake of convincing the computer that he wasn't doing anything outside of his authorized limits. Most of those trades were in single stocks; they totaled anywhere from €15 million to €135 million a trade.

Since Kerviel's manager knew the market and the trading system pretty well, Kerviel was still limited in his ability to exceed his limits. He'd spent the better part of two years trying to buck the system, only to be reprimanded if his trades got too large, even with the false hedges.

But all of that changed on January 11, 2007, when Kerviel's boss resigned his position as deputy head of the Delta One desk. He was replaced by Eric Cordelle, a man with no experience whatsoever in Delta One trading operations. It was akin to discovering a gold mine in his backyard for Kerviel, who immediately seized upon the opportunity presented by his new supervisor's ignorance.

It was a typical practice within the ranks of SocGen to move managers from one location to another, from one product line to another. It was looked at as something of a training exercise, a way to build knowledge and experience for its future top executives. Prior to coming to the Delta One desk, Cordelle had been in Japan, working in the Société Générale credit engineering and derivatives group.

At the age of thirty-four, in fact, Cordelle had no real experience in trading at all, let alone trading index derivatives and warrants. The only real qualification he could point to as a trading desk manager amongst les moines-soldats was his diploma in engineering from one of France's grandes écoles. In short, he knew nothing about his new assignment as deputy manager of the Delta One trading desk, a fact he offhandedly acknowledged when he said, "I was named to the position after five years in Tokyo spent on financial engineering."

Cordelle's limited qualifications were, ironically, exactly the help that Kerviel needed in order to establish himself among the ranks of the elite soldier monks. Not only was his new boss not familiar with the products they traded—he also had no understanding of the trade processing or risk management systems. And those were two clear advantages that Kerviel had. The way he saw it, he now had a green light to trade any way he wanted.

It's been said that sometimes it's better to be lucky than good, and Jérôme Kerviel embodied that saying in 2007. By the end of January, the first two weeks under his new, unsuspecting boss, Kerviel had built up a large short position in DAX index futures, hovering around €850 million. Within just a few weeks later, that number had mushroomed to €2.6 billion. By the end of March, Kerviel more than doubled his short position to what appeared to be a staggering €5.6 billion. Within just a few months of his new boss taking over, Kerviel's short position in stock index futures would grow even larger.

During the earliest part of 2007, the European stock markets were generally moving higher, and Kerviel was losing money, but he kept adding to his short position. It was the same story told by failed gamblers throughout the world, doubling down on bets, hoping for a change in luck. As the snowball of losses continued, so too did the size of the phantom hedges he needed to stay under the radar. Pushing through the first five months of 2007, Kerviel's losses were running around €2.5 billion at their peak.

By June 2007, Kerviel's short position in equity indexes had grown to a monumental €28 billion, and the sheer size was beginning to take its toll on the trader. "From dawn till dusk, I would stare at the screens, trading enormous amounts and hardly getting any sleep," he said. He was at the breaking point. Unless a drastic move took place, he would have to book an immense loss, not to mention losing his job. Kerviel was at the end of his rope, with everything about to come crashing down around him.

History, however, was lucky enough to repeat itself for Kerviel, who once again profited from a major catastrophe. Fears of subprime debt crisis in the United States and the collapse of the housing market led to the collapse of several overleveraged hedge funds, including Bear Stearns Asset Management, some BNP money market funds, and Sentinel Capital Management.

They were the first three dominoes to topple in the financial panic that would continue to sweep the globe through 2007 and into 2008. This time, however, all Kerviel cared about was the fact that the panic had saved him. His short DAX futures position on July 19 was just above €30 billion, and the market sell-off had turned the titanic negative into a positive. As Kerviel explained, "In July, the market had its first panic attack, and I was able to pull out with a gain of five hundred million Euros." Expecting that this initial sell-off was the depth of the crisis, Kerviel bought back the remainder of his shorts by the end of August. His timing was perfect and he made an incredible amount of money.

Kerviel's market sentiment continued to be negative, and by September, he was amassing another massive short position in equity index futures. By the end of October, he was short up to €30 billion again, and when the market continued its decline after a brief rally in October, Kerviel bought back most of his short with another large gain in November, resulting in a profit of close to €1 billion for the year. For the next two months, he worked to unwind the remaining positions in the DAX and Euro STOXX 500. "I wouldn't even go outside to get something to eat," Kerviel recalled of the last days of 2007. By the end of the year, his short positions were all covered, and his exposure was down zero.

On that December day when Kerviel finally closed everything out, his trading assistant sent him an e-mail with the subject "Valo JK + EUR 1,464,129,153." In layman's terms, that translates roughly to "Jérôme Kerviel Positive €1.46 Billion." Clearly his trading assistant knew how much the trader had made, at least on his real trades. But there was no way for Kerviel to admit that to anyone else. After a trading year like that, he could expect a year-end bonus of as much as €147 million, assuming he got paid the standard 10 percent of trading profits favored by many banks. However, in order to claim the profits, Kerviel would be forced to admit his trading escapades over the past year. First and foremost, Kerviel would be admitting much more risk taking than he was allowed, and on top of that, covering up those positions to avoid detection.

Kerviel was stuck in what can only be called an ironic twist for a trader. Rather than boast about the nearly 1.5 billion euros he made, he had to hide it, showing only a sliver of what he'd actually made. After putting through some false trades to book some losses, Kerviel reported a profit in his trading account of €18 million for the year. It still put him on the top of the list of traders at SocGen. On the Delta One desk, he had single-handedly accounted for 22 percent of the profits generated from proprietary trading and 40 percent of the profits generated from trading with customers. He had finally achieved the elusive status of elite trader and, one assumes, the respect of his now fellow soldier monks.

* * *

How can a man of modest educational achievement and background fool a system created by some of the most brilliant minds in the country? It was, at its core, where the cunning of one man was able to outwit the most advanced risk models. The risk system developed by those *grandes écoles* graduates, those *moines-soldats* who so prided themselves on their intellectual superiority, had a flaw. They didn't account for somebody falsely manipulating the system from within their ranks.

For starters, Kerviel was intimately familiar with the trade processing system and knew exactly what transactions he could easily hide. Jean-Pierre Mustier said of Kerviel's activities, "He chose very specific operations which were not involving any cash movements." Unlike some of his fellow rogue traders, Kerviel didn't steal or otherwise misappropriate money to hide his trades. He just lied about what he was doing—and the computer had no way of knowing it.

There were three specific methods that Kerviel employed to fool the SocGen system. First, as we know, he booked fictitious trades as a way of hedging the risk impact of his trading positions. Regarding those phantom trades, the computer was taking on faith that the person entering them was telling the truth. The system accounted for them as actual trades when calculating the risk and the profit and loss. It was a simple process for Kerviel, especially due to the fact that he knew the trade processing system inside and out.

Specifically, Kerviel knew that if a trade was booked as "pending," there was no need to enter the name of the counterparty. The system was programmed to check for pending trades on a regular schedule, and Kerviel knew the time of day when that check took place. So he was able to book trades right ahead of the scheduled time, and then cancel them afterwards.

The second part of his manipulation was to hide profits, and at times, hide losses. It involved booking fictitious trades to offset whatever outsized returns he shouldn't have been able to make. Kerviel booked matching buy-and-sell trades with equal quantities of the same security, but at different off-market prices. For example, on March 1, 2007, Kerviel booked the purchase of 2,266,500 shares of Solarworld at a cost of €63.00 per share, at the same time a sale of the same number of shares at €53.00. Both transactions were booked to settle at a future date, meaning they qualified as pending sales that didn't require a counterparty to be entered. The end result was a loss—albeit a fictional one—of €22.7 million with no real position in the stock ever established in the first place.

The computer system didn't identify the €53.00 share price being way off the market. Kerviel knew the forward settlement date would throw the system for a loop, meaning that it wouldn't find anything wrong with the trade. Kerviel would later cancel the trades after the system had checked for pending transactions, just like he did with the other trades. "He managed to place transactions which did not require immediate confirmations," Mustier later said, as a way of explaining the young trader's strategy.

Finally, Kerviel was able to make adjustments to the risk models to further insulate himself. By modifying the option pricing calculations that were supposed to be reserved for the trading assistants—but which did not prohibit the traders from doing it—he would change the option pricing model to fit his needs. Again, relying on the knowledge he acquired during his earlier days in the middle office, he'd adjust the volatilities used in the models to alter their calculations. Because options prices are very much determined by market volatility, changing the volatility number easily created the false profits or losses that he needed to cover his tracks.

When all of this was said and done, the amount of Kerviel's fraudulent activity was quite large. The final tally included 947 fictitious trades, 115 transactions designed to hide profits, and nine fraudulent adjustments to risk models.

*   *   *

Things began to unravel for Kerviel in the summer of 2007, when someone was doing some fact-checking and noticed that a counterparty didn't check out when they called them. Kerviel responded to the inquiry with a succinct, "No problem." He later produced a fabricated e-mail ostensibly sent from Deutsche Bank that confirmed the fake trade. Just like his reliance on booking fake trades, so too would he use forged e-mails. Whenever confronted with questions about his activities, Kerviel provided excuses that he backed up with forged e-mails.

Later that summer, Kerviel was again confronted by a risk control officer concerned with what appeared to be trades in turbo warrants that far exceeded his limitations. Again he replied, "No problem." This time, however, no e-mail was going to support his insouciance. At a meeting where his positions were collectively discussed, Kerviel produced a cleverly crafted report with charts showing that everything was actually within the limits. Claire Dumas, the deputy head of Cash & Equity Derivatives Operations at the time, said of his work, "He fooled us that way. His documents were so nice."

Eyebrows were again raised—though not enough to prompt further investigation—when Société Générale's futures broker, Fimat International Banque, regularly placed many of Kerviel's futures trades in its own account prior to moving them into Kerviel's account at Société Générale the next day.

Moussa Bakir was Kerviel's futures broker at Fimat in London, and Kerviel and Bakir had what can only be characterized as a close—and somewhat strange—relationship. One element was the fact that Kerviel paid Bakir very large futures brokerage commissions. At the end of 2007, that amount totaled approximately €6.2 million, and Bakir could be personally expected to take home as much as 40 percent of that. Combined with the fact that Bakir seemed to be booking many of Kerviel's futures trades himself, Bakir had extensive knowledge of Kerviel's activities.

Eventually, the size of Kerviel's futures trades caught the attention of the authorities at the Eurex, one of the major futures exchanges in Europe. In November 2007, Eurex sent two different letters to Société Générale questioning Kerviel's trading activities. The exchange seemed to know that something was wrong, but couldn't quite put its finger on it. On one occasion, Eurex representatives wanted to know why Kerviel had purchased nearly €1.2 billion worth of DAX futures contracts in the span of only two hours. Then, they wanted to know if the trades were booked electronically or manually. In the second inquiry, they also asked why trades were initially booked into Fimat's account instead of the account of SocGen.

The questions from the Eurex exchange led Kerviel to take additional steps to cover his tracks, steps that led him into a part of the risk control system that he was unfamiliar with. It was a risky move by Kerviel, but the letters from the Eurex had spooked him, and he didn't have the luxury of time to familiarize himself with that part of the system. In the end, that move would be his undoing.

* * *

On Wednesday, January 2, 2008, a brand new trading year prompted Kerviel to jump into a large number of DAX futures contracts. To offset his risk, he input eight phantom trades of turbo warrants on the DAX index that totaled €1.5 billion. The phantom trades were designed to be his hedge, trades he had supposedly done with Deutsche Bank. He sent the trades to the back office as "pending," including a message that read, "We will put the broker in anticipation of the counterparty conf." In other words, the trade would be finalized when the counterparty sent the confirmation. But given that the trade was fake, obviously that would never happen.

Throughout 2007, Kerviel had appeared to be spending the days and nights at his desk, trading the markets, trying to make money for the bank. In reality, he *was* trading the markets, but also working feverishly to conceal his oversized positions and book his fraudulent trades at just the right time. During the course of the year, Cordelle had suggested numerous times that Kerviel take a much-needed holiday. However, the star trader on the Delta One desk used the excuse that he was too upset by the recent death of his father. He was just happier staying around the office and working. The truth is, he was incredibly afraid of getting caught, and he knew his time was running out.

On Tuesday, January 8, an employee in the back office noticed the extremely large turbo warrant position with Deutsche Bank, which, of course, really didn't exist. Concerned that something was booked wrong, the employee asked Kerviel for an explanation. "This materializes the give up of puts made late; I owe money to the counterparty. It will be rebooked ASAP," Kerviel wrote in a cryptic reply. It was as if he'd pulled out a financial dictionary and chosen words at random. The back-office employee would later admit that he had no idea what the message meant. But it was accepted as trader-speak, something that made sense to someone smart enough to be in Kerviel's position.

Kerviel then canceled the transactions the next morning, telling the back office that they would no longer appear in the system. He then instructed his trading assistant to adjust in the options volatility calculation early the next morning, which would hide the P&L impact of his trades. The next day, everything seemed fine. The back office confirmed that the problem that was noticed earlier had been resolved. Problem solved once again.

A few days later, on Tuesday, January 15, the accounting department ran its reports for Société Générale's regulatory capital usage. Accountants noticed that there was a very large amount of capital ascribed to Deutsche Bank in OTC derivative trades: "Turbo warrants." Then, they inquired to the back office as to the source. The back office simply replied that the trades were canceled. It appeared the whole issue was a moot point.

As the day progressed, the bottom dropped out. January 15, 2008—nicknamed "Black Tuesday" by some investors—saw the global equity markets plummet. Many financial institutions saw their stocks slide on fears of the U.S. subprime mortgage crisis, as the entire U.S. housing market was under stress. The Dow Jones Industrial Average

closed at 12,778 that afternoon, but it would drop a full 17 percent—
all the way down to 10,578—in just a matter of seven days. The German
DAX followed suit, losing 11 percent of its value over the same period.

Kerviel was already on the brink of discovery, and now he had
just lost his shirt on his DAX futures contracts.

At 4:30 PM on Thursday, January 17, Kerviel was called into a
meeting. Both the risk department and the accounting department had
problems with the canceled trades with Deutsche Bank. For starters,
the accounting department claimed that Deutsche Bank had no record
of the cancellation. Kerviel had an easy explanation for it. He seemed
to have somehow booked the wrong counterparty into the system. It
was obviously his fault, and he was really sorry for the mistake. He
assured them that he'd correct the error and list the correct counterparty
for the canceled trade.

Immediately following the meeting, Kerviel got on his computer
and began an instant messenger conversation with Moussa Bakir at
Fimat. "You didn't say anything about our trades, did you? Otherwise,
you're dead meat," Kerviel warned Bakir. "Well I'm finished."

Bakir replied, "What do you mean?" It was an odd response to
the message Kerviel had sent him. When pressed by Bakir to explain
what he meant, Kerviel told him to "forget it." But obviously something
was wrong. Whatever that something was, Kerviel wasn't saying. As if
Kerviel didn't have enough to worry about, he was long the DAX to the
tune of €49 billion, and the market was crashing. Soon, he'd have no
possible way to recover.

The next day, the Deutsche Bank trade didn't go away. A person
in the accounting department was looking at the sheer size and found
Kerviel's explanation to be highly suspect. He decided to dig a little
deeper and consulted someone in risk management. She found that
Kerviel had, in fact, canceled all of the individual trades a week earlier.
There was still an issue that bothered her. She couldn't find any
evidence of a confirmation of the canceled trade from Deutsche Bank.

Together, they phoned Kerviel, who again apologized for his
oversight in listing the wrong counterparty on the trade. He then gave
them the name of a trader at another bank who was supposed to be the
correct counterparty, and hung up the phone. He must have known it
was over. Kerviel got on his instant messenger to Bakir and said, "My

last day here." Bakir returned with the suggestion to "cut the position," to which Kerviel replied, "Shit, I am dreaming of it every day."

That afternoon, Jérôme left for the weekend. Clearly, he knew he was through. He'd been chained to his desk for months, trying desperately to save himself from detection, and now he was leaving the office and going to Normandy for the weekend. His plan was to spend some time relaxing at the resort of Deauville, often called "the queen of the Norman beaches." However, by the time he arrived at the resort, investigators at Société Générale were uncovering the truth about his trade with Deutsche Bank.

There was no rest for the weary on Saturday, as executives continued to scour Kerviel's trades. They were convinced that something was very much amiss. Early that morning, a SocGen manager discovered that the reason Deutsche Bank never sent a confirmation cancellation was because the bank knew absolutely nothing about the trade in the first place. That revelation cut Kerviel's vacation short, and he was summoned back to the office immediately by the head of SocGen's investment bank, Jean-Pierre Mustier. Kerviel needed to explain exactly what was going on.

While he was in transit, the investigators finally uncovered the truth about Kerviel's earnings—specifically that he'd banked €1.4 billion in the course of 2007, an amount that far eclipsed the amount he originally reported. That in itself made absolutely no sense to anyone in the room. Why would a trader, who gets paid on his performance, downplay his own success? Confusion reigned supreme.

When Kerviel arrived at the office, he was immediately questioned by Mustier about his earnings. "If you really earned [so much]," Mustier is reported to have said, "what you did is annoying, but it's not major." In other words, he was willing to turn a blind eye to Kerviel exceeded his trading limits, assuming he made that much money for the bank. Again, the question as to his motive remained.

Another source reported that Mustier was not so enthused by the trader's actions, and was more forceful in his statement. "You have broken the rules," the source reported. "You understand that we can't keep you." That was a nice way of letting Kerviel know he shouldn't expect to be on the payroll on Monday, but the news came with a silver lining. "But don't worry," Mustier continued, "my wife works for a hedge fund. She will easily find a job for you."

Regardless of which version of the story is accurate—or if the truth lies somewhere in between—it was clear that under the best-case scenario, Kerviel had massively violated company policy, and his subterfuge was not appreciated. Worst-case scenario, his career at Société Générale was not going to last much longer.

The midnight oil continued to burn on Sunday, when an emergency meeting convened of the Société Générale board of directors to discuss the Kerviel matter. At that meeting, Daniel Bouton, the SocGen CEO, offered to fall on his sword and resign as a way of taking the blame. His offer, however, was rejected by the board. After the meeting, Bouton called all of the firm's traders into the office to tell them what had happened. It was assumed that they would keep quiet about the matter, and, it was hoped they would close out any of their own positions affected by Kerviel before the news broke. His long DAX futures contracts would be liquidated beginning on Monday, an action that would clearly drive down the already sagging equity markets.

However, it didn't take long for the news to become public. One London trader said, "By Monday, all of Paris knew that SocGen had a massive overhang and was going to be selling, although I don't think anyone knew how big it really was." Nobody outside of the inner sanctum of Société Générale, that is. At the same time, Fimat flew a flock of legal and compliance staffers to its offices in London and Paris, charging them with investigating the relationship between Kerviel and Bakir.

Bouton knew his bank was positioned precariously on the edge of a cliff with a very, very long drop. He pleaded with the Financial Markets Authority, the French regulatory body, to allow Société Générale time to liquidate the positions and to raise new capital prior to announcing the situation. "It would be very dangerous to announce this fraud without also showing an appropriate response," Bouton told the regulators. It was a request that, while veiled in sanctimonious altruism, leaned towards his own self-interest. The CEO wanted to cover his own ass before dropping this bomb on the rest of the financial world.

The request was granted, with the stipulation that Bouton and Société Générale only had three days before the stock exchanges were officially informed. While it was a temporary stay of execution, it didn't help much. Rumors were already running rampant through the markets that SocGen was liquidating a large equity position, a rumor that led to a massive sell-off in the global equity markets on Monday, January 21.

The rumors weren't something that Bouton concerned himself with, as the clock was already ticking on his three-day window. He contacted both J. P. Morgan and Morgan Stanley, who both agreed to raise the money Bouton needed. They committed to provide Société Générale with €5.5 billion in new capital.

Meanwhile, a SocGen employee named Maxime Kahn worked frantically to unwind the positions between Monday and Wednesday, desperate to unload everything before the news was made public. Kahn worked alone in a private room, and he later swore at the trial that the only positions he was selling had belonged to Kerviel.

The news was passed to the stock exchange as scheduled, on Wednesday, January 23, and the immediate response from the French government was one of outrage. When French Finance Minister Christine Legarde and French President Nicolas Sarkozy were informed, Sarkozy was furious that Société Générale executives had waited three days—five, if you counted the weekend—to tell him about the massive fraud. It was, to his mind, an unconscionable act of dishonesty.

The press got the news late Thursday, and Friday's papers carried the story to varying degrees. The *Telegraph* reported that a "mystery trader" who'd been involved with trading the European indexes had made unauthorized directional bets. Société Générale followed up with an announcement that it estimated the loss to be approximately €3.6 billion, and a trader named Jérôme Kerviel, age 31, was solely responsible for the massive debit. Even Nick Leeson of Baring Brothers infamy got in on the act, applying his own perspective to Kerviel's situation during an interview on an Irish radio station: "I would imagine that there would have been a perverse sense of relief, because he has not been able to bring it to an end himself."

Whether or not Kerviel felt any sense of inner peace was never revealed. Kerviel was immediately suspended from his job at SocGen. He holed up in an apartment in Paris and didn't leave for days. It was probably best for him to stay concealed, because the losses for Société Générale continued to mount. When the final tally appeared, Kerviel's positions had lost a whopping €4.9 billion after the liquidation. The loss also included the €1.4 billion in profits that he'd previously tried to hide. In other words, Société Générale had, at the hands of Kerviel, unloaded positions that had cost the company €6.3 billion. Jean-Pierre Mustier said of the unfortunate result, "I cannot deny that if we had not been selling, the market would have fallen less."

Kerviel was arrested by French authorities without incident on Friday, February 8, 2008. While in custody, he admitted to concealing his oversized trading positions. He claimed that he needed to hide the position because if the market had known of his €49 billion position, widespread panic would have hit the market, resulting in massive losses. The authorities were not impressed with his excuse, and he was scheduled for trial.

In what was billed in France as the "trial of the century," Kerviel attained something of an "people's hero" status. The media cast him as a modern-day Robin Hood who sought to strike out against the fat-cat bankers of the world. He was also called "the Che Guevara of finance" and the "James Bond of SocGen" by other reporters, with T-shirts depicting the disgraced banker as a revolutionary who had successfully outsmarted the greedy bankers. It was widely speculated that Kerviel wasn't the only guilty one at SocGen, just the scapegoat. Many reporters publicly wondered if his status as interloper amongst les moines-soldats had made him the perfect scapegoat. Perhaps there was a much larger conspiracy within the hallowed confines of Société Générale.

At his trial, Kerviel's lawyers portrayed him as a poor boy from the western province of Brittany, a wide-eyed and naïve young man who had moved to Paris to seek his fortune, and who was lacking in education but eager to prove himself in the world of high finance. Over time, he'd assimilated into what the lawyers called the "collective culture of faking trades" at Société Générale. He was not, they argued, engaged in an "individual intent to deceive." In other words, his lawyers said that because everyone at the bank was doing it, he shouldn't be found guilty.

Kerviel admitted under oath that he had violated company policy, but echoed his lawyer's words that it was an accepted part of the firm's culture: "I put fictitious trades in the system to hide my over-the-limits position because that's what I had learned to do as a middle-office employee and then as an assistant trader at Société Générale." He didn't elaborate as to whether it was a skill he learned from other traders or simply something he had taught himself.

Adding to the increasingly murky waters was the widely held belief that Société Générale had done everything to make lemonade from the lemons that Kerviel had given it. During testimony, it was suggested that the bank had taken the opportunity to liquidate some of its own subprime holdings, as it had been losing money throughout 2007. The suspicion was that the huge loss—a staggering figure—was a combination of both the trader's unauthorized losses and subprime losses that Kerviel was not associated with.

The court was not moved by any of Kerviel's defense arguments, and he was found guilty on all counts in 2010. He was given a five-year prison sentence, with two years suspended. It meant that Jérôme Kerviel was to spend three years in a French prison.

But Kerviel did not go quietly. To this day, he argues that two senior traders on his desk—Martial Rouyère and Eric Cordelle—knew of his activities and the size of his positions, yet stayed quiet about it. He also criticized the way in which SocGen unwound his positions, citing the fact that it chose the worst three days of the sell-off in January to do so. Because of that, he believes he shouldn't be personally held responsible for the loss. He is still convinced that the bank had taken the opportunity to unload its own holdings, bundling its losses with Kerviel's. "The bank used what it says was 'my' loss to disguise other losses on other positions," he stated.

While conspiracy theorists love the argument, the truth of the matter is somewhat less than helpful for Kerviel. If you consider that he was long about €50 billion in stock indices, coupled with the fact that the DAX was down 11 percent during the week before the positions were sold, simple math tells us that a €5 billion loss is just about right. And perhaps it was that simple math that prompted the court to order Kerviel to pay SocGen €4.9 billion in reparations. It was the final insult to the spectacular fall from grace for Jérôme Kerviel.

* * *

Following the Kerviel fiasco, Société Générale immediately raised €5.5 billion in new capital in February 2008 and spent €130 million to tighten its internal risk controls. The bank was, however, fined for its failure to properly supervise its trader. In one sense, the bank was lucky that it was forced to tighten risk controls when it did, as doing so had saved the bank from much larger losses when the market really crashed just eight months later in September 2008. SocGen did go on to take more than its share of losses in fixed-income products, just like the other banks. The French government was adamant that the bank remain French, so there was no opportunity for an opportunistic buyer to swoop in and take over Société Générale, though there was rampant speculation that the bank would not survive independently.

Eric Cordelle, the former deputy head of the Delta One trading desk and Kerviel's direct supervisor, left in April 2008, and was officially fired the next month for "professional insufficiency." That label arose from the bank's disbelief that he could sit next to Kerviel for eighteen months and not detect Kerviel's fraudulent trading activities. He pleaded ignorance when asked about that, saying, "I think an experienced desk chief could probably have spotted Jérôme's frauds." The other label that he was saddled with—that of "Kerviel's boss"—was one he couldn't shake, and it kept him from getting another job in banking. Today he runs his own whiskey distillation business.

President Sarkozy pushed for CEO Daniel Bouton to resign, telling him, "When someone is very highly paid, even when it is probably justified, you can't avoid responsibility when there is a major problem." Bouton resisted that call, saying, "The board is asking me to stay at the helm of the ship during a storm. I am a man of duty. I am not going to jump overboard." While an admirable sentiment, his stoic resistance didn't last. He resigned on April 28, 2008. Jean-Pierre Mustier followed suit and resigned on May 30, 2008.

Moussa Bakir, strangely enough, suffered no ill effects from his association with Kerviel. He is still today a futures broker with Newedge, the firm created from the merger of Fimat with Calyon Financial in 2008.

As for Jérôme Kerviel, he is age thirty-five as of this writing. He appealed his conviction, but on October 23, 2012 the appeals court upheld the sentence, and he was ordered to begin serving it immediately—though he still remains free pending further appeals. He is still portrayed as a French Robin Hood and has been elevated to the status of folk hero in his home country. One out of every eight Frenchmen believes that Kerviel is innocent and that the bank made up the scandal. The theory holds that because he was not a real soldier monk, his coworkers turned against him to hide the firm's larger losses. "My only objective," claims the fallen *moine-soldat*, "was to make money for the bank."

Chapter Seven

Thomas Hayes, RBS, UBS, and Citigroup, 2009

A friend of mine once gave me a good piece of advice for playing poker. "There's always one sucker at a poker table," he told me, "and if you don't know who it is, you're the sucker." It's easy enough to dismiss those words as an old joke, but keep in mind that he learned that wisdom from his grandfather, who had won the diamond for his own wife's engagement ring in a poker hand. So it just might be possible that the grandfather knew what he was talking about.

The thing about getting together with a group of friends and playing cards is that there's a degree of trust involved—a belief that your friends are not out to screw you out of your hard-earned money. You're there first and foremost to have a good time and enjoy each other's company. Of course, the opportunity to make a few extra bucks and earn some bragging rights is always an added bonus.

In the course of playing, a good poker player will often employ a strategy called "bluffing." It is, in the most basic sense, lying to your opponents. It's a way of making them think you've got a hand that you don't have, albeit a good-natured move in the course of a friendly game. You continually raise the bet, not too much and not too little, making your opponents wonder what, exactly, you're holding. Do you have four aces and a king, or just a worthless collection of five random cards that don't amount to anything? If you do it right, your opponents believe you have the winning hand, but if anyone calls the bluff, you're bound to lose everything.

In 2007, just when the financial crisis was taking root, another kind of poker game was played by banks around the world. It was a game, like poker, that professionals engaged in with companies they did business with. There was supposed to be an inherent trust that everyone was playing by the same rules. And just like a strategic poker game, some of those involved were bluffing. Their bluffs were a little different, however. But they weren't different in any sort of good-natured way. They were simply out to screw other people out of *their* hard-earned money.

The poker game in question didn't involve cards. It wasn't played in a casino or in a good friend's man-cave basement. It involved interest rates—specifically the interest rate known as the London Interbank Offered Rate, or LIBOR (also spelled "Libor"). That's the primary interest rate benchmark for the entire world. Trillions of dollars' worth of loans and all kinds of financial contracts are priced using the LIBOR interest rate. And while it might seem a little odd to think about interest rates like a game of cards, understanding LIBOR and how it was manipulated will make it all clear.

In the late 1970s and early 1980s, the financial landscape was changing all around the world. Banks were trading in new financial instruments, including interest rate swaps, foreign currency options, forward rate agreements, financial futures, and all kinds of new financial products. Formation of these instruments was prompted, in part, by massive moves in interest rates. Interest rates had shot up, and had then come crashing back down again. It was a wild ride for anyone in the banking industry, and it caused severe losses for many unprepared financial institutions. New instruments needed to be created to help banks hedge the risks of fluctuating rates. Borrowing at 3 percent, lending at 6 percent, and being on the golf course at 3:00 PM just wasn't in the cards anymore, so to speak.

Banks needed a standardized short-term interest rate to hedge themselves against the volatile rate changes. A benchmark was needed to match a bank's funding costs in some sort of way—something along the lines of the Dow Jones Industrial Average, but for short-term interest rates. At the time, issuing three-month and six-month Certificates of Deposit (CDs) were the two most popular ways for a bank to borrow short-term money, so the short-term interest rate index had to be something related to those two rates.

Of course, the best index for an individual bank would be an interest rate contract tied directly to its own funding costs. That would be the easiest way for the bank to hedge its own book of loans. Whereas such a contact would be great for the individual bank, it wouldn't be very appealing for someone on the other side of the transaction. The contract would not only be fragmented and illiquid, but prone to manipulation. Who'd want to buy a contract based on where a bank itself says it can borrow funds? There was, however, a lot of enthusiasm for a contract based on a general bank funding index.

The solution came courtesy of the Chicago Mercantile Exchange (CME) in 1981. The CME came up with two new futures contracts specifically designed for banks: the CD futures contract and the Eurodollar futures contract. The CD futures contract targeted banks' domestic funding costs—that is, where they could borrow funds in the United States. It was based on the CDs issued by the top ten banks in the United States and was designed to have the physical delivery of an actual CD from any one of those banks to fulfill the contract. It was, at the time, a very typical design by a futures exchange—the physical delivery of a specific commodity. And because all of the top banks' CDs traded at or about the same interest rate, the new contract was pretty plain and simple.

The Eurodollar futures contract, by contrast, was designed to mimic a bank's borrowing costs overseas. Eurodollars were originally defined as dollar deposits held outside of the United States. But there was an important difference between the two contracts. The Eurodollar futures contract was the first futures contract to be set up with a cash settlement feature. That is, no actual commodity was required to change hands when the delivery date arrived. It was a revolutionary idea at the time, and it appeared to be the wave of the future.

The CME needed a methodology to establish the future price of this unique cash settlement contract, so it came up with a bank survey. It was a system where the CME selected twelve banks at random from a larger pool, and the specific bank names were never publicizing. Then, to keep it even more secretive, the selected banks were surveyed twice a day at random times. In order to tighten up the average, the CME discarded the two highest and two lowest rates and averaged the remaining eight. After that, it published the official rate for Eurodollars.

The combination of these two new futures contracts, one domestic and one foreign, was exactly what banks needed at the time. They were finally able to do something that had never been possible before—hedge their funding costs. As an added benefit, the contracts created published information in the market about bank funding rates on any given day. The problem was solved, or so it seemed.

While both of the futures contracts were a success, one stood out a little more than the other. The domestic CD futures contract became very popular—in fact twice as popular as the Eurodollar contract, as it traded about twice the volume on any particular day. But that popularity didn't last for very long.

From 1981 to 1984, the credit quality of the banking system began to change, and that change wasn't in any kind of positive way. Bank of America was lucky, as its credit was still strong and the clearly the best credit amongst the herd. Continental Illinois Bank, however, was on the other side of the spectrum, as it was beginning to have problems funding itself and issuing CDs. That became an even bigger problem for CD futures traders. Every time banks were long a CD futures contract and took a CD delivery, they received Continental Illinois CDs, something they clearly didn't want. It was like getting the consolation prize after failing to win the big award in a game show.

Then in 1984 the credit situation got even worse, and Continental Illinois drifted into insolvency and collapsed. It was the largest bankruptcy ever in the United States at the time. Traders began moving out of the CD futures trading pit altogether, making their way into the Eurodollar pit. Eurodollar futures volumes skyrocketed, while the CD futures contract lay dormant. By September 1986 there was almost no volume left in the CD futures contract; the open interest was down to only twenty-eight contracts. It was all over for the CD futures contract, and with it came the demise of the physical delivery for short-term interest rate contracts.

With physical delivery dead and buried, cash was king, so to speak. The cash settlement feature of the Eurodollar futures contract was now cemented as the wave of the future. Why deal with messy CD deliveries in a futures contract when you could just settle at a market-surveyed price? It made things a lot easier. But there are inherent problems with any method based on surveys; as any good marketing person can tell you, surveys are not quite as reliable as you might hope. Especially when they have fluctuating opinions, as opposed to the concreteness of a hard and deliverable asset.

Capitalizing on the sudden popularity of the Eurodollar futures market, the London International Financial Futures and Options Exchange (LIFFE) introduced its own version of the Eurodollar futures contract. All of a sudden there was competition for the U.S.-based CME contract. As a consumer, you might feel that competition is good for business. But with the Eurodollar futures contract fast becoming a cash cow for the CME, that exchange didn't view the competition as very favorable.

The LIFFE futures contract was just a little different, however. Instead of using the same survey as the CME, LIFFE used the British Bankers' Association's calculation of LIBOR. The concept was about the same—an average rate of where banks borrow dollars outside of the United States—but the survey was also a little simpler. Instead of two surveys a day with a large pool of banks where no one knew which banks were included, the LIFFE survey used one survey, and everyone knew the banks involved. And, as it turned out, banks liked using the same survey for their futures contract as the one used for published LIBOR rates. LIBOR was already a quite popular benchmark rate in the first place, and its popularity was growing.

However, the survey method for LIBOR and the LIFFE futures contract did not sit well with the CME. The exchange feared it would start losing business to the LIFFE contract, which prompted the CME to switch its Eurodollar futures contract to the LIBOR survey in January 1997. Now, with the CME and the LIFFE contracts both using LIBOR, that rate was immediately established as the dominant global reference interest rate.

LIBOR is officially described as "the rate at which an individual contributor panel bank can borrow funds."—that is, an honest assessment of the bank contributors' costs of borrowing funds in the London interbank market. The banks in the panel are chosen by the BBA, and are the world's leading financial institutions in a particular currency. There are ten different publicized LIBOR currencies, including the U.S. dollar, the euro, the Swiss franc, and the Japanese yen. In 1997, when the CME switched over to LIBOR, there were submissions from forty different international banks involved in setting U.S. dollar LIBOR rates.

The importance of LIBOR cannot be overstated. It's the primary interest rate benchmark for the entire world, and it is used as a reference interest rate for a wide variety of interest rate contracts: interest rate swaps, mortgage loans, credit cards, and student loans are all tied to LIBOR, just to name a few. What many people don't know about LIBOR is that it's also a barometer of the financial health of the banking system. When investors begin to get worried about the financial strength of banks, it's reflected in their ability to borrow funds. Some might even say that LIBOR is the canary in the coal mine for a financial crisis—an early warning indicator of when investors begin pulling their money out of troubled banks.

All told, LIBOR is used to price approximately $10 trillion worth of corporate loans, floating rate notes, and adjustable rate mortgages—that's trillion with a "T." And that number isn't nearly as large as the $350 trillion in interest rate swaps contracts that are referenced to LIBOR. When you add it all up, LIBOR influences more than $500 trillion worth of financial "stuff" around the world. The slightest movement in LIBOR interest rates causes billions of dollars to changing hands globally.

In 2012 alone, about 45 percent of prime adjustable rate mortgage loans and over 80 percent of subprime mortgage loans were indexed directly to LIBOR. That's where most average people interact with the rate, albeit they're usually not aware that they're connected to it. For every homeowner out there who pays the mortgage on time, contributes to his or her 401(k) at work, and does everything that should be done by a responsible adult saving for retirement, LIBOR is vitally influential over that individual's life. The fact is, LIBOR is directly tied to people's own financial well-being, and that well-being is in turn tied to the information provided by banks that determine the rate itself. In other words, despite assurances to the contrary, John Q. Public is at the mercy of the LIBOR banks when it comes to much of his or her finances.

Calculating LIBOR commences every morning just before 11:00 AM London time, when banks report the rates they believe they would have to pay to borrow funds in the open market—the equivalent of issuing CDs. They're required to submit rates for a fifteen different time periods, ranging anywhere from overnight to a full year. The BBA officials exclude the highest and lowest quartiles (25 percent) of the submissions, and they take the average of the remaining rates for each period. That average becomes what is called the LIBOR fixing, which is the published rate for that day. The Reuters news organization publishes LIBOR at 11:30 AM London time, or 6:30 AM in New York.

It's important to understand that rates submitted for LIBOR aren't what banks specifically paid for their funding each day, but rather what they would *expect* to pay at 11:00 AM. And that brings up an important point: LIBOR is calculated, quite frankly, based on a bank's educated guess of its own funding situation. It's the interest rate the bank of a reasonable market size could expect to borrow. Banks are allowed to personally evaluate their own funding situation to determine how much they'd have to pay to borrow. As the *Wall Street Journal* reported on April 16, 2008, "The LIBOR system depends on banks to tell the truth about their borrowing rates." That statement would prove prophetic in the coming years.

The duty of reporting the bank's rate every morning falls on a trader on the money market desk known as the "primary submitter." That person is supposed to consider the overall state of the market; information acquired from interdealer brokers, futures prices, swaps prices, and cross-currency swaps can all be used to help to determine the rates. The primary submitter is specifically not allowed to consider the bank's own trading positions when determining submission rates. Obviously that part will come back later.

Given that the primary submitter is only human and that LIBOR rates are not based on actual trades, LIBOR is, again, just an opinion. From the beginning, the whole system has been ripe for manipulation. The Dow Jones average, for example, is based on twenty stock prices, not the prices at which a group of traders on the stock exchange floor think the stocks should trade. Imagine if the Dow Jones had submitters who could bias the price to the bid side or offered side of the market, depending on whether they were long or short that particular stock. It would be the equivalent of letting a tennis player at a Wimbledon championship match also serve as the line judge.

By 2007, the ability to influence LIBOR settings had actually become even easier. Due to bank mergers, consolidations, and other combinations, the pool of large global banks was much smaller. Fewer banks meant fewer participants in the surveys each day. Whereas there were forty different banks determining U.S. dollar LIBOR in 1997, that number was down to twenty by 2007. And it was much the same for other currencies, like the euro and the Japanese yen. With the LIBOR panel tossing out the top 25 percent and bottom 25 percent of submissions, those twenty banks were then pared down to ten for the average—clearly not a lot of banks determining LIBOR each day. For other currencies, the number of banks involved in the average was even less. So it should come as no surprise that traders had found a way to make millions by fixing LIBOR.

*   *   *

It's also important to be familiar with how the money market business operates around the world. When banks borrow funds each day, it generally means they're issuing CDs. CDs are the equivalent of a deposit at a bank, but on a large, institutional level. So the rate at which a bank issues a CD is, for the purposes of LIBOR, the same rate at which it borrows money. Each morning, banks send out their CD rates, ranging from overnight through one year, to their customers and the interdealer brokers. That list is what's called the bank's posted levels or posted rates. From there, the interdealer brokers will compile each of the banks' posted rates and send them to everyone else in the market. Eventually, the entire market knows where all of the CD issuers are posting relative to everyone else.

These interdealer brokers play an important role in the money market business. They serve as the matchmakers between banks or between banks and money funds, because these instruments are not traded on an exchange. They don't interact with the public in any way; they only deal with large financial institutions. Think of it this way: The CD trader at Deutsche Bank doesn't necessarily know the CD trader at BNP Paribas. They need someone to stand in between them who knows both of them. That way, there's a central liaison who can bring together buyers and sellers, and, on top of that, they're able to provide a few more perks along the way.

Knowing the buyers and the sellers and what rates they're willing to trade at is pretty important. In the course of matching them together, the brokers are able to provide their customers with a little market information too. Quite often, traders rely on the information from their broker, even though exact details of who's doing what is not explicitly allowed. Oftentimes the brokers will use code to describe a bank. "You know, the guys up in Stamford," for example, might be used when referring to the UBS office in Stamford, Connecticut, and what "the guys" are trying to do in the market.

But being a middleman and providing traders with a lot of market intel is just the beginning. Most of the interdealer brokers—sometimes called broker shops or just the brokers—are well known for their entertaining. Picture a typical broker shop, composed mostly of men with a few token women crammed fifteen to a room, an office space that would normally house about five people. They're all dedicated to one market, like CDs. The typical broker shop is made up of hard partiers who like to eat and drink.

Now imagine going out for a night on the town with a bunch of friends and spending as much money as you want on whatever you want to do. A typical broker dinner usually happens at a steakhouse, and is comprised of large steak dinners, luscious seafood platters, and expensive red wine. As my broker told the waiter at my first broker dinner, "I don't want my guy asking me if it's OK for him to take the last jumbo shrimp." There was supposed to be so much food that no one could finish it all. A trip to the local strip club until the wee hours of the morning is always a given.

The names of the broker shops range from the more formal-sounding Tullett Prebon, Tradition, Garban, R. P. Martin, ICAP, and Cantor Fitzgerald to the borderline obscene, with one shop named "GFI," which is rumored to stand for "Good Fuckin' Idea." That nickname comes from, interestingly enough, the folks at the London GFI group, not the New York one.

Entertaining in business is officially a widely accepted standard business practice. A salesperson and customer will meet, enjoy a nice meal, and maybe some extracurricular activity, like a show or a sporting event. Customer entertainment is supposed to allow the salesperson to cultivate professional relationships and to talk about business with existing and potentially new clients. That's the standard rationale for spending money on customers. Sometimes, however, entertaining can be a reward for those who are a source of revenue—that's where entertainment crosses the ethical and legal lines. When a salesperson is essentially paying back a customer for commissions, it's not explicitly a bribe, though it's teetering on the edge of it.

Brokers in New York are well known for excessive entertaining, especially with traders who generate a lot of business volume. But that's nothing compared to what they do in London. London is the excessive entertainment capital of the world, to say the least. Flying clients to Las Vegas for a weekend of gambling, or to the Alps for skiing, or to the island of St. Tropez for sunning aren't uncommon practices. And flying there doesn't always mean coach: private jets are often booked for the best clients. Prostitutes and drugs used to be a part of the culture, but that was more a thing in the 1980s. A big night of steaks, red wine, and strippers is one thing, but imagine what can be done during a whole weekend in Spain?

At one point in the history of the business, expensive jaunts started becoming part of traders' expectations, a payback for the business that those traders sent their way. As a rule of thumb, traders might expect their broker to spend about 5 percent of their total bill on entertainment. A trader doing a lot of business can generate $100,000, $200,000, or even $500,000 a month in commissions. A broker billing a bank $200,000 can mean that $10,000 a month is assumed in entertainment. Sometimes the broker is hard pressed to spend that amount at an evening at even the most expensive restaurants. Think of a broker who bills a bank $500,000 a month. Excessive entertainment became the only way to meet those expectations.

The broker-trader relationship is circular. Sometimes the entertainment comes before the business. If a big revenue-generating customer is suddenly not doing enough business, the trader would get a call from the broker saying he wasn't billing enough. It clearly meant the trader had to send more business the broker's way if he expected to be wined and dined in the fashion he'd grown accustomed. Brokers and traders and spending money on lavish entertainment all went hand in hand for many years.

Eventually, though, the money market business began to change. Spreads narrowed, banks consolidated, and some of the interdealer trading moved to electronic platforms. The environment changed in such a way that ramping up business wasn't as much of an option anymore. It started becoming harder for everyone to make money in the CD markets. Customers had access to better information about the market; that information flowed more freely. The result was that traders were making less money trading, and when they made less, there was pressure on the brokers to slash their commissions. The brokers then started making less money too. That 5 percent of $200,000 became 5 percent of $50,000. No one wanted to see the money machine that was covering everyone's livelihood stop. It didn't stop, but it slowed down. By the mid-2000s everyone in the money markets was looking for new ways of making money.

*   *   *

The first cracks in the money market business began to show in August 2007, when the CD market effectively shut down. Fear about defaulting subprime loans and illiquid CDOs spread, leaving investors worrying about which banks were overexposed. Risk management groups around the Street began cutting back on their exposure to an increasingly large number of banks. CDs were no longer deemed a safe investment, and money flowed heavily in U.S. Treasuries and collateralized transactions like the repo market. If you don't know who is holding a bad portfolio of distressed securities, the market just shuts down. Money funds just stopped buying CDs. When a broker called one of his money fund clients to ask, "Who are you open on?"—or, in more standard language, "What banks' CDs are you able to buy today?"—the answer came back: "No one." With most of the CD buyers gone from the market, nothing traded. When trades did occur, they were only in very, very short maturities.

The liquidity crisis of August 2007 had many ripples that crept through the financial markets, and one of them infected the LIBOR market. Remember, the job of primary submitters is to estimate where their CDs trade from overnight through one year—that is, the cost of funding the bank. With the CD market effectively shut down for maturities greater than one month, there was no way to know where a particular bank's CDs traded across all of the maturities. If LIBOR was historically about making an educated guess, now it became making a wild guess.

In a free market, when no one wants to buy your product, the best recourse is to sweeten the deal. The same principle theoretically should hold true for CDs, but it doesn't. You might think the bank can offer a buyer the incentive of a higher interest rate. But remember, CDs are also a barometer of the financial health of the banking system. If a bank offers rates that are too high in order to attract buyers, it gives the impression the bank is desperate for cash. And desperation is not the image that any financial institution wants, especially during a crisis.

The situation was reminiscent of Joseph Heller's *Catch-22*, in which Air Force pilots were grappling with their reluctance to fly combat missions because they were afraid of getting killed. The only way pilots could get relieved of duty was to request an exemption on the grounds that they were insane. However, asking for that dispensation proved that they really were sane. After all, only a sane man would be worried about dying in combat. It was a nightmarish situation for all involved, and one that has entered the American lexicon to describe an impossible situation, a situation referred to as a catch-22.

And that catch-22 arrived in the CD markets in August 2007 and led to the first discovery of LIBOR submissions fraud. Because LIBOR rates are also a public admission of a bank's financial health, the banks were under pressure to show a façade of strength, and the best way to show financial strength was to not post abnormally high borrowing rates. Had the submitters posted extremely high CD rates—rates where their CDs could have actually found buyers—a run on their bank would have easily ensued. Given that none of the banks wanted to submit a good-faith estimate, they just submitted their posted rates to the BBA.

The liquidity crisis didn't last very long, and buyers started returning to the CD market in October 2007. However, some people watching the markets were puzzled regarding why LIBOR rates barely moved at all during a liquidity crisis, when the CD market effectively shut down. In April 2008, the *Wall Street Journal* was looking into these inconsistencies and published an article on April 16 that suggested banks may "have been low-balling their borrowing rates to avoid looking desperate for cash." The cracks were widening in the LIBOR submission process.

In the end, Barclays was fined $451 million for its participation in the 2007 LIBOR rigging scandal. The bank's defense, albeit a poor one, was predicated on the fact that everyone else was doing it. Barclays felt it had to submit unrealistically low rates in order to avoid a panic. And while the excuse fell on deaf ears, there was a lot of truth to it. Warning signs regarding the problems associated with the LIBOR survey process were ignored. The International Monetary Fund reassured the public: "Although the integrity of the U.S. dollar Libor-fixing process has been questioned by some market participants and the financial press, it appears that U.S. dollar Libor remains an accurate measure of a typical creditworthy bank's marginal cost of unsecured U.S. dollar term funding."

Reassurances aside, it was clear that there were flaws in the LIBOR submission process, the most influential interest rate in the entire financial world. And on top of that, those flaws were easy to exploit. All it would take next was a trader with both an understanding of the system and the willingness to exploit it.

* * *

The man who would go on to exploit the LIBOR reporting system was Thomas Hayes, a brainy, socially awkward kid from a middle-class area in western London. Described as a highly educated, quiet Englishman, Hayes also had the unfortunate distinction to be referred to as Rain Man by many of his colleagues, a title derived from his overt lack of social skills. He was conspicuously absent from the excessive entertainment gatherings involving other traders and brokers; at one of the rare parties he attended, he reportedly showed up carrying an economics textbook, which he read the entire time, avoiding all conversation with the others.

Hayes studied math and computer programming in college, and then earned an MBA from Hult International Business School, where he met his future wife Sarah, a self-described "lawyer, mother to a toddler son, and avid fan of Japan." He was, in short, someone who avoided the spotlight whenever possible, preferring to show up to work, do his job, then retreat to his own private world at the end of the day.

Hayes joined the Royal Bank of Scotland (RBS) in 2001 as a junior trader in the London office, eventually moving to the Tokyo office at the end of 2002. Perhaps because of his young age, Hayes didn't dress like a typical London banker, opting instead for faded jeans, a polo shirt, and a threadbare sweater when he was at work. But he quickly managed to build a reputation as a valuable asset in the short-term rates market and funding circles, and, despite his social failings, he quickly developed an enviable network of contacts.

Founded in 1727 and headquartered in Edinburgh, the Royal Bank of Scotland Group (RBS) briefly held the distinction of being the largest bank in the world before the financial crisis struck in 2008. Once a stable company, RBS has seen its fair share of turbulence since then, when it accepted £45 billion in British taxpayer money that served as a bailout. Since that time, six different executives have held the position of CEO.

Hayes spent the next four years at RBS in Tokyo, during which time he learned his trade and honed his craft as a successful trader in the Japanese yen derivatives market. At the time, there were very few good Western traders in Tokyo, and Hayes' reputation grew on the heels of his willingness to take risk and put on enormous-size trading positions.

On the derivatives trading desk he traded Japanese short-term interest rate contracts in much the same way as the Eurodollar futures contracts traded in the United States, with the exception that Hayes was dealing with Japanese yen and Swiss francs as opposed to U.S. dollars. He traded futures and options, interest rate swaps, forward rate agreements (FRAs), foreign exchange forwards (FX forwards), cross-currency swaps, and overnight index swaps. These trades were entered into with the goal of generating profits, which were specifically not to hedge the bank's own loan positions. In other words, he was primarily a proprietary trader, meaning he was trading for his own gain.

Hayes wasn't part of the money market trading desk at the bank, whose role is a little different. Those sitting on the money market desk are primarily responsible for hedging the bank's assets and funding the bank by the issuing of CDs and other short-term products. Money market traders will scour the market each morning, looking for the cheapest sources to borrow cash on a short-term basis. They are essentially charged with making sure that the bank gets its funding in all applicable currencies, borrowing and lending funds along the way.

Additionally, some money market traders engage in speculative trading, but it's not their main duty at the bank. They buy and sell CDs, futures contracts, and OTC swaps based on their personal view of the direction of short-term rates. Their professional view of short-term interest rates is inherently important in what they are doing. And if a bank is part of the LIBOR submissions panel, one money market trader is the primary submitter.

At RBS, the derivatives desk and money market desk were initially seated separately on the trading floor, and the two desks had very little interaction. For months leading into 2006, RBS's management debated the idea of moving the two trading desks and sitting them together. Finally, it was decided that the two trading desks should be combined into one, which came to be known as the short-term markets desk. In theory, it would encourage communications between the traders, letting each group benefit from knowing what the other was doing. On paper, it certainly seemed like a good idea at the time.

The result, however, was the equivalent of putting a safe-cracker and an armed robber together in the same jail cell. On the one side, you had a group responsible for submitting honest rates to the BBA. On the other was the group vying to make money off changes in LIBOR rates. Yes, the two groups began communicating better. They did exactly as they were expected to do, namely working together. However, that employee unity had an unintended consequence. RBS's management had just magnified the conflict between the submitter—responsible for submitting honest LIBOR rates—and the derivatives traders, who were expected to make money on movements in the LIBOR market. RBS had unwittingly just created the perfect situation for LIBOR fraud, especially given that it had thrown Thomas Hayes into the cell along with all the others.

On top of that, they were all part of the same profit center, which meant that Hayes could lean over to the submitter at 11:00 AM and tell him which submissions would increase the bank's profits. The submitter now knew when higher or lower LIBOR fixings would increase or decrease the bank's profits on its trading positions. The money the derivative traders made increased and, in theory, the bonuses of the money market traders too. It was essentially the same thing as insider trading.

In the case of the yen LIBOR fixing, the submissions came from a panel of eighteen different banks. With the top and bottom four submitted rates discarded, the remaining ten were averaged. If one submitter was concerned about his own proprietary trades—as was the case at RBS—just moving the submission rate by one basis point, or .01 percent, could potentially move the overall LIBOR .001 percent. That meant that small changes in RBS's LIBOR submissions translated into real money. Lots of real money.

Over the course of the next couple years, RBS derivatives traders would make at least ninety-six separate requests to submitters for Japanese yen LIBOR and Swiss franc LIBOR fixings. They would make at least five written requests for U.S. dollar LIBOR fixings. And it wasn't just the traders in on it; one of the trading desk managers even wrote one day, "Get our boys to put higher libors [sic]."

It's important to note that RBS was not implicated in the first LIBOR rigging scandal of 2007, though later investigations would reveal that Hayes had already been involved in rigging rates. For all intents and purposes, however, he was something of a small fish at that time. But more importantly, the experience taught the young trader how easy it was to manipulate LIBOR. And he was fast adding a network of industry contacts, a network that he would tap in later years, when he really built up his scheme.

At the end of 2006, Hayes landed a job at the Swiss global financial services company UBS office in Tokyo. He found the situation between the derivatives desk and money market desk somewhat the same at UBS—it was easy to push the submitter to bias his submissions. For the first few months at the new job, Hayes kept his suggestions small, adjusting the rates up or down as he needed in order to garner the profits on his trades. But that changed in January 2007, when Hayes began recruiting his contacts at other banks to join him. He now had a network of former colleagues, including those still at RBS in addition to some other former RBS traders who had jumped ship. This network, combined with his own ability to manipulate the reported rate through UBS, meant that his influence was greatly expanding. With the network in place, on August 20, 2007, Hayes proudly wrote in an instant message, "jpy libor [sic] is a cartel now."

That cartel was made up of traders from a variety of other banks. Neil Danziger was Hayes' main accomplice and had worked directly with him at RBS, where Danziger was still plying his trade. Danziger would later have the honor of being referred to in court filings as "Yen Trader 1" and sometimes "Yen Trader 2." He was a thirty-eight-year-old South African who also had strong ties with the brokers, being widely known to enjoy all the entertainment perks that they provided. He once stated he was moving LIBOR rates up and down so much that it was "like a whore's drawers."

Tan Chi Min—also known as "Jimmy Tan"—was the head of Japanese yen interest rate trading at RBS, and kept RBS in the game of making money off LIBOR after Hayes had left. Roger Darin became another member of the cartel courtesy of Hayes's arrival at UBS. He was a forty-one-year-old interest rate trader and happened to be the LIBOR submitter at UBS. Rounding out the roster were a variety of former RBS traders who had moved on to new trading jobs or were just picked up along the way, including: Paul Robson at Rabobank, Brent Davies and Will Hall at RBS, Paul Glands at J. P. Morgan, and Luke Madden at HSBC. Of course, all the traders needed a middleman to pass the information along, and that service came courtesy of Terry Farr, their broker at R. P. Martin in London. Then, when Farr wasn't available, they relied on Mark Jones and Noel Cryan at Tullett Prebon. With Thomas Hayes as the ringleader, the cartel was up and running. Given their number of people and the expansive coverage of the banks involved, it became pretty easy to manipulate LIBOR.

Hayes became even more daring with his requests for the LIBOR submitters. Back at RBS, it was merely a situation where he leaned over and told the submitter if a higher or lower LIBOR rate would benefit his trading positions. Now he had a whole network in place sending instant messages in a coordinated effort. Messages that read "high 6s and low 3s please" or "high 3s and low 6s please" were sent to Darin on a routine basis, with Darin replying "ok" or "no problem."

Ironically enough, Hayes and Darin were still seated nearby one another at UBS, which begs the question of why Hayes wouldn't just deliver his requests verbally. As communications within the financial markets began to change over the years, Instant messaging (IM) became more popular on the trading floor. Typical traders would have multiple computer screens opened for IM chats with everyone they did business with. Instead of phone calls or just walking over and speaking with colleagues, it just became easier to do everything from the comfort of the computer. Of course, the difference between a private and quiet conversation with a fellow trader and an IM message is that the IM message leaves a record. A paper trail. It was a mistake Hayes would come to regret years later.

Messages were dug up to illustrate everything that was going on. At one point, Neil Danziger asked a fellow RBS colleague via instant message, "Do you think brokers go and tell small banks where [LIBOR] should be?" The response was, "I could imagine UBS telling the brokers to go and get all the small banks to mark LIBOR up." The RBS trader was wondering if Hayes at UBS was influencing the other banks by using the brokers. And that's precisely what he was doing.

Another IM exchange, between Danziger and broker Terry Farr, shows how accurate that trader's insight had been. Danziger asked Farr, "Has Hayes been asking you to put LIBORs up today?" Farr replied, "He wants ones, ones and threes a little bit lower and sixes probably about the same." The network was just getting going, and working like a charm.

* * *

Banks and their traders were able to benefit in a wide variety of ways by moving LIBOR rates around. On the proprietary trading side, the best way to make money was by taking positions in LIBOR-dependent swaps or futures contracts. Because those contracts settle for cash, the price is determined on the futures contract's last trading day—specifically, wherever LIBOR was set that day. For example, in the case of three-month Euroyen LIBOR futures contracts, the final settlement price is based on the Euroyen LIBOR rate announced by the BBA two business days prior to the third Wednesday of the contract month. That window falls anywhere between the thirteenth and the nineteenth day of the month. That means the final settlement price for the three-month futures contract would be the three-month LIBOR rate on the particular Wednesday. Traders were well aware of these dates and watched the LIBOR fixings like a hawk in those days. If Hayes was short the front three-month contract, he'd push the submitter for a higher three-month LIBOR submission that day.

The banks didn't just benefit in their proprietary trading books. Reset dates for bank loans were a notoriously deep well for a bank's profits. Typically, the interest rates for loans made to large corporations were spread off the LIBOR rate on a predetermined date. The bank's money market desk was well aware of when those reset dates were scheduled to occur. Oftentimes, those rates were based on the LIBOR rate on the fifteenth of the month or end of the month. When the date came due, the submitters would made sure that their LIBOR submissions were a little higher to help push the new rate higher on the outstanding loans.

In one instance, Hayes sent an instant message to Darin asking for "high 3s and low 6s." Hayes had a short position in the three-month Euroyen futures and a long position in the six-month Euroyen futures. "No problem," Darin replied to Hayes as he lowered the six-month LIBOR rate to .70 percent. RBS's six-month yen LIBOR submission fell from .72 percent the day before to .70 percent that day, then rose back to .72 percent on the following two days. It's obvious to even the most casual observer that the rates reflected their trading positions and their traders' requests, and not the price where they were actually selling six-month CDs.

Given the size of Hayes' trading positions, a .01 percent—or one basis point—movement in LIBOR could result in millions of dollars of profit or loss. Even a .002 percent movement is worth $250,000 on a $50 billion position, which wasn't uncommon. In fact, playing within the limits given to him, Hayes had positions worth up to $150 billion in three-month interest rate instruments. With such behemoth positions, any movement in short-term interest rates, even a .002 percent change, was meaningful.

Looking back now, it's even easy to understand why Hayes's larger group was so much more effective. With more banks working together, the ability to move daily LIBOR rates became exponentially easier. By convincing one or two more submitters from other banks to join in, the group was suddenly controlling three times the amount of the submissions, or 30 percent of yen LIBOR. Where Hayes was happy moving LIBOR .001 percent at RBS, when cartel members were operating together, the rate was potentially moving .003 percent. That still might not sound like a lot, but it was three times the previous amount of profits. And better yet, they were all making money from it.

Of course, none of this would have been possible without the complicity of the brokers involved. You might even say the coordination of the brokers. While the brokers were generous when it came time to entertain their trader clients, they weren't about to perform this service—an illegal service—for free. They expected to be paid for the risk they were taking. Remember, it's is a for-profit world out there. One message that Hayes sent on September 18, 2008 to a broker: "If you keep 6s unchanged, I will fucking do one humungous [sic] deal with you. I will pay you, you know, $50,000, $100,000 . . . whatever you want." It was a nice trade for the broker, all in one shot.

And while promise of six-figure commissions certainly pays the bills, the brokers weren't getting directly paid anything on actually rigging LIBOR rates. That's because the bank made money on its futures trading positions, which didn't actually result in increased CD sales for the broker. Those weren't transactions that generated commissions, so the traders had to find another way to reward their brokers, some way to throw them a bone for their efforts. The best way to do that was to put through what are called "wash trades." In a wash trade, a bank issues a CD and sells it to another bank, which in turn sells the CD back to the first bank. All the trades are arranged to pass through the broker.

If Hayes wanted to generate a little money for the broker, he'd just issue a UBS CD to be sold to another bank via the broker. That other bank would then sell the CD back to UBS through the same broker. The result was a commission for the broker on both sides of the transaction, and perhaps the broker would even buy lunch for the money market desk person who had to book the trades, as a goodwill gesture. In the end, UBS retired the CD after buying it back, and life went on as if the CD had never existed. The money market traders got a free lunch, the broker got his commission, and everyone was happy.

The wash trades were spelled out as clear as day in an instant message conversation on September 19 2008, between Neil Danziger at RBS and Terry Farr, the broker at R. P. Martin. Farr wrote, "Can you do me a favor? You're not going to pay any bro for this and we'll send you lunch around for the whole desk. Take it from UBS, give it back to UBS. He wants to pay some bro." Danziger replied, "Yeah, yeah." In this exchange, Farr asked Danziger to "take" a CD from Hayes at UBS, then sell it back to him. Danziger wouldn't have to pay any "bro," or brokerage commission, on the trade. He'd just have to buy it and sell it back at the same price.

Danziger did the trade as he was asked, buying and selling a two-year CD for ¥100 billion—a transaction that netted Farr a £31,000 commission from Hayes. For his trouble, Danziger got his lunch paid for by Farr. It boggles the mind to think of how much Hayes was making on other trades, if he was so willing to give away £31,000. When these activities were later investigated, Hayes had done twenty-three such wash trades with different brokers while at UBS, and paid out at least £119,000 in corrupt payments. And that only accounts for what the investigators were able to find. No doubt there were more payments that fell under the radar.

In total, throughout his tenure at UBS, Hayes made over eight hundred documented requests to the money market desk asking for LIBOR submission adjustments. Again, though, this number has to be taken in context—there were inevitably more undocumented cases, as he was also sitting right next to the people doing the submitting. He made over one hundred requests to submitters at other banks for similar adjustments to LIBOR. In fact, he made no secret of the fact that he was doing it, indicating at each day's morning meeting which way he planned to push LIBOR.

In terms of profits, Hayes indicated in one e-mail that the cartel could net "about a couple million dollars" for each basis point he moved LIBOR. But he wasn't able to profit from moving the rate every day; instead, they had to book trades and wait for a reset or expiration date to arrive. And while a couple of million dollars once a month wasn't bad for a start, as a truly good rogue trader, Hayes ramped up the size of his positions and moved into other currencies too, including the Swiss franc. He generated $40 million in revenue for UBS in 2007, a number that doubled to $80 million in 2008, then peaked at $116 million in 2009. Given that a trader in Japan typically expected to take home between 8 percent and 12 percent of his trading profits, suffice it to say that Thomas Hayes' foray into LIBOR led to some really fat bonus checks.

Despite the fact that federal investigators seemed unaware of the specifics regarding was going on, it seemed that everyone else in the financial industry knew it was happening. One trader, Eddy Takata, had been a derivatives trader for eighteen years in Deutsche Bank's Tokyo office. He'd been talking openly about the manipulation since 2007, but apparently nobody cared enough to investigate. One trading manager at UBS wrote another in an e-mail on December 5, 2007, referring to the "pure manipulation going on." But again, nobody seemed to care.

* * *

The first whiff of the LIBOR scandal began to gain traction on April 16, 2008, when the *Wall Street Journal* published an article titled "Bankers Cast Doubt On Key Rate Amid Crisis." In it, the writer questioned the integrity of the panel's LIBOR submissions during the liquidity crisis that had wracked financial markets in August 2007. "One of the most important barometers of the world's financial health could be sending false signals," the article warned.

The next month, things got a little hotter for the LIBOR fraudsters when the same newspaper published a study that compared the banks' 2007 LIBOR rate submissions with the costs of buying credit default swap insurance for the same time periods. The most striking feature highlighted was that Citigroup was able to issue CDs at a rate that was 87 basis points lower than the cost of its credit default swaps. That was, to put it kindly, a pretty unlikely scenario. All of the questions surrounding the reliability of LIBOR led Willem Buiter, a former member of the Bank of England's Monetary Policy Committee, to describe LIBOR as "the rate at which banks don't lend to each other."

In response to the scrutiny, RBS reversed its 2006 decision and separated the derivatives desk from the money market desk in Tokyo, making them separate business units once again and no longer physically located next to each other. And while that might not accomplish much, given modern technology's myriad methods of communication, at least it would make it a little harder.

It was very apparent that the BBA knew something was amiss. On June 10, 2008, the BBA published a new rule specifying that the LIBOR submissions had to be determined by a money market trader and specifically not a derivatives trader. "The rates must be submitted by members of staff at a bank with primary responsibility for management of a bank's cash," the paper said, "rather than a bank's derivative book." Those submission procedures were further clarified on September 15, 2008, and again on July 15, 2009. What is even more interesting is that many of the new procedures were addressing exactly what Hayes and his cohorts were doing.

In April 2010, the U.S. Commodity Futures Trading Commission formally requested reviews of reporting practices from the BBA. The BBA, in turn, requested that RBS conduct its own internal investigation about possible fraudulent reporting. In November 2010, with regulators hot on the scent of the fraud, Neil Danziger sent Hayes an instant message: "At the moment the Fed are all over us about LIBOR."

Despite the authorities looking into their activities, the LIBOR cartel didn't stop what it was doing. Instead, participants simply worked at covering their tracks better by cutting back on instant messages, e-mails, and Bloomberg chats. One trader told another—via e-mail, no less—"No e-mails anymore, after tomorrow." Another wrote via Bloomberg messenger service, "We're just not allowed to have those conversations over Bloomberg anymore." It was ironic, to be sure, that the traders were announcing their intentions to stop leaving a paper trail by leaving a paper trail.

In early 2009, Thomas Hayes was perhaps sensing that it was the right time to move on and made his intentions publicly known. Goldman Sachs is rumored to have offered him a guaranteed $3 million in annual compensation to join the firm, but Hayes declined. Then in June, Hayes had a meeting with Christopher Cecere, the head of the rates group at Citibank.

The meeting took place in a swank Tokyo bar, with Hayes and his then-girlfriend Sarah. Hayes reportedly sat mute the entire time, letting Sarah and Cecere talk as if he wasn't even sitting next to them. In the end, Hayes agreed to the terms, which included a reported $5 million in guaranteed annual comp. Hayes' boss at UBS, Michael Pieri, lobbied senior executives at UBS to counter the Citi offer with their own form of guarantee. Pieri cited Hayes's "strong connections with LIBOR setters in London" as his reason for wanting to keep the trader, but the senior executives didn't share his feelings and declined. Hayes was taking his show over to Citi.

Hayes started his job at Citi in December 2009 with much fanfare. He was introduced as "a star" to the trading desk, which would be shifting into more derivatives trading in order to take advantage of his immense talents. That same month, Citi joined the Euroyen LIBOR submission panel, becoming one of the few non-Japanese banks to be counted among that distinguished group.

Hayes didn't begin his trading career at Citi as aggressively as he did at UBS. The Citi people were a whole new group, and he wasn't sure they'd be as enthusiastic about adjusting rates as his former colleagues at RBS and UBS. The yen submitters weren't even located in the Tokyo office, as they worked out of London instead. He clearly didn't know his new coworkers well enough to even broach the subject. Additionally, there was still smoke hovering in the air from the first round of LIBOR fraud, so it was definitely smart to keep a low profile, at least for the moment. That didn't mean, however, that he didn't join in on the rigging with the cartel he left behind. Behind the scenes, things were going on just as they had been when he worked at UBS. On March 3, 2010, one broker sent an instant message to Roger Darin: "U see 3m jpy LIBOR going anywhere between now and imm?" Darin replied, "Looks fairly static to be honest." The broker then said, "Oh we have a mutual friend who'd love to see it go down. No chance at all?" Darin knew who the mutual friend was and replied, "Haha. Tom Hayes at Citibank by chance?" The broker, perhaps with a tone of comic relief, replied, "Shhh. If you cud see ur way to a small drop there might be a steak in it for ya, haha."

When Hayes finally decided to try his luck with the Citigroup submitters, he quickly discovered that he wasn't among friends anymore. After repeatedly asking the Citi traders in London if they'd be willing to skew their LIBOR submissions, one trader reported him to the Citi legal department, saying that Hayes was making "inappropriate requests." The legal department notified Cecere in July 2010 about the requests, and Citigroup immediately hired an outside law firm to comb through Hayes's e-mails, instant messages, and phone calls. The bank then sent compliance staff to Tokyo to investigate the charges.

It was, in the end, technology that did Hayes in. When e-mail first became the new communications device, it was thought to be a technological breakthrough that would revolutionize the world. And truth be told, it did. But on the trading floor, it was still a little too slow, because the markets moved faster than the speed of e-mail. The phone was still the dominant method of communication for traders until instant messaging came into being in the mid-2000s.

Instant messages are a useful tool from the perspective of traders because, as the name implies, they're instant. Traders' phone lines have been recorded since the 1980s, which meant that conversations could be listened to by a third party, and, of course, there were always conference room phones reserved for more private conversations. Those phones lines weren't tapped, but they were too far away from a trader's desk to be worth the loss of valuable time it took to get to them.

So when instant message technology became available, it became the preferred method of communications on the trading floor. And, as far as many traders thought, once you shut the conversation window on your computer monitor or deleted the last exchange, the conversation disappeared into the abyss. But it didn't. By the mid-2000s, traders' communications had become much more easy to trace. Conversations were kept in databases for years, where they could be searched in case the need arose. And that's what sank Thomas Hayes.

Following the results of the investigation, Hayes was accused by Citibank of attempting to influence both the yen LIBOR and the Tokyo Offered Rate (TIBOR), and he was immediately fired. He had gone from a star hire to unemployed within a year. Adding insult to injury was the fact that he was fired two weeks before his wedding date. After his dismissal, he reportedly told friends that he had "no idea it was wrong." Christopher Cecere didn't last much longer at Citigroup either. He too left in 2010, soon after his star hire had been relieved of duty.

It's entirely possible that LIBOR manipulation was going on for many years before Thomas Hayes arrived on the scene. It's also entirely possible that brokers used to help arrange such things over lunch or a drink or at a dinner. After all, it was pretty common for brokers and traders from different banks to socialize together after work. Whenever they did, they could be expected to talk about work. But as much as technology has advanced over the years, a couple of guys talking in a bar is still pretty difficult to refer back to several years later. And those discussions are certainly not searchable.

That possibility raises an entirely new question. Who really started the manipulation of LIBOR rates? Is it really possible that a junior trader at RBS who happened to have been seated next to the money market traders devised this massive scheme to defraud one of the most prestigious financial institutions in the world? The fact that LIBOR manipulation was so rampant and done so often across so many banks means it was clearly not a new phenomenon. It is entirely possible that the only reason it has recently been discovered is, in fact, because of the widespread use of instant messaging.

The *Financial Times* ran an essay on July 27, 2012, titled "My thwarted attempt to tell of LIBOR shenanigans." The author claims that LIBOR rates have been misrepresented as far back as 1991, when he himself was a money market trader at Morgan Stanley in London. He was trading bonds and derivatives, including the Eurodollar futures contract traded on the LIFFE futures exchange. He would watch the LIBOR fixes and CD issuance levels from banks, and he noticed that those contracts would routinely settle differently from where the banks' rates were actually trading. He regularly lost money on those contracts, and, after speaking with the more experienced traders, he learned that it was a common practice to misrepresent LIBOR rates in order to affect the futures settlements. He said he complained to the executives at LIFFE, but nothing was ever done about it.

At that time, there were no instant messages and no e-mail, so electronic paper trails were essentially nonexistent. But the lack of technology doesn't mean that human nature—with all of its foibles and negative components—didn't exist. And that nature led people then just as it does today to do things that are both ethically and legally wrong. And if you think LIBOR is the only money market rate that has been manipulated, think again.

* * *

There are, in fact, at least two other areas of the global money market business that have experienced manipulation throughout the years. The market has been commonly used by less-than-scrupulous traders and banks to make themselves wealthier.

One of these areas is in the so called federal funds rate, sometimes called fed funds rate or just funds. It's the rate paid by U.S. banks when they borrow and lend short-term funds between one another. Most of the loans are overnight, however, and they differ from CDs in that fed funds are not technically bank deposits. Federal funds are simply uncollateralized loans between banks.

The Federal Reserve—the same institution that sets our national monetary policy—uses the fed funds rate to target short-term U.S. rates. the federal funds rate is the closest thing to the overnight LIBOR rate in the U.S. market. And just like the LIBOR rate, large banks have loans and interest rate contracts tied directly to the that rate. In a way, perhaps, it's no surprise that there have been multiple instances in which banks have been suspected of rigging this rate too.

Unlike LIBOR, there is no official method for setting the fed funds rate; it trades through interdealer brokers, just like CDs. The first rate at which fed funds trades each day—usually around 8:00 AM—is called the fed funds open, and it serves as a benchmark for many other overnight interest rates and contracts. In an ideal world, the open is supposed to be the rate at which the first $500 million in fed funds trade on the brokers' trading screens.

But in the real world, the rate is notoriously easy to manipulate, and one broker, a subsidiary of one of the world's largest interdealer brokers, has a lengthy history of fixing the opening rate. It's long been open knowledge that its brokers will happily fix the rate at whatever level a trader wants, so long as there's enough trading volume to generate commissions. There are banks in the United States widely known for working with the brokers, pushing the opening rate generally higher each morning.

Most notably, one French bank is its biggest customer with regard to federal funds fixing. In the past, that bank would commonly sell funds through its broker on the bid side of the opening market just to set the opening rate a little higher than it traded throughout the day, then buy the funds back from the same bank later that morning. The result for the other bank involved was a profit on the trade, and the broker made a commission on both sides. The French bank, naturally, got an opening rate that was a little higher, and that forced other overnight loans with its customers higher. And if that process sounds familiar, it's because it was done with the same wash trades that Hayes was orchestrating with the brokers.

The other part of this rigged game happened through what is known as the league tables. League tables are the rankings of large investment banks that underwrite stocks, bonds, IPOs, and that sort of thing—that is, who underwrite the most in each category. The higher anyone's ranking on the league tables, the more prestigious the firm's image and the more additional underwriting business it is able to get. Being placed among the top ten is some of the best marketing an investment bank can get.

There are a variety of tables, each with its own subdivisions. Equity underwriting, bond underwriting, bank loans, and mergers and acquisitions are the main rankings, and they're further broken down into regions and subcategories. The catch with the tables, however, is that generally only the top ten banks are listed in each category. So if you find yourself with a number-eleven ranking, it could be worth millions of dollars in underwriting fees if you can crack that number-ten spot. Then, if you can climb your way up into the top five, suddenly you're in the position to receive even more underwriting business. There are even some underwriting clients who only sell through the top three on the list. Competition for the top spots is rampant and cutthroat, but it's surprisingly easy—and relatively inexpensive—to climb the ladder in nontraditional ways.

In the world of fixed-income trading, the criteria for listings revolve around new securities with at least an eighteen-month maturity. The requirement used to be twelve months, but it was discovered that too many investment banks were just buying one-year CDs and selling them directly to the money market funds. These days, the more eighteen-month securities that an investment bank can arrange to issue, the higher its ranking. And the best way to ensure that investors buy a new security is to offer a high interest rate, perhaps even incurring a small loss in the process. And that's where the money market business comes in; issuing short-term CDs is a lot easier than underwriting longer-term bonds. Additionally, if you're going to take a loss on something, it makes sense to lose on a short-term security rather than on a long-term one. This is how banks influence the league table charts.

It's a practice that is oftentimes referred to as dropping checks or writing checks. An investment bank would buy a bank's CDs at the bank's posted level, then add on a few basis points and sell the CDs to its clients or the brokers. The investment bank would lose a few basis points just to inflate its ranking on the league tables. It was a common practice to issue an eighteen-month CD or a medium-term note with a higher-than-normal yield. Investors would immediately snatch up the security, lured in by the high interest rate. In the end, the investment bank lost as much as a few hundred thousand dollars up front, but ended up making millions in additional underwriting fees in the long run. It is the perfect example of spending money to make money.

Like the same practice associated wash trades and fed funds manipulation, it's a circle of transactions that ends up with the security going back to the original issuer. An investment bank would announce it's selling a CD, usually from a European bank issuer at above market rates, then the word would spread through the money markets that a particular investment bank was dropping checks. Brokers immediately called their clients to show them the great eighteen-month CD rates for sale, and other market participants bought them up quickly.

Originally, the CDs ended up in some bank or money fund portfolio and stayed there until maturity. Beginning in the 2000s, competition became fierce, and the banks were just looking to buy their CDs back, then turn around and issue more. As the years progressed, buyers would sell the CDs right back to the issuer, always using the same broker in the process. Things really got out of hand when one Swedish bank trader bought and sold a total of $3 billion in CDs back and forth with one investment bank on the same day. The trader was quickly fired. A common refrain heard from the bank issuers was that they'd seen their securities trading cheaply in the market and felt compelled to buy them back. But as Bob Linton, a well-known retired CD trader of forty years, pointed out, "Banks were issuing and buying back for the sole purpose of inflating the table."

This practice, thankfully, stopped for the most part in 2009. First, with all of the bank mergers—some of them the result of individual banks collapsing—there wasn't quite the level of competition for placement on the league tables anymore. Secondly, coming off the heels of the financial crash in 2008, banks were less willing to lose money than they had been in previous years.

* * *

The LIBOR scandal that rocked the financial world was called the biggest antitrust felony in the history of the world. The Royal Bank of Scotland offices were raided by European Union officials in October 2011, who seized documents and computers. It was quickly determined that RBS employees had been complicit in aiding and abetting the manipulation of LIBOR as a way of benefiting their own trading positions.

It is difficult to pinpoint the exact amount of monetary damage that was inflicted on global financial markets as a result of the LIBOR scheme, mainly because there were so many instances of fraudulent submissions in both directions. Damage estimates in the United States alone were as high as $9 billion, including $6 billion in losses incurred by individual states, municipalities, and local governments, plus another $3 billion in combined losses for Fannie Mae and Freddie Mac. That said, it's quite possible that those groups also unintentionally and unknowingly benefited from the LIBOR manipulation, due to the fact that the fraudulent activities involved both raising and lowering the rate. But while the $9 billion estimate may or may not be accurate, the actions those traders undertook were still criminal.

Thomas Hayes was arrested on December 11, 2012, by officials from the United Kingdom's Serious Fraud Office. The arrest was made public on December 19, but Hayes was immediately released on bail. When questioned about the manipulations, he said, "Who was I to question what they were doing? I thought it was weird, but that's how they did it." He contends that upper management knew all about the rigging all along, and that it was a common practice on the trading desks. In a text message, he told the *Wall Street Journal* in 2013, "This goes much, much higher than me."

The U.S. Commodity Futures Trading Commission contends that "RBS allowed conflicts of interest to exist and affect its LIBOR submissions." The organization filed a motion in which it claimed that "RBS secretly rigged the benchmark interest rates." For its part, RBS admitted to having manipulated interest rates, further confessing to the U.K.'s Financial Services Authority (FSA), that between 2006 and 2010, staff members based in London, Singapore, Tokyo, and the United States collectively conspired to manipulate LIBOR. The U.S. Department of Justice was a little more forceful; it threatened to have RBS's U.S. operations shut down.

In order to avoid that fate, RBS agreed to pay a $325 million fine to the CFTC, an amount that was based on a $1 million penalty for each act of attempted or completed manipulation. The bank paid an additional £87.5 million to the FSA; it would have been more, but RBS was able to qualify for a discount. The FSA (which is now known as the Financial Conduct Authority) has an interesting rule: if the accused settles in the early stages of an investigation, the required payment is subject to a 30 percent discount. Had it not paid early, RBS would have been on the hook for £125 million. The fines, however, weren't done yet. The RBS subsidiary in Japan agreed to pay a fine of $50 million to the Japanese government for its role. All combined, RBS paid more than a half a billion dollars in fines resulting from the rigging scheme.

As is common practice when such an embarrassingly illegal act comes to light, the firm stuck to the tried-and-true strategy of blaming junior and midlevel managers, claiming that no one higher up knew anything was going on. In stark contrast to Hayes's accusations, twenty-three individuals at RBS who were implicated in the rate-fixing scheme—a number than included one manager—were fired, and six others were disciplined appropriately. The global head of treasury markets was also cut, as were the heads of rates trading in both Europe and the Asia-Pacific region. Three traders in the RBS Singapore office were suspended, and the Monetary Authority of Singapore announced in September 2012 that it was initiating its own probe into the scam.

The FSA, after its investigation, did not find that RBS as a firm had engaged in deliberate misconduct. Given that the firm is now owned substantially by the British government—a by-product of the financial bailout RBS received—criminal charges against the bank as an entity would have certainly put it out of business. There were those in the government who felt that the bank should be shrunk considerably, if not disbanded altogether. But those voices were drowned out by ones in support of letting RBS continue its operations. In June 2013, Stephen Hester, the CEO of RBS, resigned as a result of the scandal.

In total, $3.6 billion in penalties have been handed out globally, and the numbers are still being finalized. At UBS, two foreign exchange traders were put on leave as part of an internal probe into the manipulation of nondeliverable forwards. The bank agreed to pay a $1.5 billion fine in January 2013, and pulled out of the LIBOR panel that sets the Euribor, the Euro Interbank Offered Rate. In addition, UBS was also temporarily suspended from trading derivatives in Japan. Michael Pieri, Hayes' former boss at UBS, was fired by the bank. Deutsche Bank also fired two traders suspected of LIBOR manipulation in 2011, and suspended five more in 2013 when accusations of their involvement in rigging the Euribor came to light.

In 2013, it was revealed that J. P. Morgan had coordinated Swiss franc LIBOR submissions with RBS, which resulted in a civil lawsuit being filed against it in the United States. The suit was dismissed, but it is now reported that J. P. Morgan is in talks with the Justice Department on a final LIBOR settlement. Citigroup has avoided any fines to date, which is probably the correct course of action. Management fired Hayes as soon as it learned of his scheme, and the bank sustained a $50 million loss from unwinding his positions. Since then, the bank voluntarily withdrew from the Euribor panel.

Barclays was hit with fines totaling £290 million for rigging both the LIBOR and Euribor rates from 2005 to 2009, with the brunt of those fines resulting from its attempts to make itself appear more financially healthy during the liquidity crisis of 2007. CEO Bob Diamond was forced to resign, and the U.S. Department of Justice is, as of today, still investigating the firm. There are accusations that derivatives traders at Barclays manipulated LIBOR in much the same was that Hayes did, though the investigation is still ongoing.

Rabobank was caught up in the investigation too. It was discovered that from the period from May 2005 to January 2011, there were over five hundred attempts made by Rabobank traders to manipulate LIBOR. When one Rabobank trader asked if anyone would ever notice, the submitter responded, "Don't worry mate—there's bigger crooks in the market than us guys!" In October 2013, Rabobank agreed to pay a $1.07 billion fine, and its CEO agreed to step down. The U.S. Justice Department is still contemplating charges against its former money market trader, Paul Robson.

Gary Gensler, the head of the CFTC, said publicly on numerous occasions throughout 2012 and 2013 that he wanted LIBOR scrapped and replaced with another interest rate benchmark that's based on actual market transactions. On September 25, 2012, the BBA—while not agreeing to delete the program entirely, as Gensler wanted—announced that it would cede oversight of LIBOR to U.K. regulators, as had been proposed by the FSA. In that report, it was also recommended that an independent organization manage the LIBOR setting process, which would require that banks make LIBOR submissions based on their actual CD issuance transactions. Looking back, perhaps the cash settlement feature of the Eurodollar futures contracts wasn't really the wave of the future after all. In a strange twist of fate, the market appears to be going back to actual CD transactions, something akin to the original CD futures contract.

In December 2012, U.K. authorities blocked a U.S. Department of Justice request to interview Hayes, and the organization worked to file criminal charges against him. In February 2013, Thomas Hayes was formally charged with one count of wire fraud for engaging in a scheme to defraud counterparties. Currently living in Surrey, England, Hayes is actively fighting extradition, preferring instead to face charges in England. His wife Sarah has been vocal in her defense of Hayes, especially via social media. She has repeatedly asked, via Twitter, why it was that the U.S. Department of Justice settled with European banks, but has so far failed to prosecute any banks in the United States.

Hayes has engaged the services of the London law firm Fulcrum Chambers to advise him in his defense, and he has also reached out to David Bermingham, one of the so-called "NatWest 3" bankers, who, after being extradited to the United States in 2006 on Enron-related fraud charges, spent two years in an American prison. Bermingham runs what can only be called a niche consulting firm advising clients on extradition proceedings and negotiating plea deals with the United

States as well as how to best survive a stint in prison. He has said of his professional activities, "I would not do any deal that did not meet with the overt approval of the U.S."

*   *   *

The question now is what can be done with these megalithic financial institutions that continue to experience financial disasters. The inability to manage their operations and risks continue to send ripples through the financial markets. We've all heard the rationales posited by various groups regarding prosecuting massive banks. They're "too big to prosecute" or "too big to fail." The reality, however, is that these colossal banks have grown to a size that, in many cases, are just too big to manage. And that truism ultimately makes them too big to succeed. In other words, they're too big *not* to fail.

But until there is a complete sea change in the way they're run, these banks will never be too big to bluff at the poker table that is the world's financial system. And that means that you better know who the sucker at the table is, because if you don't, you're it.

Chapter Eight

What's Next?

No look at rogue traders would be complete without some sort of attempt to explain what ties them all together. It's easy enough to recount the stories themselves and, with any luck, discover the individual motivations that drove these traders to circumvent the law. But it has to be more than just that. There needs to be some sort of understanding, something to make it easier to prevent such occurrences from ever happening again.

Some say the answer lies with the values that we as a society place on making money. Could the root of the problem be the individuals themselves? In every case that we looked at, there was an intentional act of deceit by a trader. It's the common thread that weaves its way throughout the stories. Whether the initial justification was to hide an error, preserve one's status, make money, or save a job, the fact is that in every case, there was an intentional desire to deceive. Nick Leeson said in June 2013, "Immature people with status will do anything to protect it." So then it's possible that the whole rogue issue goes back to one's mindset.

Blinded by what amounts to the personal desire to acquire more money—call it greed, for lack of a better term—the entire banking industry is indicted by the acts of a very few individuals. The idea is that banker's greed is the driving force above all others is a little too simple, almost a cliché. The reality is that we live in a world that needs a banking industry, be it for savings, raising capital, processing financial transactions, investing, or financial planning. Those activities require financial institutions, plain and simple. There will always be employees at banks whose job it is to buy and sell investment products—that is, make money for the bank.

Anytime a rogue trader's actions are made public there is a knee-jerk reaction. Calls for more governmental intervention in the form of new rules and regulations are the most common outcries. Occasionally, there is justification for it. The Glass-Steagall Act following the Great Depression was legislation that was truly needed. But all too often, the new laws don't change as the industry changes, and rogue traders are going to be rogue traders, regardless of the laws prohibiting their actions. Case in point: Ever since the Drysdale collapse in 1982, financial services have become increasingly more and more regulated, but the new laws haven't prevented illicit trading activities. Why?

To go even one step further, there is a negative correlation between the amount of regulation and rogue trading events. The more regulators have done to try to control trading activities, the more incidents that have surfaced—and the losses have grown larger. Almost all of these stories occurred at regulated financial institutions, and losses grew larger as the years went on. Ironically enough, only one story concerned the actions of a hedge fund trader. Counterintuitive as it might seem, fraudulent trading at *unregulated* hedge funds is far less common than at regulated banks. So the answer is more than the need for new laws.

Perhaps, then, the answer lies with the regulators themselves—the people who are charged with ensuring that the banks are operating within the parameters of the law. Top-flight minds often go to work for the banks themselves because, after all, that's where the real money is. Given that the sharpest minds migrate there, it only makes sense that they can stay ahead of their counterparts at the regulatory agencies. In essence, smart people continue to develop complex instruments, and the regulators are left playing a losing game of catch-up. Regulators can keep making better mousetraps all they want, but the business schools will just keep on churning out smarter mice. Perhaps that's part of the problem, but it still doesn't explain why rogue trader events happen in the first place.

There are usually two parts to every rogue trading story—a trader with a willingness to exploit the system, and a manager or institution who fails to notice it. The next logical suggestion could be that better management is needed. In recent years, bank managers and the heads of trading groups have often been made up of career bank administrators. Promotions at banks are all too often based on politics and connections rather than experience and expertise. The trading manager is no longer the lifetime employee working his way up on the trading floor; instead, the job goes a person who is usually a lifelong management trainee being shuffled around the globe on different assignments. There is a clearly a stronger need for a better understanding of the risks a bank is undertaking. But as you might surmise, that solution, too, is only part of the problem. It still doesn't fully explain why rogue trading events occur.

One point I have stressed throughout the book is that many rogue traders operated in new markets, pedaling exotic investment products that did not even exist even a few years before. And these aren't run-of-the-mill stocks and bonds either. Remember, there are smart people creating assets involving wildly complicated math and permutations of matrices.

In the case of David Heuwetter, the repo market was a brand new financial tool just waiting to be exploited. Howard Rubin was operating in the newly created mortgage-backed securities market. Joe Jett exploited the Treasury STRIPS market and Kidder Peabody's inability to account for the transactions properly. All of those markets were relatively new at the time. The list goes on. If the head of a trading group doesn't really know what the traders are doing, how can that person be expected to adequately oversee it? The problem here is that it's hard to prevent a bank from creating new financial products. Financial innovation provides lucrative new businesses, and everyone wants in on it.

While understanding new markets takes time, perhaps the best risk management systems can overcome those risks. However, it's a proven fact that a bank can have the most state-of-the-art risk management system, one that covers 99.999 percent of all possible scenarios, but a single person who represents that .001 percent can exploit the system to his own gain. You had the best and brightest mathematical minds at SocGen developing the best risk management system in the world, but they were still outsmarted by a lowly former middle-office trader. Risk management is clearly not synonymous with fraud management.

In a global sense, there could be a problem tied to the culture of the financial industry. There is, truthfully, often little stigma attached to someone who takes monumental risks in order to generate profits and then fails in that attempt. In many cases, traders who have posted losses and have been publicly humiliated have gone on to even bigger salaries at new jobs; the logic is that their luck is bound to change, so best to get them now. In other words, buy low and sell high, the mantra of Wall Street.

Case in point: Howard Rubin landed a job at Bear Stearns soon after he was let go from Merrill Lynch. The difference here is that Howard Rubin was never formally charged with any wrongdoing, except maybe being a bad trader back in 1987. That fact flies in the face of the argument put forward by Joe Jett, who claimed that no Wall Street firm would hire a rogue trader. Of course, there are plenty of examples—including many of the people portrayed in this book—that didn't have quite the same luck. In reality, anyone who went through the legal system or was convicted of fraud does not go back to a Wall Street trading job. Being labeled a risk or a loose cannon or even a rogue is not tantamount to perpetual unemployment, but being convicted of one is.

So again we return to the question of how to fix the problem of rogue traders. How do you counteract human nature—the inherent belief that a short-term benefit is worth the potential of a long-term loss? Of course, when the short-term benefits are large enough, they can easily cloud a person's long-term view. The answer, unfortunately, is elusive at best. It's safe to assume that companies will continue to enhance and refine their risk management policies, and that there will always be someone out there wily enough to circumvent them—especially in a new market or with a new product. Just when it appears there are sufficient rules and monitoring in place, new markets are created, or trading shifts to a new venue.

One solution *du jour* is the concept of deferred compensation for traders. Essentially, the idea is to tie employees to the long-term performance of the bank by holding back their bonuses in the event that something goes wrong. It is, in a way, an attempt to bring back the business model of the partnerships that once dominated Wall Street. But there's a major difference between the two models: In a partnership, the employee is a partial owner of the business, whereas with deferred compensation, the employee is just waiting to receive the money that he or she earned. If a trader is owed a million-dollar bonus but has to wait years to get it, there is a potential to lose the entire thing to activities beyond the trader's control—like a loss in a faraway office in a completely unrelated product. So while deferring bonuses might seem like an easy fix, they're not without inherent disadvantages. Compared to having an ownership stake in the business, it's a system that is the same as the difference between chaining an employee to a post in the yard and letting the employee live in the house.

Way back when, Antoine Paille suggested giving his traders an equity stake in the business to the management of SocGen. His idea was roundly rebuffed and never implemented. The consequence was that Paille and many of his top people left the bank. The results of that failure speak for themselves.

If banks truly want to curtail rogue activities, then the suggestion put forth by Paille really has some merit. Back in the times of the Wall Street partnership, traders were tied to their ownership in the firm and their retirement package throughout the duration of their career. That situation changed dramatically as the firms became public entities, and traders benefited from an extreme upside and limited downside when they were taking risk.

Again, this differs dramatically from the idea of withholding compensation. It does, however, give the individual trader a similar carrot at the end of the stick, a goal to work towards that serves as a deterrent for everyone in a business to prevent fraudulent activities. But, as Paille discovered, that idea is not a popular one with the banks.

To my mind, then, we'll continue to read about rogue traders in the future. It's an unfortunate reality, but it's a reality nevertheless. It's entirely possible that there's nothing that can be done to protect against rogue activities. The status quo is for more rules, regulations, and procedures to police traders at banks. There's nothing imminent that might change that status quo. But rest assured, there is something the average investor—and, for that matter, the average trading manager—can do to protect against the fallout from such characters. Mind you, even the most hurricane-proof structure can be demolished by a powerful-enough storm, but any amount of protection is better than none. So while there is no way to fully insulate from the possibility of falling victim to a rogue trader, the better you defend yourself, the less likely it is to happen.

The best protection available to an investor who wants to steel himself against the calamitous destruction that can be wrought by rogue traders is education. And that's why I have written this book. So long as we live in a world that requires the exchange of currency for goods and services, people will need money to survive, which means we'll always be investing and trusting our money to Wall Street banks. Knowing the right warning signs can keep you safe. The next rogue trader might already be at work, perfecting his scheme. Your best defense is to learn from the mistakes made by others—many of whom deemed themselves too smart to fall for these sorts of things—and use that knowledge to shield yourself. As Benjamin Franklin so famously said, "An investment in knowledge pays the best interest."

For sales, editorial information, subsidiary rights information
or a catalog, please write or phone or e-mail
Brick Tower Press
1230 Park Avenue, 9a
New York, NY 10128, US
Sales: 1-800-68-BRICK
Tel: 212-427-7139
www.BrickTowerPress.com
email: bricktower@aol.com

www.Ingram.com

For sales in the UK and Europe please contact our distributor,
Gazelle Book Services
Falcon House, Queens Square
Lancaster, LA1 1RN, UK
Tel: (01524) 68765 Fax: (01524) 63232
stef@gazellebooks.co.uk

CPSIA information can be obtained at www.ICGtesting.com
Printed in the USA
BVOW08*2241040215

386465BV00003B/7/P